Run Through the Jungle

Real Adventures in Vietnam with the 173rd Airborne Brigade

LARRY J. MUSSON

Edited by: JoAnne M. Katzmarek

authorHOUSE®

AuthorHouse™
1663 Liberty Drive
Bloomington, IN 47403
www.authorhouse.com
Phone: 1 (800) 839-8640

Published by AuthorHouse 07/14/2015

ISBN: 978-1-5049-2118-3 (sc)
ISBN: 978-1-5049-2119-0 (hc)
ISBN: 978-1-5049-2117-6 (e)

Library of Congress Control Number: 2015910569

Print information available on the last page.

DEDICATION

This book is about some of my experiences in the Republic of Viet Nam from September 1969 to October 1970. It also includes episodes preparing to go to Viet Nam.

I dedicate this book to all the men in A Company 3rd Battalion, 173rd Airborne Brigade who shared these experiences with me. I also want to acknowledge and offer my gratitude with special thanks to John Chapla and Pat Welsh for the encouragement to write my experiences. Without them there would be no story...

INTRODUCTION

In May of 1965, the 173rd Airborne Brigade became the first U.S. Army combat unit committed to the Vietnam War. From 1965 to 1971, the 173rd Airborne became one of the most decorated units to serve during the Vietnam War earning Presidential and Unit Citations for various battles including the most famous battle at Dak To in November of 1967. Earlier in February 1967, the 2nd Battalion 173rd Airborne Brigade made the only combat jump during the entire Vietnam conflict.

During the entire conflict, the 173rd Airborne Brigade drew replacement forces from the all-volunteer airborne graduates of the Army Airborne School at Fort Benning Georgia. Whether the troops were returning combat veterans or newly graduated troops from the Airborne School they somehow meshed to become one of the most feared and highly respected fighting units in Vietnam.

After graduating from the Airborne School at Fort Benning, with the war supposedly winding down in 1969, PFC Larry Musson was assigned to A Company 173rd Airborne Brigade (SEP). The following account of the conflict still going on in 1969 and 1970, takes you to the rugged mountains of the central highlands and the teeming lowland rice paddies of South Vietnam as the members of A Company, 3rd Battalion 503rd Infantry do battle with a very determined enemy.

The officers and men of A Company built friendships and memories that carry on today in their hearts and minds. The bonds of brotherhood established in time of war can never be undone.

CONTENTS

CHAPTER 1

On Leave Before Vietnam/The Lion Story

It was early September; I was on leave after Airborne School before going to Vietnam. I took a long route home, which included a stop in Carbondale, IL. I was visiting my longtime girlfriend who was attending Southern Illinois University at the time. While there, I had a unique, frightening experience that is almost laughable today.

On Saturday morning, my girlfriend had an early class and suggested I meet her in the student center cafeteria for breakfast afterward. I agreed and we met as planned around 7:00 for breakfast. The cafeteria was on the lower level of the student center. It had windows along one wall that looked out along the walk that circled the cafeteria as well as the entire center. As we walked out of the cafeteria, toward the exit of the student center, we saw a man and woman dressed in what looked to be safari kakis unloading a full-grown male lion from a station wagon parked along the walk. My girlfriend and I spoke about how strange that was and then went back to our conversation of planning the remainder of the day before we had seen the lion. We did not know at the time, there was an event scheduled at the school, in the student center, which featured the lion, a young replacement for the older movie lion in "Clarence the Cross-Eyed Lion" and of the TV series "Frazier".

We continued to walk to the end of the corridor where there was a set of doors to exit the Student Center. The doors led directly outside but were two sets of solid doors both opening out, the inside being solid glass, the outside being solid metal and separated by a small carpeted vestibule. Each set of doors was equipped with "panic bar" latches on the inside, very easy to operate and ideal for exiting the building in an emergency. You could not be trapped up against the door if being shoved by a crowd trying to get out. We did not know it at the time, but very shortly, we would be in a difficult emergency in that vestibule. As we passed through the inner glass doors, I saw the arm of the person on the outside of the solid metal doors holding the leash with that full-grown lion we had seen lead the lion around the solid door. Without looking to see if anyone was in the vestibule and saying to someone on the outside "Here, just let me get rid of him while we talk", the person's hand let the lion go and he was with us in the vestibule between the glass doors and the solid doors. I immediately put my arm out and directed my girlfriend behind me and backed up against the block wall to my left. The doors to the outside were not accessible because the lion was standing directly in front of us. The doors we had just entered through had closed and they opened into the vestibule making it impossible to open them using only the handle and latch mechanism that was on the inside of the entryway. We would have to turn our back to the lion and pull the door open to exit the vestibule. We did see a crowd forming out in the corridor and some of them had very worried looks on their faces. The lion did not hesitate to pin me to the wall with his head against my chest and sniffing, probably smelling the sausage and bacon I had just eaten for breakfast! He then proceeded to sniff al l the way up to my face, his nose against my cheek. The only strange thing about this was I could feel the wall behind me, somewhere my girlfriend was back there too!

After several frightening seconds, which almost seemed like an eternity, the person that had let the lion into the vestibule opened the door to find us at the mercy of his pet! I remember his surprised comment, "Don't worry, he won't hurt you, just stay calm and don't move!"

My comment back was "That's easy for you to say".

He then gained control of the animal and was apologizing to us, almost pleading as if he was expecting a lawsuit. I was just glad I got away with all of my limbs attached. I was very frightened then, but I tell the story as a fond remembrance of the day that I came face to face with a full-grown African lion. My girlfriend was very appreciative of my protecting her the entire time, but I truly do not know where she was all of the time the lion was in the vestibule with us because all I really could feel was the wall behind me!

I thought that meeting a lion face to face was the most scared I could ever be but I wasn't thinking of the year ahead of me. What was in store for me the next thirteen months made the lion incident seem like putting out the cat for the night. There is no term to describe the extreme fear I experienced during the fire fights in the jungles and rice paddies of the Republic of South Vietnam.

CHAPTER 2

On Hold in Seattle

My girlfriend and her mother rode with my mom and me to the airport in Chicago to see me off to the war. We left early in the morning, but I did not know when I would catch a flight out to Seattle where I would continue on to Fort Lewis. I was flying military standby, which meant the airline would put me on the first flight when there was a seat available. Back then, there were not as many full capacity flights so I got a seat relatively quickly and was ready to go.

The airplane from Chicago arrived at Seattle-Tacoma airport early in the afternoon on 6 September 1969. The weather was clear and sunny; the temperature was around 70 degrees. It was a beautiful late summer day in Seattle. I found an elegant restaurant overlooking Puget Sound and watched ferries passing in the brilliant blue waters while I ate dinner. The huge ferries with their decks filled with cars and people moving through the blue waters traveling between the mainland and offshore islands creating white wakes at the stern, making a sharp contrast in the brilliant sunshine of the late afternoon. The view was magnificent and helped calm my nerves about being AWOL for one day. My orders were to report on 5 September 1969, but that was my girlfriend's birthday and it didn't seem right to leave her on her birthday. I was worried not knowing what to expect when I reported in at Fort Lewis on 6 September. I had always prided myself on being a good soldier and had never been absent without leave before. The meal, the view and the time alone to think helped tremendously to settle my nervousness. After dinner, I didn't think any more about my dilemma.

I caught a shuttle bus that ran from the airport to Fort Lewis in the early evening arriving after 6:00 PM. Check in turned out better than I expected for being absent without leave for one day. First thing, I found out my MOS, or Military Occupational Specialty, which was infantry, was on hold until further notice, a plus for me. Then the sargent at the check in desk mentioned I was a day late according to my orders, but did not dwell on it very long. He seemed to be more interested in getting me over to supply to get my issue of jungle fatigues, which was the standard uniform for all transits shipping out to Vietnam. A small bus took us to supply to get the fatigues and turn in our class A uniforms. They told us at supply we were restricted to the area around the transit barracks. We found out, that was one of the controls they used to keep their eyes on the transits making sure they made all formations and worked the details they were assigned. They did not want any transits going off post into Seattle or not paying attention to the flight status board and miss going overseas. What they did not tell us, but we found out later, that the jungle fatigues were authorized to wear at any post facility or movie house including the main post.

Back at check-in, the desk sargent assigned me to a barracks and told me where I could get on the bus that would take me there. While waiting for the bus I met the five guys I would spend the next six days with and take advantage of the Army for the first time since being inducted. One of them, a corporal who had come through Ft. Lewis before on his way to Korea, seemed to know the routine. He was a nice guy and the five of us bonded instantly. All of us were given a building number that was to be our barracks until we shipped out for overseas duty. The bus arrived and we loaded up sitting among the others on the bus that were just like us, all going to a building somewhere on post. Although it seemed like we were driving all around Fort Lewis, the bus driver knew where each building was and continued to drop off riders at different locations. I remember going through the WAC barracks area. In 1969, the Army still had a Women's Army Corps and fortunately, for us the WAC area at Fort Lewis was huge. As we passed through the WAC barracks streets, we could see the women in the windows in various stages of undress. Some of the guys on the bus yelled and whistled to which the women responded, leaning out of the widows bare breasted or in their bras. Others mooned us, enticing us with their round naked asses to come up to their rooms. They didn't seem to mind us viewing their nakedness or care how much we saw. I am sure they felt protected because they knew we were transits and the bus would not stop in the WAC area, but it was fun having a thrill while it lasted, especially those of us that had a window seat.

Finally, the driver pulled up in front of our barracks. It was a huge complex and for most of us, a different type from those with which we were familiar. As he let us out of the bus, the driver told us to stay put, not to attempt to go anywhere. The complex was a newly designed self-contained barracks with all amenities included in one building and obviously in a section of the fort that troops stationed at Ft. Lewis no longer used. The attached mess hall was converted to a large sleeping facility with rows and rows of bunk beds separated by narrow walkways. We guessed there to be about two to three hundred beds for transits to sleep while waiting to ship overseas. The six of us selected bunks in an inconspicuous spot nowhere near the front isle but not all the way in back either. Since we were the only ones in the room at the time, we started to devise a plan. Luckily, for us, we had a more experienced Army corporal in our group that had been in this situation before. The corporal took the lead and guided the rest of us on things that would follow or might happen in the next couple of days. He emphasized keeping our group together no matter what anyone might say to us or give us orders to do something to the contrary. Then the corporal and one other guy from our group of six went out to one of the post-exchange bars, leaving the rest of us to fend for ourselves. I was tired from the long day and looked forward to getting some well-deserved rest in the new barracks. The corporal and the other guy returned about an hour later with some cold beers for the rest of us. We had a beer and then decided to sleep until morning when we would make our remaining plans.

At some time in the middle of the night, a large number of new transits being herded into our barracks awakened us. The whole place filled with people dressed in jungle fatigues just like us, ruining our quiet sanctuary. An NCO standing at the front of the room was barking commands to everyone, telling them to stay inside and a bus would come for them in the morning. He was right, about three hours later another NCO was standing near the first row of bunks commanding while yelling obscenities at everyone to get up and get on the bus parked outside the barracks.

Everyone in the room but the six of us original occupants was hustling to get out there on that bus. The yelling and obscenities began to be directed at the six of us steadfast and staying put no matter what the sargent said. The corporal had convinced us not to get on the bus. Even though the NCO threatened and called us every name in his book, we held our ground and stayed in the barracks while the bus pulled away with the transits that shared our barracks for a short time the night before. We had no idea where the bus was taking those transits and we didn't care.

The corporal came up with an ingenious plan to keep the six of us informed of what was going on with all transits and exactly what we needed to know to keep ourselves out of trouble before shipping overseas. Every day all transits were required to attend a morning and evening formation and were assigned to details until their name appeared on a flight manifest for their destination. Because the corporal had been through the process before, he was familiar with the routine. The plan he devised was to stay away from doing work details altogether. In order to do that, we had to have a reason, an excuse, or already be on an assigned detail so the brass wouldn't bother us. We had to be in the proximity of the formations in order to hear our names if called during the formation. We all agreed on a place to meet after the formations. Then four of us went to find a safe spot to hang out during the day when everyone was supposed to be on details. The corporal and one of the other guys went to the formation to get information about what was going on. The scheme the corporal came up with was to use a clipboard he found with some blank paper to deceive the NCOs guarding the formation making sure no one left the formation. The plan was to tell them we were counting the broken windows in the barracks that surrounded the formation area. Those barracks were used to house the transits that were called for the flight manifest during the formation. The clipboard worked perfectly! Once we told the NCOs guarding the formation we were on a detail, they were convinced when shown the clipboard with our numbers on the paper. We were able to stay close to the formation listening for our names and not be herded off on the other details or police calls.

Later at our meeting place, the rest of our scheme came together. The hideaway we selected was a small hill in an open field next to the runway at the Fort Lewis Airport. It had good cover with trees and high grass.

We also discovered that when everyone at the formation was put on police call of the airport property, the hill was not included in the cleanup. That hill became our meeting place and proved to be a great sanctuary away from the senior NCOs that were assigning and watching work details. It was also close to the barracks where we spent our first night so we would always return to that barracks to spend the night. The barracks remained empty except for the six of us while we were on MOS hold at Fort Lewis.

We were very cautious about what we were doing during the daylight hours. We all agreed that we would be at the hideaway or stay away from the formation area and keep on the side of the fort away from the transit area. We ate all our meals at the Enlisted Men's (EM) Club snack bar, which was much better than the mess hall for two reasons. The mess hall had senior NCOs watching the transits that ate there and could become a problem if the NCOs recognized us and the food at the EM Club was much better. One evening we decided to save money so we ate at the mess hall. The chicken they served that evening was overcooked so much that it was hard to distinguish the skin and meat from the bones. That was our worst meal the whole time at Fort Lewis and we never ate in the mess hall again. The snack bar closed early so our last meal was at 5:30 PM every night. After we ate, we headed to the bus stop nearby to take us to the main post so we could take in a movie. In the Army, the main post theaters show movies for several days and you must wear civilian clothes or Class "A" uniforms in order to attend. At one theater close to the transit area, we talked to a WAC officer. She informed us they allowed transits to attend all post theaters in jungle fatigues even the main post theater. She also told us the whole fort was open to transits in jungle fatigues because we were going to Viet Nam. That single bit of information allowed us to take in a different movie every night. It also allowed us to get to the Main Post Exchange for some extras that weren't available at our snack bar EM Club.

Every morning two of us would go to the formation with the clipboard while the others would go to the hill hideaway. We would spend time there or at one of the many PXs eating chow until the evening formation when two different guys would go to that formation and use our standard ploy to gather information about flights. The job of watching for our names to appear on the flight manifest became very important and could not be neglected for any reason. Transit's names were called in the formation three different times. The first time, the NCO in charge immediately took the transit to a work detail. They told the transit that his name would be submitted for the flight list when his detail was complete. The second time a transit's name was called usually happened at the evening formation. That ensured the NCOs would have enough help for CQ duty, supply and mess duty. This time the transit was told his name would be posted for a flight. The third time a transit's name was called, the NCOs collected ID cards so transits had to report for whatever detail they were assigned. This was the time the transit's name was actually posted for a flight, and here is where the ingenious idea of the corporal paid off. We found out about the ID collection and other traps because of our clipboard detail scheme. If the transit did not report the third time his name was called, he would be removed from the flight manifest, but if he were assigned on a detail already, they accepted his ID at the office where the flight manifest was posted. We were always on a detail so they took our ID and kept our names on the flight manifest. We continued to use the same scheme until all of us learned of our flight times for shipping overseas. To our amazement, it worked every time we were asked about what we were doing and we didn't pull any details the entire time at Fort Lewis.

CHAPTER 3

On to Vietnam

On September 11, 1969, my name made the manifest list. I was assigned to a flight leaving Seattle's McCord Air Force Base on September 12, 1969. We left Ft Lewis early in the morning by bus for the short trip to McCord. The plane was a big charter, Tiger Airlines, flying for the military. There wasn't much processing, we got off the bus and onto the plane. We were greeted as most airline passengers by the stewardesses and directed to our unreserved seats. I noticed the stewardesses were mature women and not all the thin attractive females you see on commercial flights. I guess it made sense when you think about the all-male passengers and where they were heading to make the women of the flight crews less attractive, but they were friendly and very experienced. When they waited on me, their faces were smiling and voices soft and pleasant but when they got close; their makeup was covering the wrinkles in their faces and crow's feet around their eyes. Some even had a few grey streaks in their short flight attendant hair.

Once everyone was on the plane and the doors closed, we were told our route and given a specific set of rules for our flight before we took off. We headed for Alaska, Hawaii and Japan, then on to Vietnam. At no time were we to leave the airplane while on the ground at any of our destinations. That news really disappointed me: my first time in Hawaii and I couldn't get off the plane. I didn't understand at that time but someone pointed out later that it was the Army's way of controlling us and not having any AWOLs when we arrived "in country". While on the plane, in flight or on the ground, our conduct was under military jurisdiction. There would be no touching, fondling or molesting the stewardesses in any way. It was clear any attempt to satisfy any urges would land us in the nearest military prison at any of our stops. Somewhere somebody had a list of all the soldiers on that plane and units to which we had to report. Not all of us were going to the same place once we arrived in Vietnam but none of us knew anything for the time being.

As we left McCord, we turned north and flew up the coast to Anchorage. I remember looking out to the east at the coast and seeing the magnificent rugged ice covered peaks of Alaska before we landed at the airport in Anchorage. The peaks looked like gleaming shards of glass pointing toward the sky with white snow and silver ice from top to bottom, and reaching as high as we were flying. Anchorage was our shortest stop, but of course someone always tests the rules and we had a passenger that thought he had a perfect plan to get off the plane. He claimed some sort of illness, thinking they would take him off the plane for medical attention. It didn't work. A medical staff boarded the plane and treated his symptoms right there and after a short delay to our stop, we were in the air again headed for Hawaii. There wasn't much scenery, just water getting there. Nevertheless, what a beautiful view going into Honolulu airport. The day was bright with blue skies and white puffy clouds. Even the airport looked like a tropical paradise. Diamond Head, the ever-prominent landmark did not disappoint any amateur photographers on board the aircraft. It was such a beautiful day in paradise; I would have loved to have gotten out and stretched my legs if only for a moment.

Because of the rules mandated at the beginning of the flight and the length of the flight, we were served our meals on the plane. The meals were typical airline meals of the day and served to us by the flight crew. There was no choice of meals; everyone was served the same meal. By the time we landed at Yakota Air Base in Japan, everybody seemed lethargic from being fed on the lengthy eighteen-hour flight. There was no scenery to look at so we had card games, book reading and for some, napping.

Everyone perked up when the pilot announced that we were flying along the coast of Vietnam. "If you look out the windows on the right side, you can see the coastline of Vietnam."

I think to a man everyone looked! I don't know if it was nerves or anxiety, maybe fear but no one went back to sleep after that. The sea was crystal blue and sometimes aqua marine with sandy and rocky shores. There was heavy green foliage and we could detect some palm trees in there along the beaches. From our point of view, it was hard to believe there was a war going on down there. We stayed off the coast and over the South China Sea until we landed at Cam Rahn Bay, one of the major bases for incoming and outgoing troops in Vietnam. The plane came to rest on the concrete runway a short distance from what looked to be a huge quonset hut terminal and a line of hangers. One of the stewardesses opened the cabin door and we all gathered our belongings and moved into the isle to exit the aircraft.

When standing in the open exit door, I immediately felt the extreme heat, but the thing that really crossed my mind was the smell. It is hard to describe even today because there is nothing like it in the world. If I had to put it in words, it was like a combination of all these smells. Think of a high school gym locker room where nobody washed their sweaty clothes for the whole season. It also reminded me of sitting on top of the garbage dump with that fresh load of grease out of a grease trap and the decayed remains of a road kill nearby. Then there was a strong smell of an outhouse dumped right on top of it all. I can't describe it perfectly but there was no escape from the stench and I know I will never forget it. Eventually, in the weeks to come, we got used to the smell and it wasn't mentioned too much after our initial indoctrination, but even traveling anywhere in the country of Vietnam, a hint of that smell always remained.

We stepped down from the plane and filed into a nearby hanger. Here, once again we became the typical Army transient waiting in line, orders in hand with our duffel bags full of the new uniforms issued at Ft Lewis. My orders were for the 173rd Airborne Brigade working in II Corp, a large central section of South Vietnam that stretches between the South China Sea on the east and parts of Laos and Cambodia on the west. In between were white sand beaches along the coast, sometimes-extending two thousand meters inland. There were the low coastal mountains, not as high or densely foliated as the ones found further west in the Central Highlands. There were miles of rice paddies both dry and flooded among the small villages that were nestled in among the palm trees and banana groves dotting the countryside. Then of course, the Central Highlands with the rugged mountains, dense jungles, plentiful mountain streams and rivers, countless trails leading up and down along the ridgelines and the perfect hiding place for many NVA and VC. I would be attending the jungle school for the 173rd located at Cha Rang Valley. I needed to get my name on a flight manifest for a plane headed for Phu Cat Airbase. There I would be loaded on an open semi-trailer truck with other guys headed for the jungle school. All of that happened the same day I arrived. It was the quickest I had ever processed anywhere since being in the Army.

It was late afternoon when I arrived at the jungle school in Cha Rang Valley. There was just enough time to complete the essentials for anyone arriving in country. I was issued a wooden footlocker and instructed to put all personal items in the footlocker that I didn't want lost or misplaced. I didn't have much and as I remember when I picked up all my personal belongings at the end of my tour, I didn't remember having any of the articles I found in the footlocker. There was no list of the items and I guess I didn't pay enough attention to what I was placing in the footlocker. None of them was personal to me but I collected them and took them home with me.

Everyone had to write a letter home to let loved ones know we had arrived safely in country. I wrote a letter to my mom and dad and to my girlfriend. I think it was this point that I vowed to try to write my girlfriend every day. I know it was impossible to keep that vow but I did write her often. I told her things I did not send in letters to my parents. I told her about missions we went on and when someone was wounded I would write that to her so I had a record of the date of the casualty and the names. She was to keep the letters for me so I could write a book when I returned. We had also made a promise to one another to get married when I got home. She didn't want to get married before I left for Vietnam, there was too much to be done before we were ready to marry. We decided to wait, she thought that way she could concentrate on school and I could concentrate on staying alive. I bought her a pre-engagement ring, a pearl ring from a local jeweler back home to confirm our commitment to one another. She also had my high school class ring to show she had a steady guy.

All the mail from US troops was sent free and "Free" was written in the upper right corner where a stamp would normally be. Once the letters to loved ones was completed, I was assigned my first detail in Vietnam, CQ duty. CQ was in charge of quarters where one of the company's NCOs managed an all-night vigil on the orderly room and monitored the radios at Cha Rang Valley. I was the NCO's runner, doing anything he required so he did not have to leave the orderly room. Both the NCO and I missed the nightly movie shown for all the off duty troops in jungle school. The NCO had that covered, right after the movie ended, one of the cadre at the school brought the projector and film to the orderly room so we could view it there. About the only other thing that happened that night was I lost a lot of sleep.

I got off duty the next morning, and attended the mandatory formation. There I was assigned another detail for the day. I had to ride shotgun on a truck to Qui Nhon with one of the cadre mess sergeants and another guy to pick up supplies. I am now on the verge of being awake for thirty-six hours straight and at the edge of exhaustion. I was sure I could not keep up with this pace and expressed some concern to the sergeant in charge of my detail. He was OK with me sleeping on the way to and from Qui Nhon as long as I was awake and helping load supplies once in Qui Nhon.

Anytime there was travel on the roads of South Vietnam, whether in a convoy, a group of vehicles traveling together to the same place, or in a single vehicle, there was always a possibility of enemy attack or running over a land mine. Luckily, we did not encounter either hazard on our trip to Qui Nhon to supply Cha Rang Valley.

My introduction to drugs for the first time happened on this trip. It seems the sergeant had a taste for speed, the oral kind. We made a couple of stops to feed his appetite for Obisitol, a weight reduction amphetamine banned in the United States but plentiful in Vietnam. Obisitol came in a bottle about the size of cough syrup and individually boxed. The sergeant bought two bottles for two dollars each from one of the roadside markets that dotted the main roads GI's traveled. Directions on the package read, take two teaspoons once daily. Twice the sergeant drank half a bottle on our trip. He also offered it to me and the other guy, but we both refused to drink any. I didn't know the effects of speed and I wasn't going to find out by experimenting. I don't remember any striking changes in the sergeant's demeanor or physical abilities after ingesting the Obisitol, but I wasn't looking for anything in particular either.

When we returned to Cha Rang Valley, we unloaded all of the supplies and were dismissed from our detail. Since the school didn't begin for me until the next day, I had the rest of the day to do what I wanted. Cha Rang was like a mini Army post with all the amenities except everything was in tents: the mess hall, the PX and all of the quarters for the troops attending school. The tents were surrounded by fifty-five gallon drums filled with dirt for protection from a mortar attack. Thankfully, we did not experience any mortar attacks while I was there. However, when I was off duty and after chow, I went to look at a helicopter shell used as a prop for the school to practice unloading during combat assaults. While standing next to the helicopter a shot rang out and the dirt flew up about three foot from me. I didn't know what to think about it because I didn't really know what had happened. People came running from all over the school compound. I didn't even know enough to duck or take cover. The first full day I was at jungle school, and a sniper took a shot at me. That event created a flurry of activity around the school compound. I was questioned by many senior NCOs. What was I doing, where I was standing? Did I see where the shot came from? I could answer all but where the shot came from; I did not see it coming at all. I did not react to it because I did not realize a sniper fired the shot. Cha Rang spent the rest of the night on high alert because of the incident. I was lucky in two ways because the sniper missed me and I did not have to participate in the alert because my jungle training started the next day.

Once jungle school started, there were no more details or CQ duty. It was like a two week advanced infantry course with similar training like Advanced Infantry Training back in the states. The cadre, the jungle school instructors, went into more details but the classes were shorter because we only had two weeks. We went back through weapons training, grenade throwing, radio classes, getting off helicopters and securing the LZ. We went on patrols outside of the jungle school perimeter and suffered through another gas chamber with gas masks on and off. Everything in the training was more advanced with detail except for radio training. The radio training just covered the basics because not everyone carries a radio. There were medical training classes for gunshot wounds. There was also instruction about venereal diseases and how to prevent them. The instructors emphasized that the whorehouses outside the LZ's or air bases were off limits because there was no medical staff inspecting the women working in those houses. However, there were some next to the bases that were tolerated and were inspected monthly by medical staff from the base and we needed to learn the difference because the off limits houses could land us in jail or would demand disciplinary action.

After the training was over we were told in which organization with the 173rd Airborne we would spend the remainder of our time in country. I was selected to go to Alpha Company 3rd Battalion, 503rd Infantry, 173rd Airborne Brigade Separate at Landing Zone Uplift in Phu My district Binh Dinh Provence. I did not realize it at the time but that was probably the best assignment I could have gotten. I left jungle training at Cha Rang Valley on a truck headed for LZ Uplift. I wasn't happy or sad. This was my first assignment that wasn't a training assignment and I just didn't know what to expect.

CHAPTER 4

Assigned to A Company 3rd Battalion, 503 Infantry, 173rd Airborne Brigade

The truck ride from Cha Rang Valley to Landing Zone Uplift was uneventful. I do not remember much about the trip to my next assignment, A Company 3rd Battalion, 503 Infantry, 173rd Airborne Brigade. LZ Uplift, located on Highway 1, was the base camp for the 1st and 3rd Battalions working in II Corp's Binh Dinh Provence, Phu Mi District of northern South Vietnam. The helicopter-landing pad, a large black tar area in the middle of the base camp, separated the two battalions. The 1st Battalion area was fully operational and all housing was complete, including a big building called "The Steakhouse", a place where we could buy beer or soda, sit at tables like at a bar, steaks were sold for a dollar fifty with a plate of beans. There was also a church and the movie house complete with stage and a tin roof covering the bench seats. The 3rd Battalion was new to Uplift and the engineers were building parts of the 3rd Battalion area when I arrived. The only permanent buildings were the orderly rooms, supply rooms and a single building for the company platoon leaders located behind each supply room. The rest of the area was a tent city except for the large mess hall where everyone in 3rd Battalion ate. I reported to the first sergeant at the orderly room with another guy new to the 3rd Bat, PFC Thomas Simmons. We didn't know much about each other except we went through jungle school at the same time and we were both assigned to A Company. The first sergeant welcomed us and told us to report to the second platoon leader, Lt. Chapla, located in the building behind the supply room for our duty assignment. The lieutenant wasn't hard to find, and again he welcomed us to A Company 2nd platoon, or "Mike Platoon" as he referred to it. The significance of that was where the company had been operating before, each platoon had a designation, the 2nd was "Mike" and that was the radio call sign of the platoon leader. That would soon be changed, as I found out the hard way.

The lieutenant and the platoon sergeant sat together on the lieutenant's cot and sized up Simmons and me. As he looked at me he said, "You are a pretty good sized boy and I am looking for a radio operator. I think you will be my RTO."

"I wouldn't do that sir," was my reply.

"Why do you say that?" he questioned.

"Because I don't know anything about the radio," I answered.

He smiled and said, "Awe come on Private. You don't expect me to believe that do you?'

"It's true, sir, I missed the training in AIT and had to cheat on the proficiency test to pass the course", I pleaded.

"I've heard all those excuses before and I'm not buying them. What is the real reason you don't want to carry the radio?" he questioned.

I explained, "Sir, I got called out of the radio class at Ft. Polk because I had a finance problem. We had just removed the battery cover when a runner came in and told the instructor I needed to report to the finance officer ASAP. His last instructions to me were not to come back until I had the problem corrected. By the time I got back, the class was just putting the cover on the battery. I missed the whole training class on the radio."

"Well, I only have two openings, one for RTO and the other is for the M-60 machine gun," came his response.

"I'll take the machine gun. I fired expert on it!" I replied, thinking I had a choice.

Then with some emphasis, the lieutenant said, "No, I'm going to have you carry my radio. Simmons looks like he can handle the gun." And that ended the discussion.

The lieutenant then gave Simmons and me a little bit of history about the 2nd platoon and described our current job at Uplift. We were the Brigade reaction force which meant when others were in contact we went to reinforce them. We were also reaction force for the Americal Division, working close by, and the First Calvary, also in the area. A Company was always on two hour notice because we were the reaction force, but it meant we could not be more than two hours from Uplift unless on ambush or had a pass signed by the first sergeant. The lieutenant told us for the time being we were restricted to the company area because we were new and the squad leaders did not know us. The bad news about being restricted to the company area meant no movies and no steak house as long as we were restricted. The platoon sergeant took us to a tent with cots where the platoon was temporarily housed until hootches, the buildings to house the personnel in the rear, were built to accommodate us. There we met the squad leaders, fire team leaders, medic and the rest of second platoon except those on guard or ambush. They had names for us. Cherry Boy, was the one I didn't like. I knew I was a new guy and had to take a little ribbing, but there was a limit I would tolerate. Not everyone in the platoon played the name game. Some guys were helpful and genuinely interested in who we were and where we were from. The squad leader from Illinois called me "Home Boy" and was peeved that he didn't get me for his Radio Telephone Operator. Since I was platoon RTO, I was elevated above the squad level, which was a plus for me. Most RTOs start at the squad level and after carrying the radio for some time gaining experience, later move up to platoon RTO. The platoon RTO was responsible for making sure, all codes were distributed to the Squad RTOs and that the RTOs followed radio procedures. Of course, at that time I did not know any radio procedures or my responsibilities as platoon RTO. There was a down side too; life expectancy for RTOs was thirty days.

Later that evening, one of the sergeants in the 2nd Platoon, a squad leader named Sisson, approached me about attending the movie that was being shown over at the 1st Bat Area, 3rd Bat did not have a theater yet. After refusing several times, I finally agreed with the assurance that no one would know and we wouldn't get into trouble for leaving the restricted area. "After all", Sisson would say, "What are they going to do, send you to Viet Nam?"

The movie was one I was not familiar with, but was loaded with action and music. It was titled "Time Is Tight", as was the title theme by Booker T and the MG's.

The theater was a pole supported tin roof over a concrete floor with wooden bench seats. Not a high-class joint, but the movies were uninterrupted by the heavy monsoon rains when they occurred September through May. Not typical for monsoon season, this particular late September night was clear and hot with no wind or rain. Sergeant Sisson and I stood outside on the north side and watched while leaning on the heavy railroad tie sized horizontals that supported the structure until we spotted some seats near the aisle in the middle section of the theater. We had to duck under the supports on the way in to the seats because they were above waist high on us because of the concrete floor inside. We were only seated a short time when just outside to the north where we had just come from, a mortar round hit and shrapnel flew into and up through the roof of the theater. I remember seeing stars through the holes it made in the tin roof. Some of the guys that were closer to where the first round hit may have been wounded by some of the flying metal shards. This of course put everyone into a panic and the theater in complete disorder. Everyone started moving to the south away from the explosion to get out of the theater. A few sought refuge by diving to the floor and trying to crawl under the benches. I saw right away that leaving my feet for any reason would be a mistake. Everyone that stayed on their feet getting out trampled those that sought cover by getting down on the floor or tried to take cover under the benches.

By the time I made the horizontal supports on the south side of the structure, at least one more mortar round had exploded and I had unavoidably stepped on several guys on the floor. Everyone still on their feet including myself was literally being shoved to the south side of the theater. I was able to get one hand on the waist high cross member, leap over the heavy beam and get out. Some guys less fortunate than I were being mashed against the cross beams with no way for them to get over or under the beam. They were literally being crushed by the moving crowd.

Once outside I was on my own, I had long since lost track of Sisson right after the initial blast. I ran with everyone else to the east of the theater, watching rounds go off around me. At that point, someone was yelling with an authoritative voice, "Don't run. Get down. Don't run,". So that's what I did. I dove to the ground, my head buried in my arms, as everyone else continued to run or got down too. After the first round, six or seven more mortar rounds landed and the barrage was over.

As the dust settled, I saw something shiny on the ground inside my arms. I picked up a shiny cigarette lighter and then noticed three guys who had found a foxhole within about 4 feet of where I was lying. Standing up, I asked them if they had lost a lighter. After each had responded "No", one said with a sense of urgency, "Hey, get out of here, I think there is someone underneath me!" As the three sprang from the hole, they began to help a very heavy muscular individual, about 6' 4" from a face down prone position in the bottom of the hole. He needed a lot of help to get out of the hole. As the three men pulled him up and began brushing him off, they asked, "Are you OK?"

"Yeah", was the reply, while moaning and stretching. "But I don't know about the guy underneath me!"

Horrified by that remark, the three who had been crouching in the hole with only their heads above ground went back with a sense of urgency to extract a very limp, dusty individual who was semi-conscious when retrieved from the bottom of the hole. A cry for "Medic" went out and someone responded to help. They were carrying the guy from the bottom, hurting but conscious, to the aide station. It was then that I went back to the Company Area. Not until the next day did, I see the brand new Ronson lighter I found had the name "Bailey" unprofessionally scratched into both sides.

A couple of months later, I did see a guy by the name of Bailey from another company, but by then I had become attached to the lighter, as had some of my buddies. They would ask for a light for a cigarette or heat tab at chow time, "Muss, you got Bailey?" The lighter has remained a favorite conversation piece since I acquired it and even though it shows the wear from jungle use, it is still working today and the name "Bailey", remains visible on both sides. I have never replaced the wick, only flints, in the forty plus years I have owned it.

After my terrible beginning on the first night with A Company, and surviving my first mortar attack, I worked on details with the rest of second platoon, from helping the engineers build hootches, the buildings to house the personnel in the rear, to tearing down some old buildings that outlived their usefulness. I didn't have much time to think about my job as platoon RTO or being part of the reaction force to help other units in combat. The good thing about being reaction force was we were always in the rear area waiting to react to someone in combat. The bad news was we pulled many details because we were in the rear area. Soon that would change for all of Alpha Company and I would get my chance on the radio.

CHAPTER 5

Work Details and Making Friends at Uplift

The work details at Uplift were endless, from helping the engineers with buildings to guard duty along the perimeter. Each company had assigned bunkers manned twenty-four hours a day. Drawing that detail meant the whole day on the bunker until the next day when another four-man relief took over. We had details to police/pick up endless debris on the bunker line. In early October, we got some new guys in the company; Krailey, Sienkiewicz and Knox were among them. Krailey got the RTO, radiotelephone operator's job with Mangilardi, the squad leader from Illinois. Sienkiewicz took over the machine gun for Simmons. What luck. On the gun for less than a month. That was a rarity! On cleanup detail for the bunker line, we were explaining to Knox why we were finding Claymore mines with the backs broken off, a trick the troops on the bunkers used to heat their C rations or LRRPs while on guard. C-rations were the canned meals that came boxed as a complete meal and with heat; some were not bad at all. LLRPs were the freeze-dried meals designed for long-range patrols and when mixed with hot water was quite good.

Knox didn't seem to know that the C-4 plastic that charged the Claymore was not only explosive but also flammable and could be lit with a match. Knox wanted to try it out so he lit off a piece. He did not let us finish explaining that the C-4 burned very hot so only a small piece was needed to heat a whole canteen cup and once lit needed to be protected from any type of pressure, such as dropping, stepping on it or it would explode. Once he lit the C-4 that covered the entire back of the Claymore, it burnt his hand so he dropped it as the rest of us yelled and dove away from him and the flaming C-4. As we started to recover, he went to stomp on it to put out the fire. We all yelled "NO" and thankfully, he unwittingly stopped because he did not realize stomping it would set it off either killing Knox or injuring him severely. The Claymore still contained the 700 large BBs imbedded in the resin in front of the C-4. The Claymore mine was anti-personnel mine and was very devastating when set off. Hell, we were all marveling about it not going off when Knox dropped it. Luck was with us and Knox learned a valuable lesson on C-4 characteristics.

Another relentless detail was guard duty. There was no way to escape it, and everyone had to do it one time or another. I got my first indoctrination to marijuana on guard duty one night on the bunker line. The "heads" in the company would meet on the bunker and roll joints using filtered paper shells made by removing the tobacco from a regular cigarette by rolling them between your fingers and replacing it with marijuana. Then the heads put the joints back into the cigarette pack and they looked like cigarettes. It was a clever scheme to hide the marijuana from anyone looking to bust the heavy users. I kept my distance from most of the heads because I didn't smoke pot or use drugs of any type. However, I did roll tobacco out of the cigarette shells for them that one night on guard. I had to be on the bunker and it was something to do.

Monsoon season was just beginning so many of our details were rained out. When that happened we would spend time at the steakhouse where I found out you could buy a good steak with a plate of beans for a dollar fifty. The steaks served at the steakhouse came by way of the mess hall. I don't know how it worked exactly but steaks were never served in the general mess. The senior NCOs that ran the steakhouse had some deal with the mess sergeant, so if we wanted steak we bought it at the steakhouse. Every now and then, the company would have a cookout with steaks and all the trimmings. The company would trade a captured weapon for a case of steaks at the Air Force Base at Phu Cat. They were always happy to see us show up with NVA/VC weapons.

We played cards a lot in the steakhouse during the rainouts; and the guys in the platoon introduced me to a new game called "Bid Whist". It was played with partners so there had to be four people that knew how to play or at least willing to learn quickly. I was able to pick it up very quickly and that helped me get to know some more second platoon members. These guys became good friends and were easy to get along with, like Borchard, a young friendly sort that always had a joke to tell and would lend a hand when needed. Delgado and Colon were close friends themselves and always partnered when playing bid whist. I learned some Spanish playing bid whist against them, "ta ta yo tengo grande", means, "I have the big one", which means the highest trump card in bid whist. Delgado was late to the card game that day and Colon was my partner.

When the cards were dealt Colon started to sing," Ta ta, yo tengo grande."

Delgado yelled to him, "Hey, cut that shit out!"

Delgado was a fire-team leader who eventually became a squad leader. Colon, a point man and a good one, also eventually became a squad leader. Point men walked out in front of the platoon or company leading them to their objective. The "slack man" walked behind the point man and was his backup. Both men had to read a map and compass, watch for signs or markers of NVA/VC activity and had no fear being out in front. Most contact with the enemy was initiated at the point location.

One night in the hootch, our designated barracks, Doc Smith, the medic and Sgt. Thomas, a squad leader, were playing with a Bowie knife sticking it in the floorboard isle between the cots. It was very late or early in the morning and we asked them to stop because they were keeping the rest of the platoon awake. They continued the game until one of them bounced the knife off the floor into Borchard's leg right above the knee waking him from a sound sleep. The tone then turned from "Awe shut up, we know what we are doing," to begging not to be turned in for their foolhardy actions.

It is funny how things work out when least expected. Everyone in second platoon was looking for batteries, flashlight batteries, C batteries for radios or tape players. The requests for batteries were made at the A company's supply room but none were available. The supply room across the street from the orderly room was our only source unless someone got a pass to go to the Post Exchange (PX) at Phu Cat or Qui Nhon. Passes were given out sparingly because we were the brigade reaction force and needed to remain close to Uplift at all times. A trip to the PX took all day.

The second platoon got their usual details for the day, mine just happened to be at S4 or battalion supply. I spent most of the morning ripping wet OD (olive drab green) boxer drawers on a 2x4 with 16-penny nails driven in it so the S4 supply sergeant could write them off the books as damaged. No one going to the field wore underwear of ant type. The boxers would get wet, stay wet and chafe you severely if worn into the jungle environment or the rice paddies of the lowlands. I hadn't had the chance to find out what the underwear would do. I was still wearing mine and was bitching about the government wasting money by destroying perfectly good underwear. I even wrote a letter home to my dad complaining about the waste. I mean this was a whole Army storage connex 6'x 6' x 6' filled with OD green boxer underwear. Once I completed that task, I went to chow and came back to a new detail in the afternoon. I was moving different sized boxes from one connex to another. I didn't expend a lot of brainpower on either detail, but somebody had to do it. After moving what seemed countless numbers of boxes, I asked the sergeant "What is in these boxes anyway? They are awful heavy, even the small boxes."

"Batteries, "he replied.

"What kind of batteries? These boxes are all different sizes," I asked.

"Batteries for flashlights, the small boxes are 9 volt batteries, these here are C batteries," he responded, pointing out the case of C batteries.

My mind went into a whirr thinking about how I was going to get these boxes of batteries back to the barracks. When the sergeant wasn't looking, I started stuffing the waistband of my fatigues with all different types of battery boxes. I went from a trim 170 pounds to what looked like 250 pounds in just a minute or so. The sergeant in charge was at the opposite end of the compound and I yelled to him asking if I could take a break. Without looking my direction, he granted my request. Our barracks was just a short distance away and I scurried to leave the fenced compound of S4 and headed in the direction of the barracks. When I arrived I opened my fatigue shirt, removed a box of flashlight batteries and said aloud," Look what I found!" What a mistake, I was tackled instantly and relieved of all the batteries I smuggled from S4! Every off duty platoon member in the barracks piled on me at the same time. I didn't even get to keep any C size batteries for my tape player; I had to steal another case of them when I returned to the S4 compound before my detail ended. I never found out why the supply rooms did not have a supply of batteries with the quantities being stored at S4.

If we weren't on details or at the steakhouse, we used the time to learn about the weapons. I remember a session I had with Sienkiewicz and the M-60 machine gun. We came to Alpha Company about the same time and he seemed to know a lot about the machine gun. We practiced the things we were taught in training, things like checking for short rounds, clearing the gun by setting the barrel on the toe of your boot so as not to plug the gun with dirt or mud. We practiced cleaning which was more like cleaning the gun, not really practicing. There was a gas operating plug that forced the bolt back so another round would chamber, essentially cocking the gun after each round fired. The hollow plug had a small hole in one end of it to allow gas from expended rounds to enter and drive the plug to move the bolt. If the person cleaning the gun turned the plug in the opposite direction, the gun would fire one time only making the machine gun a rifle. If the gun was cleaned at night, the hole in the plug had to be located by feeling it so the plug was inserted in the right direction. All the things we practiced were good to know before we went into combat. We practiced everything but radio procedures. No one was interested in carrying the radio and there was not much interest in talking about it. Some procedures were difficult and complex and the grunts not carrying the radio left them to the RTOs, radiotelephone operators.

Ed Sienkiewicz became a good friend along with Bill Borchard and Pete Krailey; we hung out, played cards and got to know each other. We shared who we were with each other; Borchard was the son of a farmer from Iowa and always kept us laughing. He was young, but smart beyond his years, a good soldier and was always willing to help and do more than his share. He was short and someone tagged him with the nickname, Walking Poncho, because that is what he looked like if he were wearing his poncho. Ed was a tuff talking red headed kid from New York City; he worked, as a doorman in a nightclub checking IDs, the drinking age in New York was eighteen at that time. He had a noticeable scar that split his upper lip; those of us close to him teased him about being a hair lip, which he vehemently denied, claiming he got it in a car accident after going through the windshield. The latter was true, but we had fun upsetting him and watching him flail around until he realized we were ribbing him. He was stabbed with an ice pick in two separate robberies in New York City. The first time it happened, he collapsed on the street and his assailant kicked the crap out of him taking his watch and wallet, leaving him for dead. The second time he was stabbed, he said he had the same eerie feeling when the ice pick went in but he stayed on his feet and ran away keeping all of his valuables. Pete Krailey was from Alexandria, LA where his parents ran an Imperial 400 Motel. I stayed at that motel on my first three-day pass from Ft. Polk during basic training. I told him if I would have known he owned it we might have rented two rooms for five of us to stay. We talked about the theater downtown on Main Street, where we saw a movie and Herbie K's Restaurant, where I sang for my supper on the same three-day pass.

All of us in the second platoon had a very good loyal friend; his name was "Lifer". Lifer was a Vietnamese dog, a mixed breed and looked like a small German shepherd. He was brown and black and had a black face. He instantly liked anyone in the second platoon. One of the guys, Beaver was his name, claimed him as his dog and wanted to try to take him home when he DEROSd back to the states. DEROS is the date of return from overseas. Because dogs in Vietnam were susceptible to a very contagious heartworm that quarantined all dogs even the dogs that came over from the states, getting Lifer out of country was never going to happen. Lifer used to go everywhere with us as long as we went in trucks. He tried to go with us when we would go to the beach in a Chinook, but we would throw him out after we took off. It was the only way of keeping him from getting back on. The strangest thing about Lifer was he would be at the helicopter pad whenever we returned no matter how long we were gone. After we would throw him from the choppers, he would spend his days at the orderly room keeping the clerks and First Sergeant company. Strangely, on the day we would return to Uplift he would go to the helicopter pad and wait there until we landed. As we got off the helicopter, he would run to greet all of us and we were just as happy to see him. When we would take Lifer with us by truck, he just mingled with all of us and enjoyed our attentiveness.

One time we took Lifer with us while we were guarding the engineers during a road-building project. The engineers were drawing sniper fire while checking the roadbed for land mines. We walked in front of the minesweepers to protect them from snipers. It didn't make any sense to us either, who was protecting us from snipers. During a break, the Coke girls from a nearby village came out to sell us ice cold Coca Cola. Even though the Cokes were fifty cents each and we could get them at the steakhouse back at Uplift for ten cents, we gladly bought them from the friendly local girls. One of the girls brought her little brother with her, which was her mistake. Lifer did not like Vietnamese people, especially males or kids. The youngster was acting very suspicious and Lifer was keeping an eye on him, which he was more than aware of because he didn't take his eyes off Lifer either. After one of the Coke sales, the kid picked up something of ours and took off running. Beaver shouted, "get him" to Lifer who immediately responded chasing down the small thief and knocking him off his feet. We recovered the stolen item while the kid and his sister yelled obscenities at us but we figured he got what he deserved. We never saw any Coke girls after that little fracas, but Lifer proved his worth and friendship.

A little while after the road incident, Lifer was shot by the Officer of the Day (OD) at Uplift because he appeared to be foaming at the mouth. The real story was Lifer attacked a Vietnamese kid that Delta company kept like a mascot at Uplift. He was always smarting off to everyone because the First Sergeant of Delta company wouldn't let anything happen to him. He even wore US fatigues and boots furnished to him by Delta company. After chow the day before Lifer was shot, the kid was playing keep away with Lifer holding a piece of chicken just out of reach and making Lifer jump for it. When lifer knocked him down and took the chicken, he got mad and ran to his friend in Delta company complaining, crying and claiming he had been bit. Supposedly, some calls were made but after checking Lifer's demeanor, they could only continue to complain nothing was done about it. The next morning after Beaver gave Lifer a bowl of milk, the OD from Delta shot him while Lifer was on his usual roam through Uplift, because he seemed to be foaming at the mouth. He survived for three days but eventually ripped out his stitches and succumbed to his wound. He was a great dog and a good friend to all of us in second platoon.

I kept my distance from the guys that called me "cherry." It was a term used by some of the more experienced platoon members to identify the new guys in the platoon. I guess it was the way the guys said "cherry" that irritated me, almost like they were talking to some brainless individual. A medic assigned to second platoon was the most vocal in my opinion. He went home shortly after I arrived and I was happy about that. I did get a chance to observe him in the field but he never impressed me as a very caring medic. Another guy that hung out with Doc in the rear was George Taylor. He also called me "cherry", but he didn't seem as serious as the others when he said it. Normally Taylor was quiet and kept to himself. I learned to tolerate his verbal attacks and eventually got to know him. He was one of second platoon's point men, also as I would find out, a good one. Point men like Taylor and Colon got a lot of respect in the company and they deserved every bit of it. Another point man second platoon had was Wiley. He had a tattoo on his arm of Wiley Coyote. Simmons moved from the gun to walking slack for Wiley until Wiley fell on one of our operations hitting a sharp rock with his hand and almost severing a finger. He went home because of that finger injury. Right after Wiley got hurt, Simmons went home on some kind of emergency leave.

Sgt. Sam Mangilardi, the squad leader that called me "Home Boy", proved to be a great ally and was a good friend to me. He called my parents when he went home to let them know I was doing OK. Sam got a pass one day right after I got to the company and asked me if I needed anything from the PX. I gave him twenty bucks and told him to buy me a watch. At the time, I didn't own one. When he returned he gave me an automatic 17 jewel Seiko with date only in the face and two fifty in change. What a deal! That watch was very important to me and never lost a minute. I only took it off occasionally to use it for guard duty when we were in the field. Sometimes when it was returned to me after guard duty, I would find the date changed. That meant someone on guard had tried to move the time up to shorten his guard. I knew that because the stem had two set positions when pulled out to the first click position, the date could be changed. The time was changed by pulling the stem out to the second click position. Everyone was familiar with how most watches worked, pull the stem out until it clicks and reset the time. My watch was different and a lot of people didn't like it when my watch was used for guard. They didn't know the secret to change the time and I didn't tell anyone either.

The second platoon, along with Alpha Company had many opportunities to exercise their skills in the field while maintaining the reaction force status in the rear at LZ Uplift. The members of second platoon all eventually accepted me and began to trust me. In turn, I got to know them all very well. They were my friends and later when I traveled with the other platoons of Alpha Company and got to know their platoon members, the second platoon remained a sanctuary for me.

CHAPTER 6

My first Combat Assault with the Radio

Shortly after I talked to Lt. Chapla and SSgt. Andersen about my job as platoon radio operator, the lieutenant was returning to the states for emergency leave. His father was dying, and he was away arranging for going home, so the job of platoon leader fell to SSgt. Andersen. Even though he was sitting on the cot next to Lt. Chapla and heard my story about the radio. He had no idea about the consequences he and I were about to suffer as a result of my inadequacies.

The word came down that the company was going to make a Combat Assault (CA) to be a blocking force for the Americal Division making a sweep in their Area of Operation (AO). As we flew in the UH1 Huey helicopters I was a ball of nerves, scared to death and it must have shown on my face. We were the first helicopter to take off from Uplift. I was riding on the floor in the center of the bird, my rucksack with radio strapped to my back not knowing what to expect. Delgado was riding in the door but turned to look at me. My usual smile had given way to a strained worried look. When he saw my face, he tapped me on the knee and said in a loud voice so I could hear him over the sound of the chopper, "Don't worry, everything is going to be OK." He read me like a book; I was so scared, I'm lucky I never passed out. Then suddenly we were making a fast decent, the gunners on the M-60 machine guns located in each door opened up strafing the landing zone with a hail of bullets and really putting me in a strain.

We landed in a low grassy area with scrub trees on the slopes on both sides. All six choppers were on the LZ at the same time; we exited our bird and moved to the front setting up security for the others coming in behind us. The CO had landed with another platoon on the hills to our right. Andersen selected a point element and went over our blocking location on his map with the squad leader of that element. When we started to move out uphill to our left, Andersen said to me, "Stay with me." I did, sticking to him like glue. We topped the hill and moved along the ridge to our objective, which was about 500 meters from the LZ. Our movement was steady and meticulous, nobody was in a hurry, and we had been on the ground for about two hours. Andersen was getting the squads in position, telling the squad leaders where he wanted them to set up and be on line for the blocking force.

Suddenly a runner from another location came up to our position. "What's wrong with your radio sergeant? The CO has been trying to reach you for over two hours!" he asked.

Andersen turned to me, his eyes were wide, "You weren't kidding about the radio were you?"

I shook my head, but before I could say anything, the runner chimed in, "The CO wants to see you at his location right away, follow me."

As we were moving toward the CO's location, Andersen was advising me to let him do all the talking if anything was mentioned about the radio communications. I was perfectly willing to follow that order. As far as I knew, I was supposed to be carrying the radio for the platoon leader and that was all.

When we arrived at Captain Grimm's location, his attention immediately focused on me.

"Does that radio work private?" he asked

"Yes sir!" I answered.

"Why didn't you answer it when I called?" he asked

I responded, "I didn't realize you were calling me sir. I don't know anything about the radio"

"What do you mean you don't know anything about the radio private?" he emphatically shouted back.

At this point, Andersen tried to intervene in my defense, "Sir it's not his fault, he...."

The CO cut him off, "Quiet Sergeant, I'm not done with him yet, YOU are next!"

The CO began poking my chest with his index finger as he emphasized, "You will work and do whatever it takes private until you learn everything there is to know about the radio. I don't mean for you to take your time learning, you will become proficient on the radio before you leave Uplift the next time. If that doesn't happen, you will be a PFC for as long as you are in Alpha Company. Is that clear, private?"

"Yes sir!" I replied.

The CO then turned to SSgt. Andersen tearing into him with no mercy. My ears were still ringing so I did not make out a lot of the conversation, but like me, Andersen's responses were, "Yes sir".

On our way back to the second platoon's location, Andersen and I didn't talk about the ordeal we just went through. I think we were both just happy we came away with our heads on. From that point on while we were in the field, I started listening to the conversations on the radio trying to pick up some of the jargon so I could at least sound like I knew something about the radio when I had to talk.

We got through the operation without incident and saw no enemy or engaged anyone in our blocking force. The Idea for the blocking force was to stretch out in a line while another element pushed the enemy toward the blocking force, which would be cutting off their retreat. It was a good plan but it didn't always work. We secured an extraction PZ or Pickup Zone and helicoptered back to Uplift returning to our role of reaction force.

I took my ass chewing to heart and followed the CO's instructions. I talked to my buddy, Borchard and asked him for advice about who could help me. Borchard told me to talk to "Scotty", the company's battalion radio operator in the CP. Essentially Scott, was Captain Grimm's RTO carrying the radio on the battalion frequency traveling with the Command Position or CP. I never knew his first name; everyone just called him "Scotty". To me he seemed like a real cut up, never taking anything serious. He acted like the company clown all the time except when I came to him for help on the radio. There was a serious side to Scotty and I found it with Borchard's help. He became a mentor, my professor of radio and he never left anything out. Scotty told me about using the plastic bag the two-pound radio battery came encased in for a cover on the handset, making it waterproof during monsoon season. The open end of the bag tightly closed off with a rubber band wrapped around the coiled cord that ran to the radio. Scotty also told me; always carry a wooden pencil with an eraser. The graphite pencil would help the eraser keep the contacts clean. I studied the CAT Codes, the group of three letters used to replace words or phrases of a sentence were considered high security codes and required signatures when received. The CAT codes were changed at least every three months if not before because of a possible breech or loss of the codes. I learned the call signs and their meaning. The old method for identifying the CO and platoon leaders, such as second platoon leader was Mike, so Lt. Chapla was Mike, but he always stayed Mike and never changed. The new method identified not only the platoon leader but also the platoon sergeant and the squad leaders with a call sign and these changed every operation or if there was a breech in the security. Every time we left Uplift, the platoon leader in each of the three platoons had their own call sign. The radio operator was designated by adding one more word of the phonetic alphabet. For instance, SSgt. Andersen, the platoon leader for second platoon was Papa and the RTO would be Papa November. In turn, each of the squad leaders in the second platoon would also have their own phonetic call sign and for the RTO, and the squad leader's call sign would be followed by November. That way everyone knew whom he was talking to at any given time. It was a little burdensome for the RTOs because we had to learn all the call signs in the platoon and I had to learn all the call signs in the company.

We covered proper radio procedures, making sure the conversations on the radio were brief and to the point and some terms like "over" and "out". Those terms were never used together like the shows on TV use them. Over was a term used when the conversation from your end was complete but the person on the other end might have more to contribute so you were turning the airwaves over to him. He may come back with more information or just end the conversation with, "roger out", letting you know he had nothing further to say. When speaking to a superior, the proper procedure was to always return the conversation to him with "over", allowing him to end the transmission when he was done with "out". I remember one time when Scotty was not with us in the field for one reason or another, Robles was taking his calls on the radio. Robles was the Company RTO at that time and that made it easy to fill in for Scott. A call came in for the CO from the Battalion Commander, Colonel Brutus Lowery. The CO's call sign was

Tango, the RTO was Mike and Lowery's call sign was always "the Rock". The conversation went something like this.

"Tango Mike, this is the Rock, over." Lowery came onto the airwaves with his deep baritone unmistakable voice.

"This is Tango Mike, go" Robles replied.

"Tango Mike, this is the Rock, go is not a proper radio term. Use correct radio procedure on this net. Let me talk to Tango, over."

"This is Tango Mike; Tango is not at my location at this time, out." Robles replied.

"Tango Mike, this is the Rock, over."

"This is Tango Mike, go" was Robles response.

"Tango Mike, this is the Rock, you do not give me an out, I am the Rock, over." Lowery admonished.

Robles came back with, "This is Tango Mike, roger out."

There was silence on the radio, I am sure Lowery was fuming and very frustrated. It was hilarious to those who heard it, but I am sure someone paid for the word exchange when we returned to the rear. Colonel Lowery was never known to be sympathetic.

Scotty continued to educate me every spare minute we had in the rear, testing my progress as we went along until he felt I was a capable RTO. When that day arrived, he just told me to listen to all the conversations on the radio and I would pick up or be reminded of the things I needed to know. My training complete, I was feeling almost comfortable carrying the radio. The only thing uncomfortable about it was the PRC-25 radio weighed twenty five pounds with the battery and I was required to carry an extra battery which made my ruck sack twenty seven pounds heavier, sometimes I struggled to keep up in the treks through the rice paddies, mountains and jungles of South Vietnam.

The life expectancy of an RTO in Nam was thirty days. We were primary targets in firefights before the officers in most instances. If the radio communication was eliminated, help or firepower was eliminated also. I never thought too much about my mortality rate but I did some things to protect myself. Look at photos of RTOs in Vietnam. The first thing you notice is the antenna sticking out of the top and the radio is on the top of the rucksack. I always carried my radio below my ruck and tucked the antenna in under the top flap on my rucksack thus hiding it from prominent view. I could always slide it out if I was having trouble sending or receiving transmissions. I do not remember anytime that positioning of the antenna being a problem communicating.

I carried the radio for a total of ten and a half months, first as platoon radio operator for second platoon and eventually graduating to battalion radio operator for the commanding officer of Alpha Company. To me, it was the best job I could have ever hoped to have. Because of my position, I knew everything that was happening in the company and the battalion. Actually, I did not realize how much more I knew than the regular riflemen in the company until I attended a reunion with the first platoon members in 1985. There were eighteen members in attendance and someone asked the roomful if anyone remembered what we were doing on this mission or that mission. In the whole room, I was the only one who knew what the mission was and what we were trying to accomplish. The details I recalled enlightened the entire group. For that reason they named me the company historian. Even today when we get together and start telling stories, I will mention some event that reminds one of the platoon members present of the details of some encounter. At this point, I can only hope my memory remains intact for future get togethers.

CHAPTER 7

Assessing a B-52 Bomb Strike Way up North

Before Lt. Chapla left on emergency leave, he made one last CA, combat assault, with second platoon. Battalion was sending us on a B-52 bomb strike assessment. It might have been mandatory for him to go because the mission was so far from our base camp; our CO, commanding officer, did not want the platoon led by only a platoon sergeant. We went eighty-five miles north and west of Uplift to the farthest reach of our Area of Operation (AO). It was so far out; the battalion had to insert a radio relay station between the area of the bomb strike and our base camp, LZ Uplift so we would have communication with the rear.

Many things were different on this CA because of the distance out of Uplift. The area was dense vegetation including tall trees with some mountains and a river. About a week before we went, a group from battalion S-2 or S-3 flew recon missions in hueys to check the area for landing zones large enough for a Chinook helicopter. The Chinook helicopter had two huge rotors, one above the pilot's compartment and one above the tail of the aircraft. Battalion wanted to get as many of us on the ground at one time as they could; the Chinook carried thirty-three and the crew of six. Battalion felt that was a comfortable number, enough to get the job done. The day before we left LZ Uplift, the scouts finally identified an LZ large enough for the Chinook to make a safe landing. The bomb assessment was a go.

Because of the choice of helicopter, the unusual circumstances with no security on the LZ and the distance away from our base camp, they sent a gunship escort with us. A gunship escort had two or three UH-1 Huey helicopters fitted with rocket pods mounted on the sides of the huey and or mini guns in the doors instead of the M-60 machine guns normally mounted in each door. A mini gun was a devastating weapon; it had eight barrels in a circular mounted configuration and fired around six thousand rounds a minute. Sometimes one of the hueys would be scratched from an escort and a Cobra gunship would replace it. The Cobra was a sleek helicopter only three feet wide with the pilot and copilot sitting one behind the other. It had vision actuated site controls in the flight crew's helmets for the mini gun mounted in the lower front and many rockets for firepower. The battalion decision makers sent only the Hueys with us on our mission.

We left Uplift at first light because we needed to get on the ground, make the bomb assessment, report any damage and enemy body count, and then be extracted back to Uplift before nightfall. Even if everything went perfect, it would be a major accomplishment for us to pull it off all in one day. Because of the area and small size of our element, it was mandatory to complete it in one day. Captain Grimm did not want one of his platoons caught out in unfamiliar terrain with little support for more than one day. The area was supposed to be a heavy NVA traffic area; the fact they were able to schedule a B-52 strike there was proof enough of enemy activity in the area.

When the Chinook slowed the first time over our landing zone, we all got ready to exit but the crew chief on the chopper told us to hold tight - we were not landing. The key to making a CA successful was a quick landing and a fast exit after landing especially with a bird as big as the Chinook. We attempted neither the first time over the LZ. Many times that kind of delay would be reason enough to abort the mission entirely. The air was heavy and the sky overcast so we climbed to get more altitude while the crew chief explained we were not going to land we had to jump into the LZ while the pilot held the aircraft in a stable position above it, as stable as he was able to anyway. We started down into the LZ. The trees on the edges of the LZ towered about seventy-five feet. After lowering the tailgate, the crew chief ran down the center of the aircraft barking orders, "Don't jump if the bird is on the way up. Slide as far down the tailgate as you can, then drop off only when we are descending". That would make the "jump" lower and closer to the ground. With the rotors setting on the tops of the nearest trees, the pilot hovered between twelve and thirty feet above the ground. Thirty-three of us jumped out of that Chinook into an unsecured LZ. We had no ropes to repel or any ladders for an easier descent. I slid down the tailgate and went out at about twenty-five feet above the LZ, radio and all. There was no thinking about it. If there were, we all would have hesitated and we could not afford the delay. We all practiced our parachute-landing fall when we hit the ground, land on the balls of your feet with your knees together and roll on to your calf and hip. It was difficult to do that with a rucksack strapped on your back. Luckily, the soil we landed in was about six inches of soft sand, the LZ was next to the river and the banks were all sand. We only incurred one twisted ankle out of the whole platoon of thirty-three.

Once on the ground we found out what kept us from landing. The LZ was just big enough to allow a Chinook to land but the scouts neglected to see a dead tree right in the middle of the LZ. They also neglected to see the NVA hootch tucked up in the tree line above the LZ. The hootch was bamboo framed with thatched roof and probably used for an overnight stop for a traveler on the trail or a dry spot for a trail watcher. Somebody at S-2 or S-3 got chewed out for that foul up. One NVA with an AK-47 could have brought the helicopter down and killed us all. Luckily, for us the hootch was unoccupied and had no food stores for any travelers.

Right away, Lt. Chapla wanted me to establish communications with the rear through the relay station that had been set up. With my short flexible antenna, I got nothing, so I set up my long antenna known as "long john", a rigid antenna about ten feet long that broke down into foot and a half segments. I could not raise anyone with it either, so the helicopter pilot relayed a transmission for us. We were in trouble. No way to contact anyone for pickup, once the helicopter was gone we were on our own. Since we did not have a way to climb back onto the helicopter, the decision was made to go ahead with the bomb strike assessment with a predetermined time for pick up. We dropped rucksacks near the riverbank and left the guy with the injured ankle and one other person to watch them. The rest of us proceeded into the river, swollen from recent monsoon rains and running very swiftly through the high mountain valley. There was a well-used trail paralleling the river but one of the rules we followed was not to use trails because of booby traps. The river was shallow, never deeper than waist high on me but it contained some very large boulders. We all struggled with navigating through the fast moving waters especially me; I still had my rucksack because of the radio strapped to the frame. It rained on us several times and the weather was cool. The fact that we were soaked through made the trek down river a slow cold journey.

Most of the bombs hit on the mountainous banks of the river in the heavy forests; however, there was an occasional hit in the riverbed diverting the flow in another direction and creating a hole for us to navigate around. A B-52 strike covers a grid roughly three thousand meters long and one thousand meters wide. The bombs on this particular strike did not hit anything of value. We did not see any more hootches or signs of enemy activity and there was no body count. It took a long time to reach the far end of the bomb strike, longer than anyone anticipated. Because we dropped rucks at the LZ we did not stop for chow. No one had any with them except for me. We struggled going back upstream against the swift current and now the cold was bone chilling. Time was getting away from us; it was taking too long to get back. The pickup time established with the rear area before the Chinook that dropped us off went off station was drawing critically close. Unless the radio relay station heard from us before the pickup time, the Hueys scheduled to pick us up would be there before we got back to the LZ.

We were starting to crowd the pickup time at 1630 hours. The weather being the way it was we would be lucky to make it out and dam lucky if we got back to the LZ by then. It gets dark early in the mountains and jungles of Vietnam and with the clouds and rain we would be fortunate to be extracted by nightfall. The one thing everyone had on their mind was that helicopters do not fly at night unless they absolutely have to. In our case we could have been the exception because no one wanted us to spend the night this far out with just a platoon-sized element. That made us very vulnerable and put us high on the priority list for choppers and extraction.

Lt. Chapla started to solicit others in the platoon to see if anyone knew how to set up a directional antenna which he hoped would establish the link we needed with the relay station so we could somewhat get control of our destiny. Everyone told the Lieutenant no on the directional antenna except me. I remembered a class during radio week that specifically had us practice making a directional antenna. It took a piece of trip wire in the shape of a triangle with the direction established by the point with the legs on an angle and then tied into the antenna port on the radio establishing a large triangle shaped window to send and catch radio waves. LT. Chapla asked me, "I thought you said you didn't know anything about the radio?"

"I didn't Sir, but I know about a directional antenna." I answered.

With the Lieutenant's help, we got the antenna up and we hoped pointed in the right direction. I called the relay station and got a response the first try. Using CAT codes, we established a new pickup time letting them know we were not back at the LZ yet. Once we got there, we still had to eliminate the dead tree in order to get enough room for a Huey to land. The only problem we had, we were moving the pickup time back crowding the daylight window and relying on the weather to hold, time and the monsoon weather was not on our side.

We were more than an hour from Uplift by helicopter flying at top speed. We set the time back one half hour so the pickup was at 1700 hrs. We were still struggling upstream in the river in order to get back with time to eliminate the dead tree. We were moving at a snail's pace against the river's fast current. We started to rush, sometimes running in the shallow parts of the river. Lt, Chapla did not like what we were doing and tried slowing the pace several times. I guess the point element who sets the pace figured since we had already been down the river we had checked everything out and a faster pace was required to get us back on time. The determination was showing on everyone's face and we finally made it back to the LZ with little time to spare.

When we got back, we found out the guys guarding our rucksacks had an incident resulting in one NVA killed in action (KIA). The two guards were playing cards on a rucksack next to the trail when the guy with the bad ankle facing looking upstream on the trail, got a wide-eyed look on his face. The other guy had his rifle lying across his lap safety off ready to go and turned around firing on automatic, killing the NVA instantly.

Since that episode already compromised our location, we set the NVA hootch on fire with a white Phosphorus (WP) grenade and we put a Claymore in front of the dead tree and detonated it bringing the tree down just in time. The helicopters were on station asking us to pop smoke for identification. The light was fading fast and the dark gray of dusk had already set in. I do not know how the pilots were able to identify the smoke color in the light we had left. With the overcast sky contributing to the darkness, we lifted five Huey helicopters one at a time in a vertical ascent out of the LZ. We had a frigid ride back to Uplift because we were all still wet from walking in the river and soaked from the rain.

We got back with darkness setting in with just enough light to get back to our bunks. Some of us went to the showers to take a hot shower and warm up before turning in for the night. All of us hoped everything would remain quiet so we would not be called that night for a reaction force aiding one of the other units. The night passed quietly thankfully. The next morning at formation, Ascona got a three day in country R&R for his confirmed kill of the NVA on the trail.

In retrospect, so many things went wrong or could have been disastrous on this one mission. It became a learning experience for all. If there would have been better communication the mission might have been scrubbed for a better day. The rain could have caused us to stay the night in an unsecured area. If we had not been able to establish communication with the directional antenna, the helicopters would have come and gone unable to return until the next day to pick us up. We could have sustained more injuries from the jump out of the helicopter or the trek down the river. We could have had some casualties from the NVA if there had been someone in the hootch on the hill above the LZ. If the rucksack guards had not been alert, both could have been killed by the NVA on the trail. We were all very lucky on that one-day making the bomb assessment so far from Uplift.

CHAPTER 8

Blocking Force at the Beach

In order to keep from losing our edge and stay effective as a combat unit, the battalion planners devised missions for Alpha Company to participate as a combat company and break the monotonous routine of work details in the rear. There were many times Alpha Company became a blocking force for other units while assigned as reaction force at LZ Uplift. A blocking force was a unit, platoon, company that would set up in a line along the anticipated route a known enemy force would attempt to travel or escape. Another US element would attempt to push or direct the enemy force toward the blocking force. It was a trap, sometimes it worked well, and sometimes it didn't.

I remember one particular time when second and third platoons became the blocking force for the first platoon. The plans devised had the second and third platoons loading six at a time, into a single helicopter with doors closed so the troop movement would be undetected. The two strange things about the move were we only used one UH-1 Huey helicopter and we closed the doors. It was the only occasion during my thirteen-month tour that we closed the doors on any helicopter. With the doors closed the villagers and local indigenous people working the rice paddies could not see us inside the helicopter, thus they would not know we had moved two thirds of a company to Bravo Company's AO, area of operation. Bravo had been experiencing difficulty running their ambushes out of the village. They were always detected and the ambush had negative results or the VC ambushed the men before arriving at their ambush site. Bravo Company was securing the fishing village to eliminate the theft of the village's catch of fish, which was their livelihood. The problem was there were some villagers working with the VC/NVA in the area and supplying pertinent information to the enemy.

The move took all day to transport the sixty plus paratroopers five to seven miles to the village beach headquarters of Bravo Company. Once there, Bravo Company secured the village so no word of our arrival leaked to anyone outside the village. In the meantime, we had to make our way inland across the two-mile white sands and set up in a line on a low ridge covered with pine trees overlooking the rice paddies just east of the mountains known as Nui Mu's. Among the rice paddies were numerous thick hedgerows dividing them into squares and sometimes making movement between them difficult. Normally Bravo Company would secure the village and patrol the area where we were setting up our blocking force but with the recent problems Bravo had experienced, the battalion planners wanted to change things up to see if we could catch the enemy half stepping.

While we were traveling to our blocking position, the first platoon was trucked toward the beach village on Highway One and a local road branching off toward the village as far as the pavement would take them. When the pavement ended, the first platoon got off the trucks and began making their way through the rice paddies and hedgerows in single file toward the area we were securing. It was dusk when they started inland and as they began to move toward us, we saw VC/NVA movement in one of the rice paddies. There were fifteen VC/NVA with various weapons standing in the middle of one of the rice paddies in clear view from our position. We communicated what we viewed to the first platoon and gave them exact coordinates so they would be able to maneuver to catch the enemy off guard. The plan was actually working and as we watched the first platoon move to engage the enemy, there was nervous anticipation among the members of the blocking force. We were ready to surprise the VC for a change and get some confirmed kills.

As the first platoon came through the hedgerow the fifteen VC were right in front of them. The members of first platoon hurried to form a line and engaged the enemy completely catching them off guard. The VC began to flee but not in our direction. They ran parallel to our blocking force, and they were too far away for us to fire them up. The first platoon laid down a good base of fire, their M-60 machine gunner caught one of the VC right in the middle of the lower back with a tracer round. We watched as the round went into his back and came out his stomach. He dropped immediately in a heap to the ground. To everyone's surprise, the wounded VC got up and continued to run with the rest just as if he had never been shot. The M-79 grenadier took aim and put a round right between the legs of another fleeing VC. The 40 mm grenade from the breech loading M-79 has a five-yard killing radius. When it landed between the VC's legs, it went off but the VC never lost a step and escaped with the others. We were all shocked at the outcome of our trap. We felt it was perfectly executed but we had nothing to show for our efforts. There should have been at least two VC kills, maybe more, yet we had no body count. We met up with the first platoon and spent the night on the beach near the village secured by Bravo Company.

The next day we had a day off at the beach swimming and sunning ourselves along the shores of the South China Sea. Those of us that had them blew up our air mattress and paddled them out beyond the breaking waves. I wasn't able to do that myself, as I could not overcome the breaking waves before they washed me back up to shore. I tried for two hours to make it past where the waves were breaking. I probably would have quit before then but my friend Borchard kept yelling for me to come out. He was already there and just enjoying floating around in the warm water. The last time I tried to get out to him, I made it over the swell of the next to last wave and saw the last wave starting to build. I knew I was going to have to hurry to make it this time. I was stroking as fast as I could when I heard the roar of the breaking wave. I looked up to see the last wave breaking about twelve feet above me. I grabbed the air mattress and wrapped my legs around it. I knew I was going for a rough ride. When the wave hit me, it slammed me off the floor of the ocean and started tumbling me repeatedly. I held on to the mattress for dear life thinking it would eventually bring me back to the surface if I could hold my breath long enough. Finally, I stopped tumbling and I felt the water starting to move in the opposite direction. I was out of breath and knew I had to get air before I panicked so I put my feet against the bottom and pushed up for all I was worth hoping to make it to the surface. My head came out of the water; I opened my eyes and took a breath. I was standing in ankle deep water near the spot I blew up my air mattress. That was it for me. I was exhausted and I couldn't take another chance on drowning again. I slept the rest of the day on my air mattress. The only repercussions I had, my nipples were sore from rubbing on the rubber air mattress. They were so sore I couldn't touch them for about a week. Since our attire for the beach was total nudity, we didn't have any type of swim trunks and we didn't wear underwear, I guess that was a small price to pay. The next time we went to the beach, I kept my tee shirt on.

That night it was back to running ambushes, giving Bravo a hand cleaning up their AO. Each platoon took a different area to ambush. The second platoon split into two different elements and selected a site just before dark. Sgt. Mangilardi had one group, and SSgt. Andersen and I went with the other group. We lined up behind a hedgerow with a trail on the other side. As we started to lay out our gear for the night, we heard the handle from two grenades release and the grenades landed in our ambush line. One fell right in front of Delgado who was only feet from me. He got to his feet, yelled "grenade" and ran two or three steps then jumped to the ground. The only thing I could do was cover my head in my arms and pray. The first grenade went off about fifteen feet away sending glowing red-hot shards of metal up into the air. Then the second grenade went off about four feet from me. I was shocked no fragments hit me. I guess when they told us the best place to be is right next to a grenade when it goes off is true. I saw the red-hot fragments go up and over me but none hit me. We had two wounded from the first grenade but luckily, none was serious. Once the excitement from the explosions settled down, we all were firing our weapons through the hedgerow. While we dealt with our aggressors, Mangilardi's element had their position swept by AK-47 fire. His element had two injuries from gunshot wounds. One of them was serious. The guy's arm was shattered from the elbow down, and the other wound was a gunshot to the heel; both individuals would get a ticket home. We called in a medevac for all the wounded, then moved our ambush sites to new locations. The remainder of the night passed without incident.

Because of the activity in Bravo's AO, the battalion planners wanted us to stay in the area and run ambushes. The first platoon got the job of escorting the captain and the rest of the CP around. The CP was the command position, which included the captain and his two RTOs, the "Top Doc" medic and any forward observers (FOs), either artillery or four duce mortars and their RTOs. For some reason the captain favored the first platoon when in the field with the company. For that reason, the first platoon often stayed in the same position for several days. We sometimes viewed that as an advantage, but after I was there a while, I learned it could be hazardous also.

It was monsoon season and one of the nights we spent out by the coast, it was pouring and when we set up our ambush, we were in a rice paddy in water about knee deep. Once I settled in for the night, I had to inflate my air mattress half way, bend it in half and lay on it in order to keep my head above the water. Normally we were not allowed to use the air mattress inflated but this time it was keeping me from drowning. When I slept, the water was chest deep on me. The only thing that kept my chin and mouth out of the water was my half-inflated air mattress. The rain continued to pour down throughout the night. When stand to, everyone up and awake, came around at 05:00 in the morning my hands, fingers, feet and toes were so wrinkled from being in water all night they were sore to touch. They remained sore all day and the following day.

We also tried out a new optical device for seeing in the dark, the Starlight Scope. It supposedly magnified light from the stars to allow images to be seen at night. It was difficult to use during monsoon season because of overcast skies and few starry nights. When it was working, everything appeared green but images of humans could be detected. I only remember using it on this particular mission. It had its drawbacks: it was large and heavy so no one wanted to carry it. It was made to mount on a rifle but that defeated the purpose of sharing it on guard. It was signed out of the company supply so it was expensive and must be accounted for by the carrier. It had no value in the triple canopy jungles we worked in. It had to be protected from the rain and kept dry in order to be effective. It became easier to leave it in the rear than hump it to the field.

One of the days after the first platoon fired up the VC in the rice paddies, we captured a wounded NVA soldier that must have been with the VC. Through our Chieu Hoi, a captured enemy soldier converted to our side, we learned he was only twelve years old and had been drummed into service out of his home in Qui Nhon. In the skirmish, the top of his left shoulder had been blown off by an M-16 round. It took a piece about six inches long and two inches deep the full width of his shoulder. He winced from the pain but was very cooperative and answered all of our questions. He informed us there was another casualty up the mountain in a cave with a stomach wound. We figured that was the VC we saw hit by the M-60 tracer. Before we moved out, our medic treated the boy and we had a chopper from the rear pick him up for interrogation. Many of the enemy we fought was just like this young boy, not really committed to the cause but forced into service with lies about American aggressors. They were more scared of what we would do to them if they were captured than dying. Once they learned we were not going to hurt them, they became cooperative. Of course, there were others, which were hard-core, would not give up, and fought to the death. They believed all the propaganda the VC/NVA put out about the American soldier.

Once the helicopter relieved us of our prisoner, we started up the slopes of the mountains. We climbed in a column with a point element leading, the rest of us weaving in and out of the granite boulders that dotted the slopes. I remember after climbing for a time, I smelled the palm of my hand and could smell the enemy. The oil from their skin was left on the rocks and rubbed off on our hands as we used the rocks to assist our climb. The smell was a fishy smell, probably from their diet of fish for almost every meal. It was the same for us since we couldn't use any aftershave, deodorant or soap with fragrances in them because they could smell us. It was like the battle of the senses. Nevertheless, anytime we were in rocky areas I smelled the palms of my hands to see if the enemy had been there first.

About half way up, one of the machine gunners thought he saw someone above us and opened up with a large volume of fire. Those of us in front of him were lucky we weren't hit by the rounds that zinged by our heads. Once we convinced him to stop firing SSgt Andersen organized a small patrol to climb up to see if we could find anything. Andersen must have gone on this patrol because I was there also. Normally I went where he went. I remember I was following Colon, our point man. Colon was teaching me a little about walking point. He ducked into a cave created by two boulders that overlapped one another. As he went into the opening he thought he caught a glimpse of someone above us on the left. He immediately turned in that direction and began firing on full automatic.

I was in the entrance and watched as the bullets ricocheted off the granite rocks all around us. When he realized it was a shadow and nothing was there, he turned to me to see if I was all right. I was, just scared is all.

We continued to the top where we discovered a huge cave that was used for a hospital. There were freshly used bandages soaked with blood but we didn't find any casualties or anyone treating casualties. We called the discovery into the rear and were told to locate a LZ. Once we secured the LZ, an element from Bravo Company arrived and we were extracted back to Uplift. The next issue of Stars and Stripes, our Army newspaper had a big article with pictures and the story of Bravo's uncovering a huge hospital complex in their AO. Alpha Company got no credit for finding anything at all. Such was the plight of Alpha Company on this and many other missions.

CHAPTER 9

PX Trips and General Population Assessment

While in the rear area, occasionally I was fortunate to get a one-day pass to visit a PX. Uplift did not have a Post Exchange at the time so we had to travel to LZ English, Qui Nhon or Phu Cat. Usually a one-day pass would be good for LZ English or Phu Cat, both twenty-five miles away but stretching the forty miles to Qui Nhon. Travel to the PX was up to the individual and was mostly done by hitching a ride at the gate from Uplift on Highway 1 to the intersection going to Phu Cat Air Base. Highway 1 was a two-lane blacktop considered a major highway running the full length of Vietnam. It was a protected highway, meaning all the bridges had guards and the road was gated at some firebases. LZ Uplift had two of the gates, which closed the highway running right through LZ Uplift at 1800 hours every night.

Sometimes if we were lucky, we could find someone going south to Phu Cat from Uplift, skipping the stop at the intersection where Highway 1 continued on to Qui Nhon. Qui Nhon was also south of Uplift but since it was forty miles, a dedicated vehicle was required to make the trip in one day. LZ English was to the north and was home to the 2nd and 4th Battalions of the 173rd Airborne Brigade. LZ English was a much larger base than Uplift and had more of the conveniences offered to troops at larger base camps: PX, swimming pool, volleyball court, and a runway for fixed wing aircraft.

There was a world all its own waiting at the intersection to Phu Cat Airbase. For a price, we could buy almost anything from the locals hanging out at the intersection. The favorite of most GIs was the local whorehouse, with their variety of women willing to boom boom, Vietnamese slang for fuck GIs for a meager five piasters or five dollars in military payment currency or MPC. MPC was the printed currency for US military in Vietnam. The US did not want regular currency used in Vietnam. Even five and ten cents were paper MPC.

While standing at the intersection waiting for a ride, usually a young boy would approach and ask, "You want girl?" If the answer was "Yes," then the boy would take the lucky guy to where the girl was waiting and payment was handled off the road. There was not supposed to be any exchange of MPC with the Vietnamese but most GIs never took the time to convert their MPCs to Piasters, Vietnamese currency for dollars, even though the conversion rate was four dollars fifty cents MPC to five Piasters. In addition to a girl, it was the place to buy drugs, including speed, marijuana and though not drugs, American cigarettes. It was stupid to buy cigarettes there if making a PX run because the local price was fifty cents a pack or you could buy a carton at the PX for one dollar and fifty cents. Usually during the business with the girls, the drug transactions were discussed if the clientele was interested. I was an exception to the usual business; I did not do drugs or business with the local girls. Even the so-called pretty ones were not really that good looking and I wanted to remain faithful to my girlfriend back in the States. Sure, I would talk with them and occasionally look down their blouse, but when it came to discussing business, I would tell them I was "Cherry Boy" and that would drive them away yelling, "You number 10, GI." Besides, the complication of venereal disease was always present and their age was always questionable. Some were probably only fourteen or fifteen years old and chances of getting an older woman was negligible.

I remember one day stopping at the Phu Cat intersection and one particular tall girl caught my eye. She was unusually tall for a Vietnamese woman and her hair was done up differently than most whores at that intersection. I am guessing my attraction to her was probably because of the sheer outfit she was wearing which showed her breasts; she did not have a bra on and the thin white slacks she was wearing revealed her white bikini underpants. I guess I looked at her long enough; the mamasan told her to come over and offer to take me inside for some boom-boom action.

I could tell she was resisting, but she finally crossed the road to where I was ogling her. She grabbed my hand and started pulling me toward one of the hootches along the road.

I gave her my standard answer. "No, I am cherry boy" and after a few more tugs, she finally left me alone.

Later at Uplift toward the end of my tour, I was talking to a friend in Bravo Company I had gone through training with in the States. He insisted on showing me a picture of a nice looking Vietnamese girl he had been seeing and spending some nights with when he had overnight passes. He claimed he wanted to marry her and take her home. He was submitting paperwork to do just that. I didn't have the heart to tell him his girl was the tall girl that approached me at the Phu Cat intersection.

Traveling along Highway 1, weather to Phu Cat, Qui Nhon or Phu Mi our financial office was located at the latter; one could see a wide variety of local people doing all sorts of things. The locals showed no modesty when mother nature called. It was nothing to see women squatting with their pants down on the side of the road pissing right in full view of anyone traveling the road. There were all kinds of things to see on the roadways of Vietnam.

The bridges on Highway 1 were built with single planks on top of the support beams on one or both sides of the road. These were there for the people traveling the road by foot. They crossed the bridge on the plank there by avoiding being hit by vehicles crossing the bridges at the same time. One day as we drove along the highway, a woman stopped in the middle of the plank on the bridge, pulled down her pants and squirted a banana yellow colored runny stream of shit into the water below. Just downstream, about thirty feet, was a family either bathing or swimming in the stream. It was not a pretty picture, and confirmed there were not many concerns for sanitary conditions throughout the whole country. I never saw anyone wipe himself or herself when finished relieving themselves or defecating and there were no outhouses or latrines anywhere in any of the villages or roadside stops.

Occasionally as we passed through villages on vehicles, we saw couples engaged in various carnal acts in a hammock or bed in full view from the road. Once leaving Phu Cat Air Base, in the village connected to the base, I saw a Vietnamese woman washing her ample breasts. It was a nice view of the twins on a woman probably in her forties. I don't know if she realized she was exposing herself or if she cared if she did know. That particular village was a nonstop village so no one would be able to approach her for any more favors anyway.

There were other things on the roadways: the Lambrettas, a three wheeled cross between a motorcycle and a mini truck, loaded over capacity with local people traveling from village to village. Once a vehicle I was riding in was passed by a 1957 Plymouth Fury loaded with Vietnamese going like a bat out of hell. There were motorcycle gangs of Vietnamese in varied sized groups just out joy riding. These gangs were not like the motorcycle gangs you might envision in the US. They wore white shirts and black pants or shorts, and most were on Honda 90s or scooters, probably school kids out looking for trouble. They harassed the GIs in the trucks moving down Highway 1 because they knew the trucks could not stop on the open road without a reason.

One night just before I DEROSd, (date of expected return from overseas), I was in charge of a bunker assigned to A Company not far from the road when a group of motorcyclists approached the gate at Uplift. The road was closed for all travel at 1800 hrs. However, this group was threatening to crash the gate; they wanted through. The MP's at the gate turned the unruly group away with a warning and then alerted the bunker line to be ready if they made a run on the gate. I got everyone on top of the bunker and instructed them if the motorcycle group made a run on the gate, we would fire over their heads to turn them away. If that did not turn them, we would fire directly at the leaders to stop them. Once I finished the instructions to the group on my bunker, the group of motorcycles made a run at the gate. Everyone stood there hesitant to open fire until I fired the first burst of M-16 rounds on full automatic; then they all fired too. The group of motorcyclists turned rapidly and headed away from the gate. Most of the guys on my bunker were new so I told them I understood their hesitance to engage the motorcycles but I also explained the importance of maintaining the security of Uplift and following orders. If they would have shot anyone, we could have been in trouble. Thankfully, they listened to my instructions and our deterrence of the motorcycle group was a success

Several times when I was traveling Highway 1 in the back of a duce and a half truck, GIs riding with me would pull the pin on a hand grenade and throw it into a rice paddy we were driving by. Sometimes I knew the guy who threw the grenade sometimes I did not know him. It was a foolish game they played, not meant to hurt anyone, but still hazardous for everyone.

There were other games played that were not as serious, like one time when a bike rider wearing a pith helmet going in our direction got it lifted by the guy in the passenger's seat of our cab. The driver moved close to the edge of the road as we came up behind the biker. The man on the passenger's side leaned out and snatched his hat without us slowing down. The biker yelled great obscenities at us, shook his fist furiously but there was nothing he could do. As we traveled down the road, we came up on another bike rider without a hat. The driver again moved close to the edge of the road and the man on the passenger's side leaned out once more with the pith helmet in his hand. As we passed the old gentleman, he placed the helmet on the old guy's head. When he realized what had happened, he gave us the million-dollar smile.

I rode along with Borchard once to LZ English to get the company supply of cokes and beer for a cookout we held on occasions when the company was in the rear area after a combat mission. My friend from Iowa got a rear job. He became the company armor after extending his tour and coming back after a leave at home. The First Sargent sent him and he asked me to go along for the ride.

We had steaks at the company cookouts supplied by the Air Force at Phu Cat after a trade was made, steaks for an AK-47 we captured on one of our missions. We would take the AK to one of the Air Force mess halls and negotiate with the mess sergeant or the person in charge for a number of cases of steaks he was willing to part with. We never had to give up more than one weapon for enough steaks to feed the company of one hundred plus men. No one in the Army was allowed to take an automatic weapon, AK-47, home but the Air Force did it somehow without restrictions.

Borchard and I secured our load of sodas and beer in the back of the jeep and headed out the gate from English on to Highway 1, turning south toward Uplift. After traveling for a short time, Borchard and I came upon a whole group of trucks and jeeps pulled over with everyone out of their vehicles looking into the tree line along the left side of our travel route. As we approached, they were waving frantically for us to stop because a sniper was shooting at vehicles traveling that roadway. As Borchard started to slow down he asked, "Do you want to stop or should I drive on?"

"Drive on!" I yelled

As he sped through the group of surprised GIs cowering behind their vehicles, Borchard said, "I'm glad you felt the same as me. If I had stopped, we could have been late for the company party." Then he grinned and gave a familiar chuckle I had heard many times before. We drove on at a little higher rate of speed, putting some distance between us and the sniper. We both quipped light heartedly about the incident the rest of the way back to Uplift.

"It looked to me like they already had enough people to handle one sniper"

"Yeah, they didn't need us to add to the body count; besides I'm signed out for this jeep and if there is any damage to it I'll have to pay for it. How much do you think one of these costs anyway?"

"Don't tell the first sergeant about this, we don't want him to know we skipped out on those guys, just in case they didn't make it."

The joking was all clean fun because of a small altercation with an invisible sniper. It let us poke fun at a serious situation, sometimes we did have a morbid sense of humor about things we encountered. We didn't receive any small arms fire as we drove through the stopped traffic. We returned to LZ Uplift unscathed in time for the cookout and had a great time with all our friends in Alpha Company.

For a country at war, there were always many local travelers on the roads. Sometimes it was hard to tell what most of them were doing on the road. There were some obvious travelers, those taking a load of charcoal to market, or maybe a daily catch of fish. Some carried puppies, a favorite Vietnamese delicacy. The vehicles, bikes and backs of people were loaded sometimes with different manufactured goods also sold in the markets of the larger towns. One thing for sure, none of them could be trusted. They were all suspected or potential collaborators with the enemy, or at least sympathizers. If there was after hour socialization with locals, your life was at risk. Many GIs didn't heed the warnings and wound up casualties because they were visiting overnight outside the protection of a base camp. The Stars and Stripes, an Army publication for GIs in Vietnam was full of the stories of GIs being murdered and found somewhere outside the wire that surrounded the basecamp.

There were certain Vietnamese that worked for the companies at the basecamps like LZ Uplift. They were issued work permits and had to produce them to anyone looking for Vietnamese to work details on the basecamp. The Vietnamese workers on permits usually filled sandbags, or burned shit from the latrines scattered around the basecamp. A few worked at the laundry and the steakhouse, but those jobs were steady and the same Vietnamese were hired every day for those jobs. Their work also included KP or kitchen details helping the cooks prepare all the meals served each day in the mess hall and cleaning the pots and pans after the meals were served. The mess hall was like the GI cafeteria. There were two sides to the mess at Uplift: the general mess where enlisted men were served their chow and the NCO/Officer's mess where all the NCOs and officers were served chow.

One day as I was walking through the buildings at Uplift, I noticed a Vietnamese standing against the outside wall of one of those buildings or hootches as we called them. I stood behind the corner of an adjacent hootch and watched as the Vietnamese stepped off the distance between that building and the next. He then moved along the side of the hootch, still counting steps. He was finding distances for a mortar attack on Uplift. I went to the MPs, Military Police, and pointed him out to them. The MPs confirmed my observance and took him into custody. He was obviously one of the trusted workers that had one of the steady jobs because he was unsupervised and walking among the hootches on his own. I never heard what happened to him but I became a celebrity for a day or so. That episode convinced me not to trust any Vietnamese, on or off the basecamp.

Whether traveling the roads or walking the dike walls or through the rice paddies, it was easy to see the local Vietnamese were about a century behind the US. The working of the fields was all done by hand and tilling the rice fields was done by water buffalo pulling a single bottom plow while one of the workers steadied it walking behind the buffalo. Planting rice was work for women, women and children herded cows as well. Most of the villages off the major roadways had only dirt path access to them. There were no sidewalks of any type throughout the whole country. There may have been something in big cities like Saigon, but I could not verify that because I was never in Saigon.

The people were poor; they had nothing but an existence. If they did have something, the VC/NVA took it away from them. Yet the people sympathized with the communists and helped them, which complicated the US role in South Vietnam. For the most part, we could not tell one Vietnamese from another. During the day, they were farmers and villagers eking out a living off the land. At night, they became soldiers fighting against the US. Sometimes they were a very formidable enemy force. Often when we would search villages, part of our normal routine, there would be a conspicuous lack of men in the village leading us to believe the village was a VC village. If we conducted interviews with the women in the village, they knew nothing or the men were working the fields. However, if we looked at the fields there were no men there either. The general population in Vietnam was very hard to read and to know if they were telling the truth. We did not trust them or the information they provided us.

Once while on bunker guard at Uplift, the guards detected movement in front of their bunker on the south side, opposite of where I was on guard. Even though after six o'clock we were a free fire zone, standard procedure required us to request permission from our command to open fire on any movement unless the movement was a threat or was about to breech the perimeter of Uplift. After getting that permission, the south side bunkers fired up the area where they saw movement. It didn't affect us, but we went on alert in case the movement escalated to an attack. Nothing else happened for the rest of the night, but at the morning formation we had after every guard duty, we found out that a girl was killed on the south perimeter. She was the movement that was detected from the bunker line. Her grandfather showed up with the Red Cross for the formation and they were asking all of us for donations to help out the family. No one asked or explained about what she was doing out there in the middle of the night, but the Red Cross was claiming it was our fault she was killed. Some of the guys put money in the hat that was passed for donations. I just passed the hat on when it got to me; I didn't feel sorry for the girl at all. She was sneaking around in a place she knew she could be killed. We all wondered how the Red Cross was able to be at the 0700 formation the next day asking for money. Even though there were several incidents similar to the one I described, the connection with the Red Cross was never explained, nor did we figure it out. It just happened. I always thought the American Red Cross was on our side but after that day, I did not like them. I thought they were trying to take advantage of us in a situation that was beyond our control.

CHAPTER 10

Setting the Trap and Friendly Fire

Alpha Company participated in at least two major combat assaults involving the entire third battalion; this is one of the most memorable. Still in the second platoon at the time but more in tuned to the radio and its procedures, I was following SSgt. Andersen our platoon sergeant and acting platoon leader at the time.

The company was picked up at LZ Uplift in Huey, UH-1 helicopters and flown to a designated LZ somewhere north of Uplift. When we arrived, it looked like every Huey in Vietnam was on that LZ, a huge valley selected for the large number of helicopters landing there for this operation. There was a cemetery near where we landed, and though we had to walk through it to receive our instructions, it was off limits to helicopters landing to participate in this huge battalion combat assault.

When we got off the slick, Andersen said, "Follow me."

We were on our way to a high-level meeting with the battalion commander, usually a lieutenant colonel, and all the company commanders and platoon leaders participating in the combat assault. That meeting took place right in the middle of the LZ. If the enemy would have known, they could have killed all the major leaders in the battalion. I remember seeing a full bird colonel in the group. I do not know who he was representing, but it was very unusual for such a high-ranking officer to be in the field.

I was not privy to what the officers discussed, but when Andersen was done, we went back to where the company was waiting with a strange announcement for second platoon. It seems we were going to an area where the NVA were very active, according to our intelligence people, looking for a fifty-one caliber machine gun that had been shooting at aircraft in the region.

"We are going to be inserted by Chinooks; I have marked our LZ on my map. Squad leaders make sure you note the coordinates for your map," Andersen told the rest of the company leaders.

Shortly after that conversation, we moved to a location on the LZ where the Chinooks picked up all of Alpha Company. There were at least three, maybe four Chinooks, the large double rotor helicopters that carried about forty troops including the crew and four gunships escorting us, three UH-1 Hueys and a Cobra. Just as quickly as the whole battalion had come together there in that huge valley, we all loaded on some kind of helicopter and were on our way to designated LZs. Every company in the battalion was represented.

As we approached the landing zone in the mountainous jungle, the gunships escorting us went to work on it, sending rockets and heavy machine gun fire into the surrounding triple canopy jungle. The Chinooks descended, heading for the LZ as soon as the gunships made their last run. Our particular LZ looked like a dirt spot right in the middle of the jungle; there was no vegetation growing on it at all. It was like a rain puddle in the middle of a cornfield after it dries, the ground all cracked from holding the water, then drying rapidly.

Our descent into the one Chinook LZ was slow because of the tall jungle trees surrounding the dirt spot. The rear tailgate lowered as the first Chinook sat down. I was sitting about midway back on the right side of the aircraft and once the bird came to a rest everyone was up and moving toward the rear. There was a serious problem. We found out the LZ was a bog, the top was dry but underneath was sticky black muck. There was a backup getting off the aircraft because when we stepped off the tailgate, we sank up to our knees in mud. The supposed dry spot in the middle of the jungle put everyone in Alpha Company in jeopardy. What would usually be a swift exit putting thirty plus troops on the ground in a matter of a couple minutes, left us exposed and struggling to move in the black quagmire and get to the cover of the trees safely out of the way of the next helicopter. It was a slow process and put the Chinook helicopters at risk of being downed by enemy small arms. They moved more slowly than the

Hueys and were a huge target. Luckily our LZ was absent of any enemy. We found out Bravo Company went into a hot LZ only ten klicks away and came away with ten men wounded. A klick is short for kilometer or one thousand meters, so Bravo's insertion wasn't that far from where we were inserted. If that had been our situation, they would have probably killed everyone on the first Chinook and more than likely downed the aircraft and killed the crew. We got lucky again.

After what seemed like an endless struggle through the muck, we reached the tree line and offered security for the remaining aircraft. Once everyone was on the ground, we started to look for signs of the enemy presence in the area. When there is a whole company involved with a search and destroy mission like we were on, logistics becomes a problem. Stealth is not an ally when moving that many people through the jungle, they make a lot of noise. The platoons stay together and everyone moves in a column one behind the other with an acceptable space between individuals. A company consists of about one hundred GIs but we fielded around ninety on this particular trip, an average of thirty per platoon.

First platoon started out on point with the Captain and the rest of his CP traveling in the middle of the first platoon. Second platoon followed the first, and then the third platoon brought up the rear of the element. Not too far from where we were inserted, we found an old trail. It was wide and in its day, it was well used, but we found no new signs of anyone moving on it for some time. The size would fit the reason for us being on this mission. The NVA were supposedly moving a fifty-one caliber machine gun on a cart with bicycles. The fact that Bravo Company had contact when they were inserted and they were only ten klicks away from us, kept us in the area looking for that fifty-one caliber machine gun for some time.

The fifty-one caliber machine gun was a powerful weapon in the NVA arsenal. Its design was mostly for anti-aircraft, but it could be used against infantry or ground troops. It was similar to the US 50-caliber machine gun. Its effective range was 1800-2000 meters. An advantage of the fifty-one caliber machine gun is that it could fire the US made 50-caliber ammunition. For that reason, and that the US ammo was armor piercing, most US firebases guarded the ammunition to an extreme limit. The US rounds could pierce one inch thick steel at two hundred fifty meters. We did not want the powerful 50-caliber ammo to be used against us.

After several days of scouring the mountainous jungles, cutting trails and sometimes-breaking rules and using the existing ones, digging foxholes for nighttime laagers and not finding any recent signs or traces of enemy activity, the scuttlebutt came down that our mission was changing. As often happened on the missions, command in the rear had no patience or tolerance for negative results so we would end one mission and start another. Usually a mission was fifteen days in the field and then a three-day rest in the rear. Unfortunately, for us, that almost never happened. We were lucky to end up with twenty or twenty-five days out and maybe three days in the rear to pull guard and work details. We had already been out for ten days. I do not know how they calculated the numbers when we moved from one mission to the other with no break in between.

They picked up the entire company in Hueys and transported us to an area being worked by the Americal Division. When in the rear as reaction force, we supported other Army units like the Americal Division, 1st Calvary Division and of course other elements of the 173rd.

We set up as a blocking force for the element from the Americal Division who would push the enemy toward us. At the time, we had no knowledge of the size of the elements we were working with from the Americal Division. All three platoons of Alpha Company had a separate area to set up and block for the Americal units. When working with other units, communication was both important and difficult. Important because we had to talk to each other and be on the same frequencies to make that happen. Difficult, because the frequencies had to be communicated to all units participating, which took time and had to be confirmed. There was also a radio slang that could differ between units and sometimes took time to learn. It was important that everyone on the mission was on the same frequency. There was a lot of traffic on the radio with everybody communicating positions and acknowledging transmissions. There was no room for error so an RTO had to monitor all transmissions and pay close attention to the radio.

When we were all in position, the Americal units started to push toward us. One particular Americal unit sent out word on the radio that they were coming in from the south traveling north. The transmission went something like this, "Be advised Bravo Foxtrot, we will be approaching your position from the Sierra, over." Something seemed strange about that because it put them in a position behind us. No one should have been behind us, but nobody questioned the transmission from the Americal unit. Now the tension started to take over: we had Americal units supposedly pushing the enemy toward us from one direction and another Americal unit coming in from behind us.

Alpha Company's first platoon set up their blocking force in some dense jungle overlooking an "L" shaped trail. Their main body was parallel to the vertical of the "L" but could only see the corner of the short leg clearly. They strategically placed a Claymore mine, a devastating anti-personnel mine, at the corner of the "L" to cover the blind spot. As they intently watched for any movement, one of the guys spotted a boonie hat above the brush on the short leg of the "L", and then another boonie hat came into view moving toward the corner and the Claymore mine. Boonie hats were a soft hat with a wide floppy brim like an old cowboy hat. The first platoon radio operator from Alpha Company got on the radio and verified that there were no friendlies in the area. As soon as they received confirmation from all units, it was time to blow the Claymore and they did. After that Claymore went off, first platoon found themselves in one hell of a firefight. The ambushed element, assumed to be enemy, was pouring return fire into the positions of the first platoon. As usually happens in those situations there was a lot of yelling taking place. Suddenly someone realized all of the yelling was in a language everyone recognized, American.

Frantic screams of "Cease fire, cease fire" sounded from both units involved. Once the shooting stopped, everyone was scrambling to see what had happened. The other unit involved was the Americal unit that had reported they were approaching our position from the south. They were in error because they approached the first platoon from the north. In the initial contact, the Americal lost their point man, killed instantly by the Claymore mine. His legs were gone from the waist down. The second man or slack man took most of the blast from the Claymore in the chest and head he was also KIA, killed in action. No other injuries were suffered in this horrific friendly fire encounter.

Anytime there was a friendly fire incident, there was always an investigation. In this particular case, there was a lot of finger pointing. It is a horrible thing to kill people on your side in a war. The final outcome on this incident was both units were to blame: Americal for the false information on the direction they were traveling and Alpha Company first platoon for not having positive identification before engaging the unidentified element. Also, it reaffirmed the fact that boonie hats were not to be worn in the field, a lesson we had learned from prior incidents with someone engaging another element by identifying the boonie hat and not the nationality of the person wearing the hat. It was a great tragedy, especially when the method of contact lends to such great irreparable carnage. We learned from the incident and we moved on, hoping to never repeat it.

CHAPTER 11

Monsoon

Monsoon season started in late September or early October and lasted until April or May, and the rains began. If we were in the rear area it meant the work details were fewer except for guard duty and rain related details, including digging small trenches for water runoff, but the time spent at the steakhouse increased. It was the place to hang out, play cards, drink beer, and have a Coke. We also had steak for lunch with a plate of beans to go with it. I am sure the monsoons made the senior NCOs running the steakhouse happy, as their profits were up. But, attendance at the mess hall suffered, nobody wanted to get drenched going to the mess hall for possibly a hot dog when the steakhouse offered steaks for lunch. I am not sure how the program worked but the Vietnamese girls serving at the steakhouse had steady work. I heard they spent the night with some of the NCOs running the steakhouse and it made sense because they were unapproachable from the general troop population. They would smile and be friendly but if anyone asked for a date or rendezvous, they would immediately dummy up and get away from the individual asking. In addition, if one of the senior NCOs was around they did not seem as friendly to any of us. I think the senior NCOs had a good racket going on but it was secret and tough to learn anything about their business.

If we were in the field, monsoon season made everything more difficult. The constant downpours reduced visibility, already impaired by the thick jungle. The sound, which usually carried in the jungle, changed drastically because of the rain constantly drumming off the broad leaves of the tropical plants, making it more difficult to hear. And moving around became inherently more difficult; the slopes were slippery even if we were following a trail or cutting brush, and we slipped and fell frequently. Falls were dangerous in two ways. Injury of course was prevalent but falling also broadcast our presence, which could be hazardous to us all. No matter how hard we tried, we never prevented either scenario from happening. We traveled without any protective rain gear. Even though supply issued ponchos and we all carried them, we could not use them because they made too much noise when moving through the jungle. The Army made two types of ponchos. The original was OD green and made of heavy rubberized material with a hood. Then they developed a new style for the jungles of Vietnam, a lighter waterproof material with a rip-stop design, which unfortunately did not work. One walk in the jungle in the newly designed poncho and it was in shreds. If carried only to use as a shelter, it needed protection from being caught on branches that would rip it to pieces. Other than being lightweight, it was not a very practical solution for rain protection. So everyone was used to being soaked through all day long.

At night, the rain caused additional problems. The listening posts, two or three people selected to move out in front of the perimeter to listen for the enemy, or become the early warning system for the perimeter detecting approaching enemy, are awake all night and have to remain alert. The rain plays tricks on the eyes and ears in the jungle. If you can see at all, everything appears to be moving and the water dripping and running off makes sounds like someone is out there walking around. If it starts to pour, someone could walk right by undetected.

Making camp or laager as we called it, at night in the rain meant stringing a hammock under a poncho or rigging a tent out of a poncho. It was a place to get out of the rain and dry out. Normally if you wrapped up in a poncho liner, a light nylon camouflaged blanket, your clothes and the poncho liner would dry, at least until it was your turn for guard duty. Everything got wet all over again moving from your dry spot to the unprotected guard post. We could only construct tents or string hammocks in the jungle where there was cover. In the lowlands or rice paddies, we had to lie down and just cover up with a poncho. When we laagered in, we always dug foxholes, fighting positions dug chest deep on the tallest man using that fighting position. For that reason, the shorter guys liked to band together because they did not have to dig as deep to meet the tallest man requirement. The tall guys like me spent more time digging in because our holes were deeper. In the rain, the foxholes rapidly filled with water and became more of a swimming hole rather than protection from enemy fire.

With the continuous wetness came sores, which we called "jungle rot". All you needed was a scratch or small cut, maybe a blister on the foot, or the place where a leech attached to the skin, and the unremitting wetness would not let the sores heal. Without medical treatment, the sores remained open, got deeper and sometimes became infected. More times than not, they got bigger and worse before they got better. I was still treating several jungle rot sores on my legs five months after I returned home, and the scars still show.

The sores were not the only problems caused by the rain. The leeches were all over the place. They thrived in the wetness and sought out warm blood. Usually there was no way to detect them once they attached themselves until they have filled with blood. Then their anti-coagulant begins to make the attachment itch and they can be discovered. They were not particular where they attached themselves either. I saw leeches on arms, legs, in the small of the back, on the neck and some on the cheek. Two of the strangest places I saw a leech was squeezing through a hole about the size of a small needle in the vent on a jungle boot and another crawled inside a guy's penis. A squirt with insect repellent or a lit cigarette on their body would remove them very quickly once detected. I do not know how the guy with the leech in the penis got rid of his. No one wanted to help him with his dilemma. I saw the medic looking at his problem and that was enough for me.

Even though the temperature was eighty degrees or higher, the rain of the monsoons made it seem cold, especially in the mountains. We had special clothes like jungle sweaters, a heavy knit wool OD green sweater for warmth but there was a price if the weather warmed up, because it added weight to the ninety or one hundred pound ruck I was already humping. The lightweight nylon poncho liner kept us warm at night, although when I pulled mine out of the waterproof bag in my ruck, it was always wet until my body heat dried it out overnight and I put it back in my ruck in the waterproof bag in the morning. That only happened if I was able to find shelter under a poncho somehow to stay dry all night, a hammock with my poncho rigged, as a tent over me was my favorite. To rig a tent out of the poncho I tied shoelaces in the center eyelets of the poncho and then tied the laces to a tree above where my hammock was tied off. Then I simply cut two tree branches for either end of the poncho and stuck them in the two outer eyelets on either end of the poncho. It was a perfect triangular tent very easy to assemble and take down. Then there was guard duty in the middle of the night; the rain soaked your fatigues until guard was over and the poncho liner and shelter dried them once more. There were also the times we could have no shelters of any type and we settled for finding or clearing a spot on the jungle floor and just pulling a poncho over us to stay as dry as possible.

The monsoon rains also created problems for the helicopters flying us into LZs or resupplying us once we were in an AO, or area of operation, searching for the enemy. We never knew for sure if we were going on a combat assault the day we were supposed to or if resupply would come every four days like it was supposed to. The weather always dictated our flight times and resupply. Our combat missions would overextend our fifteen days and our resupply days would always go one to two days over during the monsoon season.

Occasionally we would get a break in the weather and get to see the sun, which was definitely a welcome sight in monsoon season. The problem with that was the sunny days were too few and could not be predicted. We did not count on any days of sunshine for sure, if it happened we were grateful and we left it at that.

One of those days, we were between clouds and sunshine while the company was searching for the enemy on top of a ridge somewhere north of Uplift. We were not high enough to be out of the tree line that often gave way to high grass in the upper elevations of the jungle in South Vietnam. We had been out beyond our fifteen-day mission and turned out negative results; just a bunch of old used trails with no enemy contact. There was a call to the CO and the word was passed down to the platoons. Bravo Company was coming in to relieve us and we needed to find a LZ for the choppers to pick us up. The only place convenient for a pickup was in the valley two thousand feet below us. It was mid-morning and we were told they would pick us up if we could get to the valley floor before nightfall. We knew that making the valley would be a formidable task but, anxious to get back to the rear, we ran downhill through the jungle toward the valley floor, hoping we could make it while it was still daylight. We were taking a chance but since our mission turned up no signs of the enemy, our focus shifted to making it back to Uplift before the end of the day.

We stopped for a short respite near a stream where a beam of sunlight made a rainbow in the mist. We could see the water from the stream running off the top of the mountain far above us. It was falling so far by the time it made it to where we were it was just a mist and reformed into a stream then continued to flow down the mountain. The mist was so fine that it would only dampen our fatigues if we walked through it. During the break, we took pictures of guys standing in the rainbow in the mist. After the short rest, we continued down the mountain finally reaching the valley floor about 1400 hours.

The Command Post, CP, made contact with the rear to tell them we were in place and had secured a LZ for extraction. The word was passed on to everyone our extraction would take place after Bravo Company was inserted. After a two hour wait, we watched Bravo Company's insertion by a number of Chinooks high on a grassy ridge at the far end of the valley. Then the word came down to us. We were too far down the valley for the Chinooks to extract us. The pilots did not feel comfortable coming in with no one left for securing the LZ after the last of Alpha Company was picked up. We needed to head toward the end of the valley closer to where Bravo was inserted. We could not understand how Bravo could help us with security when they were way up on the ridge. Even though we protested, command insisted we move to the other end of the valley. We were all tired because we had just run down the side of a mountain and now we would have to run the length of the valley if we were going to make it out of that AO before the end of the day. We did not think we could make it, but the lure of being out of the field and back at Uplift that night forced us to continue on to the end of the valley.

After dealing with jungle terrain through the entire trek to the valley, the scenery finally gave way to tall grass and cane breaks next to a shallow river broadened by the monsoon rains. The banks of the river were sand and large round pebble rocks close enough together to be considered paving stones. They made it hard to walk in a hurry, but we were managing.

Second platoon was on point as we traveled through the center of the valley toward our pick up point. As luck would have it, the point element made contact with some VC/NVA. The group up front just behind the point team dropped their rucks along with the point team and SSgt. Andersen and began to pursue the VC/NVA. Since SSgt. Andersen went with them, I also had to go only I could not shed my rucksack because of the radio. We probably ran the length of a football field before breaking off the search. The VC/NVA had simply disappeared into the cane breaks and was gone. They left no traces or signs as to which direction they took when they vanished. The group of us talked and decided to give up the hunt and move back to the rest of the company's location.

We ran down the mountain with little or no rest, we stopped for only two hours before we began hastily moving down the valley on difficult terrain, then we ran to chase the VC/NVA we spotted and now we were backtracking to the company only to return to the same area while continuing to our LZ. All this time I was humping the radio, an extra twenty-five pounds. I was exhausted, wet and looking forward to our return to the dry buildings at Uplift. This was a constant problem since I had to carry the radio.

We linked back up with the rest of Alpha Company and then traveled back to the area where we had lost the VC/NVA and continued our trek toward the LZ with no further distractions. It was getting late so once we arrived at our pick up LZ, the rear command was notified immediately. To our chagrin, we were told there was not enough time to extract the whole company before nightfall and rather than leave a smaller element in the field for the night, the company would remain intact until the next day and be extracted then.

We dug in for the night and posted guards around the perimeter relieving them every two hours until stand to or wake up at 0500 hours. Beginning then, everyone cooks chow and has coffee or hot chocolate to warm them up from the overnight chill. The morning was gray and looked like the rain would continue, possibly delaying our extraction. We continued to prep for extraction regardless of the weather. We filled the foxholes and packed whatever was removed from our rucks back into them. No one wanted to miss another opportunity to return to the rear so by 0700 everyone was ready to go. Second platoon would secure the LZ for the Chinooks that would pick up the first and third platoons. Then Hueys with gunship escorts would pick up the second platoon last. At 0830, the first Chinook came in and picked up the first platoon. We were finally going back to Uplift for a well-deserved rest.

CHAPTER 12

The Big Lie

Once back at LZ Uplift, everything went back to normal. The rain kept the duty light but there was still guard duty and other details. I was on a detail tearing down the old TOC, Tactical Operations Center, where all activity in the battalion came through. It was the center of all radio transmissions and was manned twenty-four hours a day. It was so cold and rainy on that detail, I wore my field jacket for the only time in Vietnam. After we tore down the TOC, I remember we patched holes in the roofs of all the other buildings, both old and new on Uplift. The tin the engineers used for the roofs of the buildings they were constructing had been used before and had many holes that leaked. We patched the holes with tar, which seemed to do the trick as a stop leak.

The rumor mill was working overtime at Uplift and the word was out that Bob Hope was going to be at Phu Cat Air Base for his Christmas show on November 4, 1969. When that got out everyone was in the First Sargent's office at the orderly room wanting a pass to go see Bob Hope. Of course, the fair-minded First Sargent canceled all passes for that time. Since he could not let us all go, no one would go.

We all decided the solution was to go AWOL, absent without leave. After all, how many times do you get to see Bob Hope's Christmas Show in Vietnam? That was our plan and everybody I knew was in on it. We were going. Our attitude was to hell with the consequences!

Little did we know, the Battalion Command had another plan. I can tell you now it was a fabrication of the truth when they told us it was a special mission for the whole Battalion and all companies would be involved. It already sounds suspicious, doesn't it? Starting November 2,1969, we were going out to a large tabletop mountain somewhere and sit for seven days. There was supposed to be enough room for all the companies in the Battalion to set up on top of the mountain. Finally, 2 November came, and there was no denying it; we were going out to the field.

Since this was another battalion operation and we were leaving from Uplift, we had plenty of time before we loaded onto helicopters for transport to the tabletop mountain. Charley Company was the first one to load up and go. I used the extra time to go to the steakhouse and buy a case of Coca Cola to cover me for the next seven days. I strapped it under the flap on the top of my ruck and was set to go. With the extra weight of the Cokes, my ruck was very heavy. Fortunately, my plan was to get off the helicopter and find a spot to laager in and enjoy a Coke now and then.

When it came time for second platoon of Alpha Company to go, I sat on the floor of the Huey in the door with my feet on the skid, leaning back and resting against my rucksack. Next to me was SSgt. Richardson, second platoon's acting platoon leader for this mission.

I found SSgt. Richardson to be a very competent senior NCO with a no nonsense attitude in the field. He was a man of few words but clearly made his point when he spoke. I never saw or heard of him making a bad choice or wrong decision. SSgt. Richardson was with the second platoon when I arrived in country and was second behind SSgt. Andersen by seniority only. Both were equally capable leaders. I can remember watching SSgt. Richardson practicing karate in the rear at Uplift; he was good at it. He would come out in his sweats and do his routine workout. I guess it was a way for him to stay in shape, he was a head shorter than I was but had a muscular build. I watched him use his karate once in Qui Nhon when we were at Red Beach. One of the privates got drunk and jumped a young Staff Sergeant Ranger. The Ranger wanted nothing to do with the private but could not shed him because he was not willing to hit him. Richardson waited until they were separated, took the private out with one kick, and the fight was over.

The helicopter flight out to the tabletop mountain took some time and was a cold flight. The birds swept in and landed about in the middle of the unusually large flattop mountain. Once on the ground we moved off the LZ past some rows of poncho hootches or tents full of Charlie Company troops. The hootches had one or two people to each one. The guys sitting in the small shelters began to heckle me about carting a case of Coke. They kept saying things like, "You might as well give those sodas to us now. You aren't going to be able to hump them where you are going."

At the time, I was sloughing off their comments because I did not understand why they were making them. Later I would learn, Charlie Company obviously knew more than we did about this mission. SSgt. Richardson was called for a briefing with all of Alpha Company's platoon leaders. When he returned to our location, I found out why Charlie Company was making those remarks.

We were not going to just sit on top of the mountain. Every company but Charlie was moving down off the top of the mountain to run search and destroy missions. Each company was assigned a different section in different directions over the side of the mountain. The mountain was huge and flat for as far as the eye could see. There was room for at least a couple of long runways for an airport. If it had been more accessible, or a road built to it, there probably would have been some kind of base on it. Its cover was all waist high grass so we were well above the tree line. It somewhat reminded me of the escarpment from the old Tarzan movies with Johnny Weissmuller.

The sun was shining brightly, unusual for a November day during monsoon season, but it was very cool. As we stood on the edge of the mountain overlooking Alpha Company's AO assignment and figuring out our avenue of descent, someone spotted a large group of NVA moving along a ridge in the distance. We reported the sighting and several minutes later a group of jets came in and dropped napalm along the ridge where the enemy had been traveling. Napalm is gelled gasoline packed into a capsule like a bomb so it can be dropped from a jet. When it hits the ground, it spreads out in the direction traveled by the jet that dropped it. Napalm burns very hot with intense flames for a long time and is a very effective mechanism for eliminating a large group of enemy in the open. It was too far away to determine if there were any casualties, but we learned there were NVA in the vicinity where we were going to be searching for them.

Before we started our descent, the guys from Charlie Company made one last attempt to wrestle my sodas away from me. I told them, "No way", I was sure there were guys in Alpha Company that would help me drink them. That's the very thing that happened on the way down the mountain. When we took our first break, my ruck felt like it weighed a thousand pounds, so I asked if anyone wanted a Coke and passed them out. I would have rather enjoyed a Coke sitting on top of the mountain while writing a letter to my girlfriend. I could still write the letter, Coke or no Coke, and I was enjoying the camaraderie with the guys of the second platoon.

Once we went over the side of the mountain, we were back in jungle terrain. It was thick, slippery, and steep. There were many vines hanging from the trees that grabbed our rucksacks and hung up the progress of decent. There were also the "wait a minute" vines that caught us around the boots and took about a minute to untangle, thus the name, "wait a minute". We stayed in platoon-sized elements for our security because the size of the NVA element we dropped the napalm on before we started down was estimated as company sized. All three of Alpha Company's platoons operated in a different area of the section identified as our AO.

The terrain was mostly wooded ridges coming off the tabletop mountain. Second platoon laagered in early the first night in a bunch of trees. It was cold and a heavy mist moving in made it feel even colder. The routine in the perimeter was the same as usual: everyone setting out Claymores and trip flares early and then taking turns pulling guard monitoring the radios until stand to in the morning. Stand to meant everybody was up and awake just before first light. That was the favorite time for the NVA to attack so we were all awake just in case of an attack. The first night was uneventful; we had no contact or breeches of the perimeter. I woke up with an earache and went to talk to the medic, Doc Espinosa, about some medicine to treat it. He didn't have anything to treat an earache so I contacted the CP on top of the mountain to see if the Top Doc had any, but he didn't have any either.

I put the earache medicine on our list for resupply, which would be in two days. What I didn't know was the Top Doc put it on his list also. I started to run a fever with my earache, so Doc Espinosa was giving me aspirin for that but it did not help with the pain in my ear. The weather was still cold or raining and cold.

On the move through the thick jungle environment, traveling up and down ridges slickened from the dampness in the mist or rain, the point man Wiley slipped, hitting a rock with his hand on the way down and almost severed a finger. We medevacked him out to a hospital and found out later he returned to the states because of the serious nature of his injury.

Back to the search and destroy mission, as we topped a wooded ridge about noon the day before our resupply, the point element came in contact with some wild hogs. They fired them up but unfortunately for us, their aim was poor or the hogs were too fast for them, and they did not kill any. We could have had a feast with a fresh roasted hog.

The night before our scheduled resupply was a rough night for me. I felt sorry for SSgt. Richardson. He and I were sharing the cover of a poncho we strung about eight inches off the ground to keep the heavy dew off us and get a little protection from the wind. The wind we referred to as the "hawk" was bitter cold that night. I tossed and turned all night, sometimes moaning in a half sleep from the pain I was experiencing in my ear. I don' know how SSgt. Richardson tolerated it, but he never said a word.

Sometime before morning stand to, a trip flare went off. Of course, the normal reaction from everyone was to start shooting. The perimeter on SSgt. Richardson and my side where the trip flare went off lit up with small arms fire. When I rolled out of the shelter, I grabbed for my weapon I had left leaning against the tree to which one corner of the shelter was tied. The rifle was gone! I could not do anything but lie there and watch as everyone around me laid down a base of fire. As most of the second platoon fired their weapons, we heard the wild hogs running and breaking branches getting away. Our perimeter was probed by a herd of wild hogs and after a check in the kill zone, we did not get any again. There were no NVA bodies either so we just chalked this one up to the hogs.

As daylight came upon us, one of the squad leaders that had positioned himself next to me during the fracas asked me, "I noticed you weren't firing your weapon. Why was that?"

"Because I can't find my weapon," I responded.

I could see the look of disgust come across his face, then he lit into me, "You can't find your weapon." Where is your weapon? Where did you leave it?"

SSgt Richardson stepped in at this point, "Hey, leave Musson alone. He had a bad night!"

I thought when Richardson stepped in, it would end there, but the squad leader kept it up. "You need to find your weapon right now, troop."

I started to answer, "I left it right here against this tree…" but then I noticed the corrosion around the pin on the squad leader's weapon. That pin hinges the weapon open in order to clean it and the weapon the squad leader was carrying looked an awful lot like mine. It was a common thing for an older M-16 to have corrosion of the cast aluminum because of the jungle environment, but mine was unique. Then I finished my sentence as I pulled the M-16 from his hands, "And here is my weapon right here. Where is yours?"

He was dumfounded and did not respond immediately but finally came back with, "Well where is my weapon?"

I replied, "I don't know, but you can't have mine!"

SSgt. Richardson had the final say, "You need to find your weapon, now, Sergeant."

He found his rifle right next to where he was sleeping when the trip flare went off. Why he left it when he ran across the perimeter, no one will know. I guess he took mine because he looked stupid not firing a weapon. He was saved from embarrassment for a while, and I looked stupid for a while. We both continued with our job, and did not mention the incident again.

I was always appreciative of SSgt. Richardson sticking up for me that day. I don't know how he was able to do it after the way I had treated him that night. I know he did not get any sleep either, but he certainly endeared himself to me. I will never forget how good it made me feel when he stepped in to defend me. When I met him forty-four years after that event, we hugged, and I told him so too. He is a great friend.

When the resupply bird came in that day, I was anxiously awaiting the package for the medic that would contain the medicine for my ear. As we combed through all the supplies, distributing the food for everyone and cigarettes for those who smoked we came up short on the medicine. Once again, I contacted the Top Doc in the CP on top of the mountain. It seems the rear decided of the two orders for ear ache medicine they had, the Top Doc would need it more than second platoon, so with only one bottle in the rear supply, they sent it to the Top Doc on top of the mountain. Since there was no clean way to transfer the medicine to second platoon, Richardson made the decision to send me back to the rear on the resupply bird. The only other way was to call in a dust-off, a medevac helicopter to take me back to Uplift. The resupply bird was the lessor of two evils and nobody had to explain anything or fill out paperwork.

The next day after I arrived back at Uplift, I reported in at the aide station first thing in the morning to see the battalion Doctor. He took my temperature and a look in my ear, and then wrote up orders for me to report to a specialist at the 67th Evac Hospital in Qui Nhon. Since I wasn't dusted off or medevacked, I was on my own for transportation to the hospital. I went to the gate at Uplift and caught a ride going straight to Qui Nhon right away. I found the specialist's office and he took me in right away. He diagnosed me with an inner ear infection. Then he told me he was going to stick a probe, which was like a long fine needle in my ear beyond my eardrum to clean out the infection. He told me I had to hold very still and not move my head, even though the procedure was intricate and painful. Boy, was that a huge understatement! The only thing that kept me from passing out due to the pain was the doctor told me I could not move my head. I never felt pain like that before or since having that procedure done. He gave me some kind of antibiotic pills to take for about two weeks and sent me on my way back to Uplift. I was fortunate that I was able to accomplish all the travel and treatment in one long day. As far as where the ear infection came from, I am sure it had something to do with the weather. Even when I was a kid at home I used to get earaches, in the late fall in cold weather. Although I never had any of this magnitude when I was a kid and I attribute that to the delay in getting the medicine for my ear. If Doc Espinosa would have had it or we would have gotten the medicine in second platoon's resupply, the trip to the rear and to the hospital may have been prevented.

I was detail free while I was at Uplift for the next two days, which gave me a chance to send a tape home to my girlfriend and see a movie. After this letter tape home, I had to give up sending tapes. I could not carry the recorder in the field and my friend Hendricks from Headquarters Company kept it with my duffle bag in his room at Uplift. I did not want to expose him to scrutiny by having him dig out my duffle bag every time

Alpha Company came back to Uplift. It was not legal for him to have my duffle bag and his duffle bag according to regulations and any exposure would put him in a bind. The tape recorder remained unused from then on.

I went back on the next resupply to a location near where I left second platoon. The battalion was on its eighth day of a supposed seven-day operation and it was still on going. I do not remember how they finished the seven-day mission, but we moved around as a company to different AOs on different missions and with the exception of first platoon who went back, to secure Uplift in January, Alpha Company's second and third platoons never saw Uplift again until March 19, 1970.

Just before one of those moves, our resupply loaded us up with all kinds of different things we didn't normally carry. Everyone was mandated to carry more ammo and grenades than normal. The weirdest thing they wanted us to carry as many as we could was the LAW, M72 Light Antitank Weapon. It was a shoulder-fired, 66mm rocket with a one-time disposable fiberglass launcher. I was carrying a LAW and two hundred extra rounds for the M-60 machine gun besides the radio. We were going on a mission to block an unknown force of NVA and unfamiliar to us our objective was only 500 meters from where we were inserted. The brass figured the extra ammo would not hurt, traveling that short distance.

We also had a new platoon leader, Lt. Harrold. He was the one that knew where our objective was located. The problem was his map reading skills were somewhat lacking. After walking for hours, moving out of a jungle into a swamp and finally struggling over jagged rocks in a swift river, we took a break on a dry pile of rocks just off to the side of the river. While the NCOs and Lt. Harrold were discussing where they thought we were, I was monitoring the radio trying to figure out why I couldn't hear any chatter on our net. Then I heard a chopper pilot talking to someone.

"Roger, I'll see if I can make contact with them on your net, over."

I did not hear any response, just the pilot's next transmission.

"When was your last transmission from them?"

There was no response over the radio again.

Then the pilot said, "Roger, I'll fly in a circle and we'll see if we can find them, over."

I called out for Lt. Harrold, "Sir, I can hear a pilot talking to somebody on the radio, and it sounds like they are talking about us."

"About us?" he quizzed. "What are they saying about us?"

I was still monitoring the pilot's half of the radio transmissions and I said, "It sounds like they think we are lost."

Then the pilot came onto the net saying. "Papa Tango", my call sign. "Papa Tango, this is Casper six two on your net. Do you read, over?" Casper was a helicopter company, one of many, that was assigned to haul the 173rd into and out of combat. They had a Casper the Friendly Ghost painted on the nose of each helicopter. They were always a welcome sight coming in to haul us out.

I answered the Casper pilot, but I only had my short antenna on the radio and my transmission only cracked the airwaves.

The pilot came back with, "Papa Tango, this is Casper six two, if you read me pop smoke, over."

I yelled for someone to, "pop smoke", while I put up my long john antenna to get better communication. When I had the long antenna up I transmitted, "Smoke out."

"Roger, smoke out," the pilot replied, but he was too far away to identify any smoke.

"Papa Tango, this is Casper six two, I have negative smoke, can you see my aircraft, over?"

By this time, I had the military compass my parents had sent me and was looking at directions in anticipation of guiding the distant chopper to our location. "Casper six two, this is Papa Tango, I have eyes on a helicopter to our north, over."

At that point, the pilot must have turned toward us because the profile of his helicopter almost disappeared from view. "Roger, Papa Tango. Understand you are to my south. Pop smoke, over." Then I heard the pilot contact the CP to inform the captain he may have located us. I still could not receive the CO's reply even with my long antenna.

I threw a smoke grenade out and spoke into the handset of my radio, "Smoke out, over"

The helicopter was still not close enough to see the smoke, "This is Casper six two, I have negative smoke, over."

As the helicopter came closer we tried one more time, "Casper six two. This is Papa Tango. I have smoke out, over."

The pilot responded, "Roger. I identify purple smoke, over."

For all of us relieved to be found, I replied, "Casper six two. This is Papa Tango, roger on the purple smoke, over."

Then the pilot again contacted the CO at his location telling him we had been found. The sad news for us was, the pilot gave us our coordinates and we were twelve kilometers or klicks for short, out of our AO, area of operation. When we got off the helicopter earlier in the day we were five hundred meters from where we were supposed to be. The lieutenant would have a lot of explaining to do when we got back which the CO relayed through the pilot was to be before the end of the day. We gathered our gear and after the typical bitching about being lost, humping extra gear and ammo, we moved out back toward our AO.

We did not want to take the same route back so we stuck to the river as long as we could. Everyone wanted to ditch the extra ammo and LAWs especially after we found out how difficult the route we chose was. It was even tougher than our earlier trek and we did not quite make it back inside the AO before night set in on us. We did have radio communication with the CO though and when I relayed the message we weren't going to make our objective, I could sense the disappointment on the other end.

The CO wanted to talk to Papa, the lieutenant, and expressed his disappointment in their radio conversation. The only reason the CO allowed us to remain outside the AO was he did not want us traveling at night. Outside the AO, there were countless hazards that could be detrimental to a small unit alone. One thing it usually meant was that the artillery set up for our protection would not be available because they could not reach outside the AO. Another hazard was a small unit like one platoon left alone with no protection could be cut off and annihilated by the NVA. The fact was that a rescue attempt, if something happened at night, also doubled the risk for everyone involved. We were not in a good situation and the CO was not happy about anything that happened to second platoon on this mission.

When we got back the next day to our intended location, the opportunity for success on our mission had been lost so we made a combat assault to another area. We went in to a hot LZ, when the bad guys are shooting on the way in. Thankfully, no one was wounded or killed and the choppers that hauled us in also made it out unscathed. The LZ was actually still burning from the tracers and rockets fired by the gunships prepping the LZ before they inserted us. It seemed there was no end to the perils and surprises on the extended seven-day mission the Battalion had assigned to us. Funny, Bob hope never missed us not being at his Phu Cat Christmas performance but we sure missed him and we remembered the lie that prevented our attendance at the Bob Hope Christmas Show. One thing for sure, we weren't headed back to Uplift for a long time.

CHAPTER 13

Lost for Christmas

When the holidays came along, we were still in the field, working our way through the mountains and the jungles north and west of Uplift. The rains continued to soak us every day as the monsoons carried on. The big news was the cease-fire for the Thanksgiving and Christmas holidays. The US put a moratorium on bombing the north and the Ho Chi Minh trail, but that just let the enemy move more munitions, troops and equipment down from the north. Every break in the bombing always put US troops at risk because of the increased activity of the VC/NVA; they never honored any cease-fire.

We got a treat for Thanksgiving: our first hot meal delivered to the field. Our normal diet consisted of C-rations or LRRPs, long-range reconnaissance patrol freeze-dried meals. Everyone had their favorites but we doctored every meal with something extra to make them palatable. Therefore, when we got hot turkey delivered to us in Melamine cans, everyone was ecstatic. The story that was passed down to us as to how the meal happened went like this. A general who was making a holiday tour to base camps in our area stopped by Uplift for dinner. On his tour through the mess, he asked the mess sergeant a question.

The general asked, "What are the troops in the field eating today Sergeant?"

"I don't know, C-rations I guess, sir," the Mess Sergeant replied.

"That was the wrong answer, Sergeant. If I am eating hot turkey on Thanksgiving, so should the troops in the field," the General admonished.

The next thing we knew, the rear was contacting us to get to an LZ so they could bring in a hot meal and resupply us. That first hot meal set precedence and from then on, we had at least one hot meal a month when we were in the field for extended periods. We did not carry mess kits like those back in the states so everything we ate with or on was brought out on the helicopters with the hot food. We also had to make sure we dug a sump to throw trash in once the meal was finished. We did not want anything left over to fall into the enemy's hands.

Wherever the VC/NVA went during the holidays, it was not where we were looking in the mountains and jungles. All we were turning up was old used trails with no contact with the enemy. At one time, there must have been plenty of activity on some of the trails. We found a punji pit that was three foot square and about fifteen feet deep. The cover had been off for a long time so it was an easy find. A punji pit was a hole dug into a well-used area, usually about two feet deep with sharpened bamboo stakes in the bottom. The bamboo was strong enough to impale a person in the foot even penetrating the protective plate in the sole of our jungle boots. The punji stakes in the bottom of the fifteen-foot pit we found were about five feet long and three inches apart. Those punji stakes were intended to impale and kill the person that fell into the pit.

Sometime before Christmas, the company made another combat assault or CA for short, to a different area. Actually, we split into platoon-sized elements and were inserted into different areas with a plan to unite for Christmas day and celebrate with a hot meal.

Second platoon was inserted into an area of woods and jungle so dense; shortly after we were inserted, we were lost. The jungle was so thick we were not able to identify any terrain features to read a map. The lieutenant decided to call for an artillery strike to determine our location. We had the co-ordinates of the location where we were inserted. We knew the direction we moved away from the LZ where we were inserted and we estimated about how far we had moved from the LZ. With that information, we worked up a co-ordinate to call in for an artillery strike. Normally artillery will not fire if a unit is between the firebase and the target, in case there is a short round. A short round is an artillery round that lands short of the target. I do not know if the artillery firebase in this instance did not know our location was between the firebase and the target co-ordinates or if they fired because they knew we were lost. The artillery fires a volley to allow us to get a reading on the map so we would know where we were. Since we know the co-ordinates of the artillery barrage we take a compass reading and follow it back along a line, the back asmyth, and our location should be somewhere on that line. A simple example would be if the heading on the compass reads three hundred sixty degrees, then the back asmyth is one hundred eighty degrees. If you draw a line on the map your position should be somewhere on that line. To get a better fix, a second round of artillery could be requested and using the same method for marking the map with the back asmyth, where the lines cross should be your location. It is a guess but it is better than nothing. We wanted the artillery to fire two volleys to get our location right, but this time we stopped at one because in the initial volley we took a short round. It missed us but the sound of an artillery round coming in is frightening. All the rounds went over the top of our location, cutting and whistling through the air as they sailed over us. The short round was tumbling repeatedly, we could hear it cutting the air, "shoop, shoop", and then it hit the ground not far from us and exploded. It was close enough for us; we decided to go on until we could get to an area where we could see some terrain features to read the maps.

We regretted that decision shortly after making it and having to cut our way through the jungle brush. It was so thick everyone took turns at the point. We had three men working the point element: one with a machete cutting the trail, the second dragging the cut brush off and stacking it to the side of the trail, and the third watching with an M-16 to make sure there was protection in case the point made contact with the enemy. It was hot so we rotated the assignments every ten to fifteen minutes then changed the whole point element. Everyone got a turn except the lieutenant and the platoon sergeant. We worked for eight hours straight but had moved only one hundred meters. After moving that short distance, everyone was so exhausted we laagered in for the night. In a usual night laager position everyone forms a circle making a perimeter for security and guard positions are established in critical locations. I think that was the only time we laagered in a straight line with a platoon-sized element.

Finally, out of the thickest jungle I experienced during my entire tour, we were still having trouble figuring out where we were and locating the remainder of the company for our Christmas Day celebration. The platoon broke into smaller elements; I remember Mangilardi was out away from us with his squad. We tried to identify where he was by popping smoke once but no one saw any smoke at all. Not wanting to give our position away, we just kept struggling along. I do not think Mangilardi was lost, I think we were. The terrain was hills and elephant grass, occasionally a stream would appear. We saw no signs of any enemy activity of any kind. I think both the first and third platoons had already linked up and were waiting on the second platoon to start the celebration.

Christmas Eve we moved across a stream and up a small hill with scrub trees and grass on top. We made our night laager there and passed the night with no incidents. We were so lost even Santa could not find us. The next day at stand to, I was organizing a water patrol to go back down the hill to the stream to get some water and take a swim. Not too many people were interested at 0500 in the morning on Christmas Day. Four of us went for water meaning everyone needing water gave us their canteens to get water for them. Some guys just wanted to sleep in and did not care one way or the other. Those guys never gave us any canteens.

My interest in the swim was because the stream was perfect for it. When we crossed it the day before, I noticed a boulder with a thin sheet of water flowing over it right in the middle of the narrow rapid flowing stream. The boulder was huge and formed a dam in the stream. The water behind the boulder was ankle deep and skinned over the rock about a half-inch deep. Then it cascaded into a pool of crystal clear water about fifteen feet deep. After we retrieved our water, we removed our clothes, leaving one guy on guard and had a blast sliding over that boulder into the deep pool of water. That boulder was twenty feet in diameter, so it was a good drop into the clear pool after sliding over it. The water stopped sheeting over the rock and a waterfall made up the last six or eight feet before we went back into the water of the deep pool. Once the first guy had his fill of all the fun, he relieved the guard and we all got refreshed and clean on Christmas morning. When I got out, my boots were missing and I asked if anyone had taken them. Of course the answers were, "No, we didn't take your boots."

I was sure the boots left on the bank with my clothes were not mine. For one thing they seemed newer and had more polish on them than mine. So I persisted, "Well these are not my boots I am sure of that." As I looked at the Lieutenant's boots, I asked, "Sir, are you sure those are your boots? They look like mine."

"No, Muss, these are my boots. They fit me good," he answered.

"Well what size are they? These are size 12 narrow and I wear 12 regular," I persisted pointing to the boots I was holding.

"I thought these were my boots but you may be right. Those look more like my boots. Let me try them on," he replied. As he slipped the first boot on, he said, "I think you're right. These are my boots. They feel much better."

I had to keep my mouth shut but I was thinking, no wonder we are lost all the time, he can't even find his boots.

With the boot exchange done, we went back up the hill to where the rest of second platoon was just fixing morning chow. A few of the guys who weren't interested in a swim earlier wished they had gone after we told them about the water slide. We were nice and refreshed but it was too late for them. We had to finish chow and press on.

Later that day as we were traversing the side of a steep mountain, the trail we were making was just a narrow path only about a foot wide. The jungle bushes and vines to our left offered us some handholds to keep us balanced on the narrow pathway. To the right was a very steep, almost cliff-like slope, covered with jungle vegetation for as far as the eye could see. The word passed back along the column to take five, meaning to take a break in place. The side of the mountain was so steep I just leaned back on my rucksack as I squatted down with my ass planted on the narrow footpath. The lieutenant was in front of me and I watched as he removed his ruck, pulling his map from his pocket and sat down. Our respite lasted long enough for us to get a drink from a canteen, rest our leg muscles which had been straining hard traveling the narrow path around the side of the mountain, and for Lieutenant Harrold to check his map.

When the word came down to get ready to move, I carefully stood up to put on my rucksack. I always slipped my ruck on as if I was putting on a coat, one arm in a strap then the other. Usually there was no need to adjust it other than making sure the pads on the shoulder straps were not twisted or out of place. With the radio, it was heavy enough that if anything was a little out of place I knew it immediately because I was in pain almost instantly. Some of the other guys, including the lieutenant,

RUN THROUGH THE JUNGLE

put their ruck on by picking it up over their head and letting it slide along the back of their neck, putting their arms in the straps as it slid down their back. Even if I was not carrying the radio, I doubt if I would employ that method because it just seemed painstakingly awkward and cumbersome. I watched as the lieutenant accomplished the first phase of slipping into his ruck. Once he had it on his back, he would bend forward, hunching his shoulders and propelling the rucksack higher up on his back. As he did that, he would pull the quick release straps taut and then straighten up to make final adjustments. This time as he bent forward and hunched his shoulders, the rucksack went over his shoulders and his head and dragged him off his perch, causing him to somersault down the side of the mountain. We lost sight of him almost immediately after he fell away from the trail. All we heard was the screaming on the way down and the jungle brush cracking and swooshing as he went through it. The noise continued until we heard the lieutenant come to an abrupt stop. Then there was a certain amount of moaning: not the," I'm hurt" kind, more like "What did I do?" kind.

I called out to him softly because we were practicing noise discipline, "Sir, are you OK?"

"Auh ah, I think so," he replied.

"Do you need some help?" I asked.

"No, I think I can make it on my own," he said.

As I looked around, those who saw the lieutenant fall, knowing he was now OK, were silently laughing their asses off. Even I could not keep a straight face after witnessing him somersault off the trail. I do not remember if this event caused him to be called, "Weird Harrold" but it was one of the many that contributed to him getting the moniker. We all calmed down when we saw the lieutenant crawling and scratching his way back up the side of the steep mountain. His glasses were oddly placed on his head because one of the earpieces was bent in an odd configuration. He remarked later that he was lucky he did not lose his glasses in the fall. We estimated his fall was about one hundred meters, longer than a football field, and he was lucky he didn't break his neck.

After the lieutenant rejoined us and we got back under way, we finally topped the ridge we had been paralleling and got into some dense triple canopy jungle. In triple canopy jungle, very little light penetrates to the jungle floor during the day. It appears as if the sun has just set and the gray light of dusk is the only light available. The trees were tall and full of the dark green foliage blocking out the sun's rays. The soil of the jungle floor is dark black and rich from the plant decay. Strangely, there is little or no grass growth, just the broad leaves of plants that are indigenous to this jungle region.

There was an old well-used trail about three to four feet wide on top of the ridge. We considered not using it, as was the practice we normally followed but after all we had been through getting here and still not linked up with the rest of the company, we decided the lesser of two evils would be using the trail. Cutting trail in this jungle would have taken forever to get to the location of the first and third platoons. We proceeded to use the trail with extreme caution, checking for booby traps, punji pits and ambushes. Luckily, we found none of those and at long last linked with the rest of the company to start our Christmas celebration.

After arriving at the selected spot for the LZ to bring in a hot meal, we joined the other two platoons in removing the trees so there would be room to bring in helicopters. We had axes dropped in and went to work cutting the giant trees and removing them to clear the space required to land the UH-1 Hueys that would bring us our resupply and hot meal.

Unknown to us, the command back at Uplift had a special treat planed for us. They had held all the packages sent from home for about two weeks before Christmas and planned to present them to us on Christmas Day to make it extra festive. It was a nice gesture but once we were resupplied, had a hot meal and opened the care packages that we usually shared because one guy couldn't eat all the cookies and candy he received, we had too many gifts to share. Almost everyone in the company got at least a dozen chocolate chip cookies. There was no one to share them with since we all had cookies. There were other things that individuals received that were special to them. Delgado got homemade flour tortillas from his mother. I remember they were separated by squares of newspaper. He shared them with us and they were good. I received some packages of my favorite black licorice. I got two packages from my mother and two from my girlfriend's mother. I shared with the others but sparingly. It was my special treat and I didn't want to give all of it away.

There was another surprise from the Salvation Army: a ditty bag for everyone that had many things we did not often see. One of the items was a washcloth, the only one I ever saw while in Vietnam. Some of the other things were a bar of soap, a toothbrush and toothpaste, a needle and threads with buttons for our uniforms, a writing tablet and a ink pen to write letters, and some candy fit for a high-heat jungle environment, bull's eyes and caramels. That little dark blue bag had the Salvation Army emblem on it in red and I never forgot the kindness it represented. Unlike the Red Cross, the Salvation Army never asked us for any donations. The bag was a gift from their heart. Sometime before Christmas, the Salvation Army also distributed some Christmas cards. We were allowed to take as many as we wanted with the stipulation that we would write the person who sent them and thank them for their kindness. I selected five cards because each one had interesting unique handwriting. When I wrote my thank you letters, three of them sent a letter back and we started a correspondence that lasted almost to the end of my tour. I wrote letters home to my girlfriend every day, but I couldn't get enough return mail so the extra mail was welcome.

First platoon set up a Christmas tree, a bush they decorated with ammunition from different weapons. The weather was cold enough to be Christmas. Somebody took a picture of me wearing a jungle sweater; I don't remember carrying it but I saw the picture at one of the first platoon reunions. Besides cold weather, we were still having a lot of rain, heavy downpours. That made the mountainous jungle gloomy and guards had to stay very alert. Not only could we not see anything but also it was impossible to hear anything but the rain pouring through the broad leaf plants. We stayed a few days at the Christmas laager. Then we moved up hill to the next mountain about a klick, or one thousand meters away. Once we were settled in at the new laager, we found out one of the other platoons had a guy go AWOL. That was unheard of in the field especially in the jungles of Vietnam.

We called in artillery in on our old Christmas laager to try and mess it up as much as possible making it unsuitable for the enemy to move in and have a readymade basecamp. We watched from our new hilltop location as the rounds exploded all over the LZ we had worked so hard to complete for delivery of a hot meal and mail from home.

After that, we started searching for the guy that went AWOL, sending out patrols in all directions to try and find him or signs of him. We ran those patrols for about a week remaining at our second laager while doing so. That made many people nervous; we never spent that much time in one area. Just as the discussion was leaning toward us moving out, the word came to us from the rear, Perry the AWOL had been found. He walked into a South Vietnamese Army Base Camp miles from our location. His condition wasn't good; he hadn't been eating very well since he left us. I never heard what his problem was and he never came back to the company.

We continued to run our search and destroy missions in the dense triple canopy jungles right into the New Year. I was on guard the night the year changed. All the rear areas held a mad minute when they fire their weapons, throw grenades, and shoot off star clusters to celebrate the New Year. For us, 1969 passed without any fanfare and no shots were fired. I guess we were thankful for that.

CHAPTER 14

Walking Out of the Mountains to Firebase Abbey

We heard through the news radio on AFVN, Armed Forces Vietnam that one of the famous psychics from the states had predicted that US soldiers with service numbers that contained the numbers 5 and 4 together would be killed in battles throughout Vietnam in the next two months. Some of the guys believed it and started to become a little paranoid. It seemed to be the hot topic on any break we took, and at chow time. Anybody with a radio had it tuned in to see if there were any updates. The psychic had made the prediction as one of her New Year predictions after the first of the year. Even though that included me, I didn't believe the prediction and did not take any extra precautions to prevent something from happening to me. It turns out I was right and she was wrong.

Alpha Company continued on search and destroy missions in the same areas where we had already found nothing but old signs and we made no contact with the enemy. The morale of the troops was low due to no action or contact for some time, and it seemed we were just walking around in the jungle achieving nothing. The weather remained cold and damp or cold and raining. Some nights seemed bitter cold but we had no way of recording the temperature to see how cold it really was. There was a lot of fog that hindered our searches and we had to be extra cautious maneuvering around. We were trying hard not to surprise anyone or have them surprise us in the fog. Most of the low morale came from the fact that we had been in the field for a long time. Two months without a break was too long.

Because of the all the confusion of being lost several times on this mission, I had asked Lieutenant Harrold if I could order a set of maps for myself. When he found out I could read a map he gave me the OK to order a set. The maps were renewed only when we changed our AO enough to require a new set. When it came time for everyone else to change maps, I ordered and received my set. I was happy about getting a map set for myself. I already had a lensatic compass my parents sent to me. They went to the Army Surplus store and got a US Army issue compass. Now I was in business and felt that I could help when we were trying to figure out where we were.

One of the days as we moved through the jungle the point element came upon a US Army APC, armored personnel carrier. It was like a tank capable of carrying a six or seven man squad in addition to the crew. We certainly did not expect to see one in the jungle mountains on this mission. We also found some Bangalore torpedoes another strange item to find in the high mountain jungle. The Bangalore was usually used to take out objects that blocked the way such as walls or concertina wire. It was a round tube filled with explosives about 2 inches in diameter that could be screwed together in a series and slid under any blockage then detonated to remove wide obstacles giving ground troops access through the obstruction.

About the time we found the APC, we got word we were moving out of the mountains to secure a firebase overlooking the river that runs through the An Lao Valley. We spent one more night in the jungle and early the following morning, we were standing on the ridge overlooking the valley. The fluffy cumulus clouds were slowly moving by below us. Standing there overlooking the river valley with the clouds made a perfect photo opportunity. The sky was even a pretty shade of blue, unusual for monsoon season. After taking in the view for a short time, we started down the ridge into the valley below. By late afternoon, we were paralleling the river and moving toward Firebase Abbey, the location we were supposed to secure. An artillery unit attached to the 173rd was already there, but they needed reinforcements to secure the entire firebase. The firebase was two small hills, thirty to forty meters high separated by the helicopter pad located in the middle of what we referred to as the saddle connecting the two hills. All together, the firebase was about four hundred meters long.

As we moved toward Abbey, we found some huge tiger tracks in the sandy banks along the river. We scared up a large deer in the tall brush right after seeing the tiger tracks and the whole company fired up the area thinking it was the tiger. We sent out a search patrol to see if we killed anything but the results were negative. When the patrol returned, we continued along the river until we came to a shallow rapid where we crossed to the other side and approached the firebase. The company CP made radio contact with the artillery unit on Abbey and we entered the firebase without incident.

Once inside the wire on Abbey we found out some news that was important to some in Alpha Company. The first platoon would leave the field and return to LZ Uplift to provide security for our basecamp. They were picked up from the helicopter pad at Abbey before we even settled in. The company commander, Captain Grim, went with them because we were getting a new commanding officer. Some in Alpha Company didn't like Grim; he seemed unfriendly and aloof with the troops in his command. Because of the dislike, he was "fragged", meaning grenades were thrown in on his location, three times since I arrived in September. The entire grenade throwing incidents happened on three separate occasions when we were back at Uplift. The closest his adversaries came to injuring or killing him with a grenade was when they threw the grenade through the front door of the orderly room. It rolled to the door in front of Captain Grim's room and went off. Fortunately, for Grim, he was just returning from washing up for the night and was entering through the back door of the orderly room when the grenade exploded. The only damage was to Grim's office, bunk, and the floor in front of his office. He was unharmed by the explosion and continued to be unfriendly and aloof.

I don't know when the new CO arrived on Abbey but my role in Alpha Company was about to change for the better. The change in command made the remainder of the troops in Alpha Company feel better too. We also learned the APC we found in the mountains was driven off Abbey when a unit from the First Calvary was overrun by the NVA while securing the firebase. The NVA took a lot of equipment including the APC and the Bangalore torpedoes we found.

After being in the mountains where the nights were cold, we were looking forward to the more pleasant temperatures at Abbey. As we walked in the valley next to the river, the temperature was a pleasant eighty-five degrees. Once on top of the hill, darkness settled in on us before we were completely ready, leaving some guys without shelter in the bunkers we were assigned. So much for the pleasant weather. When the night moved in so did the cold and wind. It was colder on Abbey than in the mountains because there were no trees to break the wind that blew straight down the valley. Despite that, we would go swimming in the river during daylight hours washing, cleaning our clothes, and cooling off from the 85-degree days.

Alpha Company took over the bunkers on the entire south end of the perimeter. The CP, command position, was in the first bunker next to the helicopter pad on the east side of the hill. It was the largest bunker on our end of the perimeter. The flat top on the bunker was made up of sandbags laid three deep on top of six by twelve treated wooden beams and made a nice observation deck to look out at the old road that came down the valley. Second platoon CP, Lieutenant Harrold, Sergeant First Class Amick, Doc Espinosa and I were in the bunker opposite the company CP. Doc and I pulled five hours of guard every night we were on Abbey because the lieutenant and SFC Amick refused to stand guard. We took turns having first guard swapping every night. After first guard, we made relief in the bunker. Whoever was first would wake up the next guy and begin to crawl in the bottom of the bunk we shared while the guy going on guard climbed out the top of the covers on the bunk. We conserved the body heat stored in the bunk that way and the one coming off guard was able to go right to sleep in the warmth of the covers. No one else in the company was pulling five hours of guard a night except the Doc and me. We had no coats or blankets on guard duty, only one poncho liner with a poncho to break the wind. I don't know about the Doc but I spent all my nights on guard shivering with my lips turning blue and my teeth chattering all night. At stand to, Doc and I discovered our bunker on the west side of the hill was overlooking an old abandoned French plantation nestled up against the not too distant mountains just to our south. We also saw the thin film of ice that had formed on the water puddles around our bunker. That meant the temperatures at night were reaching near freezing. That was a big temperature swing from days to nights: eighty five to thirty-two degrees. What a country!

As the sun came up the view of the old plantation became more picturesque. The plantation main house probably rivaled the plantations of the "Old South", in its day. It had large round white columns all along the front and a huge balcony with a wrought iron railing in the middle above the double doorway into the main hall of the house. I imagine there was a massive staircase leading to the second floor just inside those doors. The frames of the doors and windows were painted red, but the double doors were missing. I envisioned they were red also at one time. The roof of the tall white mansion was red-orange clay tile laid in perfect straight rows and surprisingly still intact covering the entire expanse of the front in a sloped rectangular shape. The enormous windows in the front of the mansion still had tattered white curtains hanging in some of them. They looked tall, stretching from the floor to the ceiling of the old mansion. There was no glass in any of the framed panes that were left; the others were just rectangular black holes into the interior. The front yard had grown over but some of the palm trees remained to add their beauty to the landscape. The road up to the main house was still there but it was a single well-used footpath. Even though the old plantation house was in some disrepair, it would have made a nice picture with the white mansion and red roof contrasting the plush mountain greenery behind the house. Even the servants quarters located at the bottom of the hill and very close to Abbey had the red and white colors of the main house. They looked like an old sixties era motel, a straight line of rooms with one door and one window with a stoop in front of each door. It still had the red-orange clay tile roof and white stucco walls. There was a group of banana trees growing by the well at the end next to the river.

After we ate chow, C-rations or LRRPs, we started to work rebuilding the perimeter around Abbey. Over the next several days, we added two rows of razor concertina wire stacked two high. There were two rolls of wire on the bottom and one on top of those. That made two six-foot high razor wire fences around the perimeter of Abbey. We also installed a pattern of barbed wire called tangle foot in two places around the perimeter, one outside the second row of concertina wire and one in between the two rows of concertina wire.

The second day we were on Abbey we learned that there had been a rocket attack on LZ English, the second and fourth battalion basecamp about twenty five miles north of Uplift. They lost almost every officer on the LZ in one rocket explosion. They were playing volleyball; a direct hit from one rocket on the volleyball court killed them all. They also lost all the refrigeration units for the mess hall on English. Because they had no refrigeration, they had to give all the meat stored there to other units. They passed out all the roasts, steaks, chops, sausage and hamburger to other bases in the area. They didn't find any takers for the bacon they had. For some reason no one wanted any. One of the mess sergeants came up with the idea to send it out to the field to units that would take it. For us it was a goldmine! They brought it out and stacked it on a table telling everyone we could take as much as we wanted. There were five-pound slabs of bacon stacked so high we couldn't see the guy passing them out. Almost no one took less than five pounds. I didn't take any because I didn't want to hassle with having to build a fire to cook the bacon. There was enough that if I wanted some, I could find someone willing to part with it.

They also brought a colossal amount of ice cream. The Army ice cream was the best. They had five-gallon pasteboard tubs of it and were dishing out giant bowls to everyone. It seemed like we hit the jackpot for food and entertainment that day because a couple of Red Cross Donut Dollies also showed up to hand out coffee and donuts. I went to the area where the Donut Dollies were talking to the guys and watching everyone enjoying the donuts, coffee and their company. I was standing in the back of a large bunch of GIs thinking to myself how the tall brunette Donut Dolly warming up the troops looked a lot like my girlfriend back home. Then I got the surprise of my life, she started talking to me.

"You've got a nice smile. Where are you from?" she asked but I didn't answer.

"You there, the tall guy in the back, where are you from?" she repeated.

I still wasn't sure she meant me, so I put my finger on my chest and asked, "You talking to me?"

"Yeah you," she said with a big grin. "Anybody ever tell you, you have a nice smile? Where are you from?" she asked again.

"I'm from Illinois," I answered a little embarrassed.

"Well, Illinois, I am from Indiana so we are neighbors." She went on, "Did you get any donuts and coffee?"

"I don't drink coffee, but I had a donut," I replied.

About that time, she got distracted and someone came by me talking about the ice cream that was being given away. I went over to the table where they were handing it out and found out it was my favorite flavor, banana. The Army had the best banana ice cream ever. It was a bright yellow color and tasted like a bowl full of bananas. I took my bowl of ice cream and my plastic C-ration spoon that I always carried in my pocket and went back to where the Indiana Donut Dolly was still talking with the troops.

When she saw me this time she asked, "What do you have there, Illinois?"

"Ice cream," I told her. "Do you want some?"

"That would be nice," she replied.

As I started to move away I said, "I'll go get you some."

"No, you don't have to do that. I'll just have some of yours if it's OK with you," she said as she came up close to me.

"I don't mind if you don't," I replied as she reached for my spoon, filled it with the banana ice cream, and slowly pulled it off the spoon with her closed lips.

"That was good," she said. "May I have another bite?"

"Sure help yourself," I said, as she again took a spoonful of ice cream and put it in her mouth.

At this point, she was really making me think about my girlfriend and her actions reminded me of something my girlfriend might say or do.

"Thank you for sharing your ice cream. I really enjoyed it. Take care of yourself, Illinois." She turned to go back to where I first saw her talking to the other guys.

As she walked away, she looked back over her shoulder at me and smiled. I felt refreshed, as if I just had a visit from my girlfriend. I was a little homesick too; her looks, her voice and all the things she said to me reminded me of my girlfriend. I returned to my bunker next to the helicopter pad and talked with Doc about who was taking first guard that night. Shortly after that, I saw the Donut Dollies loading on the helicopter to return to the rear area. As the chopper flew over my bunker, the tall good-looking brunette saw me, smiled, pointed at me, waved and threw me a kiss. I don't know if she knew it or not but when she turned her legs back in toward the center of the chopper, she gave me a good view all the way up her lite blue Donut Dolly dress. At that time, I wish I had asked her for her address. I realized she might have been flirting with me all along. If it seemed to her like I was flirting with her, it was because she reminded me so much of my girlfriend back home.

That night there was the smell of bacon being cooked all over Abbey. During Doc Espinosa's guard there was a couple of bursts of automatic weapons fire. Somewhere down the bunker line from us, the guards saw a tiger inside the outer row of concertina wire. They fired their M-16s to scare him off and it worked but the perimeter was on high alert for the rest of the night. That bacon smell must have gotten the tiger's attention and brought him in close.

The next day, the tiger inside the wire was the topic of talk on the firebase. However, not too far from my bunker another event was being implemented. Sergeant Garcia, the platoon sergeant for the four-duce mortar platoon that had been traveling with the company for a while was taking bets whether he could put a mortar round down the well at the bottom of the hill. That was the well by the servant's quarters on the old French plantation. I was interested in the conversation but not the bet. The sergeant claimed he could do it with one shot; he would set the tube up and fire it himself. When the guys betting against him put a time limit of fifteen minutes on the event from start to finish, Sgt. Garcia became a little hesitant. I guess he wasn't sure he could do it within fifteen minutes. By the look on his face, he was deep in thought, considering the consequences if he was not able to make the time limit. Finally, Sgt. Garcia agreed to complete the entire task within the fifteen-minute deadline. A time keeper was selected and a person to hold the money for the bets. The words ready and go put Garcia in motion. He was like a person possessed with no hesitation or wasted motion. He dragged the base plate in an open area and set it in place shoveling some dirt around it. He mounted the tube to the base plate leveling everything as he went. He started looking through what appeared to be a scope mounted on the side of the tube. As he looked through the scope, he was adjusting the tube. He grabbed a mortar round and was removing bags of black powder as he hung the round at the top of the tube. The timekeeper announced twelve minutes and Garcia dropped the round. It went down the tube and back out, all of us watched as it went out of site. There was an eerie silence for a while. Then we heard the round cutting the air. We watched as it went down the opening of the well and exploded causing some damage to the well and throwing up a fountain of water from the depths. He did it; everyone's mouth was wide open, captured by the shock and amazement of it all.

I went to see Garcia after all the furor died down and asked him how he did the trick of putting the mortar round down the well. To my surprise, he did not have a problem sharing the secret of his success. He told me the scope on the side of the mortar tube is just like a scope on a rifle. Once he had the tube set and the cross hairs of the site scope on the center of the well that is where the round would go. He never doubted for a minute that he could do it. It seemed so simple after he explained it. He won a lot of money on that simple trick. I did not share his secret with anyone else on Abbey and shortly after his demonstration, Garcia and the rest of the mortar platoon went back to Uplift.

Later that day I had to go to the CP bunker to find out something for Lt. Harrold. While I was there, a helicopter came in with a one star general on board. I knew he was probably headed for the CP bunker so I made a hasty exit starting back for my bunker with Lt. Harrold's answer. By the time I got under way, the general was already making his way to the CP bunker. I saluted the general as we passed one another. At the same time, his helicopter began to lift off the landing pad. The engine revved up to full power. As the chopper lifted off, it pulled a poncho liner off the CP bunker into the air with it. The general and I both stopped to watch as the poncho liner drifted toward the chopper. When the chopper made a left bank, the poncho liner caught and folded over one of the props. The helicopter hesitated as if it wanted to stall and made more of a turn toward the ground. The engine groaned and I became worried about the disaster that was about to happen, but when the blade rotated from the top of the helicopter to the bottom, it spit the poncho liner off the blade and the engine recovered sending the chopper on its way with full power. As my luck would have it, the near miss was over for the pilot of the helicopter but not for me.

The general turned and with a loud voice exclaimed, "Hold on there soldier! Do you realize what just happened there with your poncho liner?"

"Yes sir, but that wasn't my poncho liner." I replied confident I was in the clear.

"Really? And how do you know that it wasn't your poncho liner? It came off your bunker didn't it?" the general bellowed.

"No sir, that's not my bunker, I was only visiting that bunker," I replied.

"Listen to me, I don't give a damn if that is your bunker or not. That poncho liner could have taken out my helicopter and you should have done more to prevent that from happening. DO YOU UNDERSTAND!" he ranted.

"Yes sir," was my short reply. I figured if I said any more I would have been in more trouble.

"Good, now get out of my sight, and don't let me see you again while I am on this firebase,." he warned.

I didn't answer or salute, I just turned and walked away wondering how I always get in trouble for somebody else's mistakes. That general did not have a clue about that poncho liner nor did he care about knowing to whom it belonged. Once he started chewing my ass about it, he had to finish with me so he didn't look bad. Hell, he probably gave himself a medal for saving the pilot for all I know. Some officers were like that, and their staff just made out the paperwork to get it done. That's the way my luck has always been and still is. I guess I am used to it by now.

CHAPTER 15

Change in January/A New CO/The Tiger Story

After we moved on to Abbey, Alpha Company's commanding officer changed. Captain Grim went back to Uplift with the first platoon and the ceremony to replace him took place there. The rest of the company continued to work repairing and installing new defensive measures on Firebase Abbey. Unceremoniously Alpha Company's new commanding officer, Captain Patrick J. Welsh appeared at Abbey. There was a brief introduction and then he got down to business making the changes he saw that were necessary to make us more effective as a combat unit. One of the things he observed right away was that the whole company needed haircuts. We had been in the field longer than two months without benefit of a trip to the barbershop. Capt. Welsh had a barber flown out to Abbey and we had haircuts in the field. The captain also wanted everyone to shave. We had all become a little lax in our appearance; some guys were even sporting beards and were instantly disappointed by the abrupt change made by the new CO. Even though my hair was long and I had regrown my civilian long sideburns, my face was clean-shaven and the mandate didn't bother me. I looked at it as our return to the Airborne unit we were supposed to be. Therefore, when I sat on the makeshift barber chair, I had the Vietnamese barber cut my hair short in the tradition of the Airborne. It was the first and last time we ever had our hair cut in the field.

There was a lot of activity on Abbey, with the details installing the concertina wire and the tangle foot, a low web of patterned barbed wire causing anyone crawling toward the firebase to either stand up or dig under the barbed wire. The tangle foot was a preventative measure for sappers, an enemy soldier carrying bagged satchel charges designed to destroy artillery or buildings and sometimes bunkers on US bases. Others were either swimming or washing clothes in the river below and of course, every detail, working or swimming had someone pulling security watching over them. We also had some patrols out hunting the large deer in the valley to supplement the fresh meat supply at LZ English.

As night fell upon us, this was the second night the scent of cooked bacon drifted thick across the firebase. Every fighting position must have had a slab of bacon cooking over an open fire. Sometime during the night, around midnight, the tiger made a second visit to the firebase. This time before he announced his presence, he made it all the way inside the defensive rolls of concertina wire and near the bunker line. Still undetected he let out a mighty roar heard all over the firebase, awakening one of the guards who had dozed off. To the surprise of the guard, the tiger was only ten feet from the bunker he was positioned atop. The guard opened up with an M-60 machine gun loaded with a two hundred round belt of ammo. He fired all two hundred rounds, hitting the tiger once just above and slightly behind the right shoulder blade bringing the huge cat down with what was apparently a heart shot. We identified the wound from the small trickle of blood about one and one half inches long that had seeped from the bullet hole. Other than that the pelt or carcass was undamaged. Once the word spread of the dead tiger the next morning, we were told to get the animal to the helicopter pad for transport back to the rear. We suspected some general wanted it for his trophy room. Eight of us volunteered to take on the task of getting the monstrous cat to the helicopter pad for extraction. This turned out to be a major chore for just eight of us, much more than we expected anyway. We estimated the tiger weighed about six hundred pounds. To record his size I used the only measuring device I had: my hands and body. His teeth and claws on his front paws were as long as my index fingers or about four inches. His paws were as big as my hand spread out which is about nine inches in diameter. I measured his length by lying next to him on the ground. I estimated his length at eight feet without his tail. I am six feet three inches and he clearly dwarfed me. His fur was as soft as any house cat and very clean. There was nothing clinging or hanging off his fur anywhere; we found no burrs or ticks. He was definitely eating well because his body seemed thick and well nourished, probably from feeding on some of the many deer in the area. In order to get him to the chopper pad, we cut a pole about six inches in diameter and tied his feet together around it, letting him dangle below. We lifted the carcass and shouldered the pole. Even with eight of us, we were struggling to carry the load. Because he was so big, we could not get his head off the ground. We did not want to damage the carcass in any way so I dropped off the pole and held his head off the ground to prevent it from dragging. What a chore that was. His head was huge, as big as my arms encircled with only fingertips touching. By the time we got him to the helicopter pad to be extracted, I was exhausted. Shortly after we had him on the pad, the helicopter was there to pick up the carcass. The gunners helped us load him by dragging his body onto the floor in the aircraft, and then he was gone. I would like to see the rug that is more than likely adorning the floor of someone's home, office or den. I regret not having a camera to take pictures. What a magnificent animal!

Although I had already been face to face with a lion, neither I or anyone in Alpha Company could imagine being face to face with this tiger. I suppose the fact that the guard was asleep didn't do much to impress our new CO in a positive manner. With the tiger and the long hair, we were zero for two in the good score department. I didn't know a lot about what went on in the CP yet, but I was about to find out.

Scotty, the battalion radio operator, was getting ready to DEROS or go home. He was the guy that helped me learn about the radio over two months ago. Captain Welsh went to Scotty and asked him about helping select a replacement for his position.

"With you going home soon, I am going to have to replace you here in the CP. Who would you recommend to take your place as battalion radio operator?" the CO asked Scott.

"I'd have to say Musson is the best radio operator in the company, Sir," Scott replied.

Not knowing me or anything about me, the CO told Scotty, "Ask him if he wants to come to the CP and take your place."

Scotty came to the bunker I shared with Lt. Harrold, SFC Amick, and Doc Espinosa. The Doc was out at the time. Scotty stood in the door and talked to me.

"The CO wants to know if you want to come to the CP to take my place on the battalion radio," he said.

Before I could answer, the lieutenant sat up and asked, "Hold on, Sergeant. What's this all about?"

"Sir, the CO sent me to ask Musson to replace me in the CP," Scott replied.

"Well, Sergeant, you tell the CO if he wants Musson in the CP he needs to see me about that," the lieutenant informed Scott.

"Yes sir," Scott said as he turned and walked out of the entryway.

A short time later, the CO was standing in the door to the bunker. "Lieutenant, when I send someone to have an individual report to me, I expect to have your full co-operation and without questions,." he declared as he looked at Lt. Harrold.

"Yes sir, I understand but I don't think Muss wants to go to the CP, do you Muss?" the lieutenant said as he looked at me.

"With all due respect, I do want to go to the CP, Sir," I answered with all the military style I could muster.

"Well, Sir, I am surprised, I thought Muss liked it here in the second platoon. I'll have him report to you right away," the lieutenant responded to Captain Welsh.

"There is no hurry, I have a radio operator until Sergeant Scott leaves. You can hang on to Muss, is that right," as he looked at me confirming my nickname, "until you can find a replacement for him." Then the CO turned and walked away.

After that conversation the CO never called me anything but "Muss" right up to and including the last time I saw him in May of twenty fourteen. On the other hand, SFC Amick and LT. Harrold acted as if I just slapped them both in the face. It surprised me that they changed their attitude so quickly. It was almost as if they were bitter about my decision to better myself. I looked at it, as not being lost in the jungle with second platoon anymore, at least I hoped not anyway.

I spent the rest of the day talking to everyone in the second platoon letting them know I accepted the battalion radio job in the CP. Of course, I took the usual ribbing about being a suck-ass or captain's pet. I knew they wished me well no matter what they were saying about me. A plus for me was my friend Borchard had already gotten the company radio operator's job in the CP and we were still close friends.

Late that afternoon the CO saw me and asked me to come and see him. He wanted to know if I would go on a patrol he was organizing for that evening. I would be the only radio operator going on the twilight patrol. We would leave after evening chow and return to Abbey before nightfall. I told the CO I would be happy to go. He then asked if I wanted him to intervene with the Lieutenant to make sure he was OK with me going. I told him I didn't think that would be necessary; I could explain the patrol to Lieutenant Harrold. I think the CO was aware of the change in climate I was experiencing in the second platoon CP. I am sure this was going to be a get acquainted with some of the people working for the CO type patrol. I went back to the bunker, ate chow, and talked over the opportunity to go on the CO's patrol with Lieutenant Harrold. Afterwards I donned my ruck with the radio attached and headed for the CP bunker.

We left the wire through one of the gates that were incorporated in the concertina in various locations around the perimeter of Abbey. Taylor from second platoon was on point as we descended the hill and crossed the river at our daytime swimming location. As long as we stayed in the rapids the water at that location never got over knee deep. Once on the other side we paralleled the river walking on the rocks and sandy bank next to the trees that hung over our path blocking some of the remaining daylight. We stopped for a break and there was some discussion involving the time. I don't know if the group was discussing the time we had been out or the time we needed to be back inside Abbey's wire, but I heard Captain Welsh tell everyone to synchronize their watches.

"Who has the correct time?" the Captain asked.

With that, several answers came back, and all were different times.

"Let's agree on a time and set our watches, who thinks they have the correct time?" the captain asked.

"Excuse me, Sir, I have the correct time," I chimed in looking at my Seiko seventeen-jewel watch Mangilardi got at the PX when I first arrived in Alpha Company.

"OK, Muss. What is the correct time?" Captain Welsh inquired.

"The time is nineteen ten hours, Sir," I answered.

"Everyone set your watch to nineteen ten hours." The Captain directed the others.

After that we went on with our patrol and had negative contact with the enemy. We did see more tiger tracks but could not tell if they were made earlier from the tiger we killed or they were from other cats that may have been in the area. Everyone was hoping it was the first scenario because none of us wanted to think about meeting a tiger in the wild, but it was hard to believe a cat as big as the one we killed would have been the only one in an area this size with all the food sources available.

I made a radio call in to Abbey to let them know we were on our way back. The CO wanted to make sure they knew we were coming because darkness was creeping in on us and he wanted no incidents of friendly fire. We moved through the gate in the concertina wire and actually were challenged for the password from the guards nearby. If challenged, the point man would give his name, how many individuals were with him, and the password.

I wasn't sure what kind of impression I made on Captain Welsh until he came looking for me the day after our patrol. He sat with me and we talked about general things, where I was from, where he was from and a little of our family background. He told me he was from Louisville, Kentucky, the youngest son of a large family. I let him know my grandfather was originally from Kentucky and had owned and raised horses in his youth. Some of my grandfather's sisters were still located in Morgantown, Kentucky and we had some relatives over in Pikeville. It was like having a conversation with one of my friends in the platoon not the company commander. After continuing our general discussion for a while longer, he abruptly went to a question about the patrol.

"So, Muss when we were talking about what the time was on the patrol last evening, you seemed pretty sure your time was the correct time. Why was that?" he asked me.

Well, Sir, I set my watch by AFVN Radio, and I check it whenever I can get near a transistor radio." I answered. AFVN was the Armed Forces Radio Vietnam station made famous by Robin Williams in the movie, "Good Morning Vietnam".

"That's interesting, "he said. "I'll have to check you out on that one of these days."

"Ok, Sir. Anytime," I answered.

With that being said the CO moved on satisfied with my explanation of the time check. Of all things, my watch was one of my prized possessions and it never failed me during my tour in Vietnam. I never removed it unless we were using it on guard duty. I wore it when I swam and when I took a shower. It was never off a minute of time. I still have it today and it still works when wound and worn for a while.

Before we left Abbey, I was sitting on top of the CP bunker talking with Borchard and listening to AFVN on a transistor radio someone had tuned in. The DJ on the air said, "At the tone the time will be exactly twelve hundred hours."

Captain Welsh just happened to be nearby so I said to him, "Here we go, Sir. Check this out." I held my watch out for him to see. As he looked at the face of my watch, the tone went "beep" and the second hand swept across the twelve and the watch was reading twelve noon or twelve hundred hours.

The captain looked at me and said, "Muss, I will never question your time again." And he never did. I do not know why or how the hands of my watch, including the second hand were on the exact time of the radio station but it gave me some bragging rights from then on.

Even though I was a part of the CP, I had not started to work in the group yet. I continued to be housed in the same bunker with the lieutenant and the rest. I continued helping install the tangle foot barbed wire and pull the nightly five-hour guard. Then a strange command came down from Battalion. We were abandoning Abbey, so we had to start dismantling everything. We removed the concertina wire, the bunkers, and the metal PSP or pierced steel planking, for the helicopter pad. Hell, we hadn't even finished the tangle foot and we started pulling up the stakes and rolling up the barbed wire. We went to an awful lot of work building the perimeter at Abbey for nothing. It was all gone in just a couple days.

One of the most memorable things that I recall during the disassembly was the helicopter we used to pick up the bundles we created from the materials we were dismantling. The Army called it a crane because of the powerful lifts it was able to make. We referred to it as the mosquito because it looked like a huge mosquito. The body of the crane was just the cab in the front of the aircraft for the pilot to have a place to sit. The rest was just a frame or shell with a large engine and huge overhead rotors in order to make the heavy lifts required. I got the job of hooking a couple of sling loads onto the monster aircraft. In order to be able to do that, I had to wear a pair of goggles to keep debris out of my eyes from the strong prop wash. The prop wash was so strong I found it difficult to stand on top of the piles of material and get them hooked up. I am surprised the strong wind created by the prop did not rip the clothes off my body. No one else could be near the location of the lifts and had to locate behind some kind of cover in case the crane would pick up loose rocks and propel them through the air. It was known for slinging inch and a half diameter rocks like bullets with no trouble.

We even helped load the artillery pieces and ammunition to clear it off Abbey making it a clean sweep. Once that was done we waited for extraction helicopters to come and transport us to our next assignment. It was an AO in the heavily wooded mountains not far from LZ English. Because the first platoon was still guarding LZ Uplift, the two remaining platoons of Alpha Company split into two platoon-sized elements. This is where I parted company with all my old friends in second platoon, at least for the time being. Captain Welsh attached the CP to third platoon and I started making many new friends from third platoon.

I had to learn new duties as the battalion RTO in the CP. For one thing, as platoon RTO, I would call our location to the battalion RTO when laagered in at night. Now as the battalion RTO, I had to receive the locations of all the elements of Alpha Company whether platoon or squad sized and then transmit them to the rear TOC or Tactical Operations Center. The same principle applies when gathering resupply lists: the platoon RTOs send them to the Company RTO who then gives them to the battalion RTO to transmit to the supply sergeant in the rear. Then the supplies on order are sent out every four days, the normal resupply interval. The company RTO and the battalion RTO in the CP break the resupply down for each platoon if the company is together for resupply; otherwise it was the responsibility of the platoon RTO to take charge of the resupply for his platoon.

There was also a sundries pack, a box of supplies or SPs that weren't put on the resupply list. These were supplies like various brands of cigarettes, cigars, different hot weather candies such as, Chuckles, Bull's

Eyes, caramels, bootlaces, writing tablets, envelopes, and ballpoint pens. For personal hygiene there was bar soap, Ivory brand because it floated, toothpaste and tooth brushes, combs and buttons with needles and thread to sew the buttons on our uniform. The SPs were sent in a large cardboard carton to each resupply area. The hard part about them was breaking down the cigarettes so smokers got their fair share of their favorite brands. I eventually memorized the brands for everyone in the company. There sometimes had to be substitutions for the more popular brands to stretch them enough so the guys got some of the brand they liked. For example, Marlboros were very popular so were Winstons. If there happened to be five guys that smoked each brand that meant only two packs per person. I would take the carton of L&Ms and add a pack each to the other two brands, and each guy got three packs of cigarettes. Sometimes if I had the carton of Kent left I would add them to guys that were short and they might end up with four packs each. Some guys that smoked the odd brands like Pall Mall, the unfiltered brand, with luck might even get a whole carton. I know the guys that smoked were just looking for cigarettes and I hardly ever got complaints from my ration methods. I did not smoke and that helped too because the guys knew I was not hoarding any cigarettes for myself.

When we left the now deserted Firebase Abbey, the third platoon and the CP made a CA into a flat valley surrounded by wooded hills and mountains. The second platoon made a CA on the top of the ridge overlooking the valley we went into. The second platoon moved along the ridge and made contact shortly thereafter. The point came up on a small camp with a cook-fire still burning and a makeshift hootch near the path they were following. The camp seemed deserted but as they looked around, they discovered a VC/NVA in a bedroll inside the hootch. As the guy that found him yelled, "Chieu Hoi," meaning surrender, the VC fled down the path and the shots from second platoon's M-16s missed their mark. The CO was disappointed the second platoon had missed the opportunity to record a confirmed kill with such a close encounter with the enemy. He was also worried about the platoon's lack of alertness in not finding the VC right away. The CP reported the incident and second platoon moved down the trail in the direction the VC fled.

CHAPTER 16

Wood Cutters Ambush Site

As we unloaded from the UH-1 Hueys, the CO and the third platoon leader Lt Jensen got together and decided our route. We began moving toward the end of the valley where it narrowed down and became a trail between the slopes of the hills on either side. It was heavily wooded with tall trees and thick ground vegetation on both sides of the trail running through the narrow valley. Someone pointed out a good spot to set up an ambush site where the narrow valley widened just a bit to allow a squad to blend in to the jungle vegetation and be hidden from view in any direction. We dropped off one of the squads from third platoon to do just that, lay in concealment and wait for the VC/NVA to happen along. The rest of the platoon and the CP turned to the left opposite the ambush site and headed uphill to find a suitable laager site. The hill we chose was two hundred meters high. The top was flat enough to make a decent perimeter for the third platoon and the CP with a place in the middle that would make a suitable LZ if we needed or wanted to make one.

After we settled in, there was an unmistakable sound coming from the jungle forests surrounding us, the sound of a woodcutter chopping wood. It could have been a local villager cutting wood for the home fire or cutting wood to make into charcoal to sell in the markets in Bong Son. It was a lot of activity for the area we were in, so we stayed alert in case it was VC/NVA cutting wood for their campfires.

I received and called in all the laager positions for the night for second and third platoons including the ambush site at the bottom of the hill. I completed the guard list and made sure everyone knew who was on guard before them and who followed them and the time their guard started. As a courtesy, I always gave Captain Welsh his choice of either first or last guard. That way he would get the longest sleep possible unless something happened during the night. In this instance, he chose the first guard. Normally, as in this case, I would assign myself second guard. That way the CO would know exactly where to go to wake me up and not have to look for one of the platoon members he may not know as well. Again, also as a courtesy I would go to Lt. Jensen and ask him if he wanted last guard or just be included in the rotation with everyone else. If he would prefer second guard, I would relinquish my post and then assign myself to last guard. Sometimes last guard worked better for me because with all the work I had gathering laager sites and notifying every one of guard times, I was usually into the first or second guard times by the time I finished. Lt. Jensen took last guard in this case so the rotation after me went to whoever was next to me in the perimeter and so on until we got to next to last guard. I would make sure that person knew he had the next to last guard and he had to wake up the lieutenant after his watch was complete. I made sure all the platoon members, the CO, and the lieutenant knew where the guard post was because during the night the guards monitored all the radios at that post. The guard post was usually at a prominent point of the perimeter. In this case, it was near the trail we cut when coming up the hill to the laager site. To avoid a lot of talking on the radio at night, the person on guard at the CP location would ask for a "sit rep", situation report every hour from the platoons and ambushes. When their call sign was heard on the radio with "sit rep", they would reply by breaking squelch twice on the radio if everything was normal or OK.

The first night passed without incident. Lt. Jensen was waking up everybody for stand to and some guys were already heating water in their makeshift stoves for their morning coffee. I was gathering up the radios to return them to the radio operators from the guard post. At the ambush site, the squad was also getting ready to eat morning chow and then, after being relieved by a fresh squad from our location, the squad would spend the night with us. As our morning meal began, automatic weapons fire rang out from the trail below our position on the hill. After the gunfire stopped, we got a radio transmission from the squad at the ambush site.

They killed a single VC/NVA with a weapon walking on the trail. Now the squad relieving them put on the hustle to get down to the ambush site to lend a hand. The enemy KIA, killed in action, was searched for documents, ammunition and any additional weapons. He was then dragged off the trail and buried in a shallow grave so the ambush site was not compromised. The squads made their relief at the ambush site and group that claimed the kill that morning came to our location with their version of what had happened on the trail below. They came into the perimeter and found a location in the perimeter to spend the night with us on top of the hill while the squad that relieved them manned the ambush site below. The rotation at the ambush site would be repeated each day so all four squads of the third platoon would get a chance at the ambush site.

Early that afternoon automatic weapons fire again erupted from the ambush site, resulting in another confirmed VC/NVA kill. This ambush was starting to pay off big time; we had two confirmed kills in just a few hours. The CO made the decision to stay in the area as long as our efforts were rewarded. I started revising the guard list because the names of the squad that had been on ambush the first night were not on the list.

Just before dark, one of the guys, Bill Smith, asked if he could borrow my Bowie knife to remove some brush and improve his night laager position. I got the Bowie knife just before Christmas when some of the platoon members ordered ten for twenty dollars each from The Western Knife Company out of Colorado. After they received the delivery, they had an extra knife and needed a buyer. I had originally wanted one but missed the order date cutoff. I gave them the twenty bucks and I had the knife and the leather sheath to hold it. This knife is the one Paul Newman wields in Butch Cassidy and the Sundance Kid. It was a very solid well-made knife. I always kept it sharp enough to cut a two-inch sapling with one swipe. It definitely came in handy in the jungles of South Vietnam. I loaned it with the stipulation that he watch and not chip the blade. He assured me he would be careful not to damage the knife. He brought it back to me after dark and I slid it back into the sheath and did not think any more about it. The night passed by silently with no incidents and no contact at the ambush site.

The next morning at stand to, the squad relieving the ambush decided to go early and eat their chow at the ambush site. By doing that, it allowed the men from the ambush to eat their morning chow at our location where security was plentiful and they would not have to eat in shifts while watching the trail. Bill Smith was a member of the squad going on the ambush that morning.

Once they relieved the squad on ambush, the fresh squad went about getting into position and making chow for the morning meal. In order to do so, they put two squad members on OP, observation post, watching the trail on either side of the ambush. Bill Smith was assigned to the forest side of the ambush site and he positioned himself where he could see the trail just as it made a slight bend. As he looked beyond the bend in the trail, Smith saw a VC/NVA stop on the trail and move the M-1 Carbine he was carrying slung over his shoulder to ready arms as if he may have heard activity from the squad at the ambush site. Smith alerted his squad leader who joined him at his OP position and they discussed a course of action. They would allow the VC/NVA to approach their position until he was within ten feet and then both would engage him with their M-16s.

Their plan worked to a point. The VC/NVA approached stealthily, suspicious of the noise he had heard. When he was within ten feet of their position, Smith and his squad leader, Sgt. Happel, fired their M-16s. Some of the rounds struck the enemy soldier in the head obliterating completely the left side of his face and head. As fate would have it, he fell forward, an uncommon phenomenon for having half his head blown off. As he fell, he squeezed the trigger of the M-1 Carbine he was holding, firing one round, which hit Smith in the upper right shoulder just below his collarbone. Since Smith was lying in the prone position, the bullet traveled down to his heart or lungs, killing him instantly. Happel immediately called for help from the remainder of the squad. Whoever was on the radio called the CP position for assistance. We responded with the medic and a number of riflemen plus Captain Welsh and Lt. Jensen. The medic gave Smith a shot of some type and began CPR. When he breathed into Smith's mouth performing mouth to mouth, an eerie moaning sound came out. The medic shook his head. He could not help him. Smith was dead. On February 5, 1970, William Smith became the first casualty in Alpha Company since I arrived in country. The irony of it is an enemy soldier who was already dead took his life. The enemy soldier was carrying a US made weapon, the M-1 Carbine, and had only three rounds of ammunition for the carbine on him.

We moved Smith's body and gear to the LZ where we were inserted. After identifying the smoke we threw out, a single UH-1 Huey helicopter landed long enough for the stretcher-bearers to load his body on the floor of the chopper and they were gone.

Even though there was a more solemn atmosphere in the third platoon, they continued to man the ambush site. Everyone felt bad about Smith but the US Army thrived on numbers and we had just killed three enemy soldiers in three days. Despite the loss of one of our own, the odds remained in our favor.

I noticed a huge nick in the blade of my knife after Smith's squad had started down the hill toward the ambush site so I did not get to talk with Bill about the damage to my knife. I still have the Bowie knife. It is displayed on the wall of my bedroom and the nick is almost undetectable. It is a grim reminder of the mishaps of war.

The next day, our fourth in this location, was also resupply day so in my new capacity as battalion radio operator, I started to prepare for resupply. I got head count from each of the platoons in the field so I could figure the number of rations I had to order. The rations were both C-rations and LRRPs. The LRRPs were long-range recon patrol freeze-dried meals in waterproof pouches. The C's were canned meals and came in boxes with the names stenciled on the top. The LRRPs were the most desirable but were limited in number otherwise, we would have ordered all LRRPs. I also had to find out if there were any special needs such as uniform replacements, either part or full replacement. We were limited on uniform replacements also, usually a complete replacement for the entire company was only once a month. The other special need was the SPs and the head count and location of the resupply. The head count determined how many boxes the rear sent out to us.

The second platoon was supposed to come off the ridge and link up with the CP and the third platoon for resupply. They got lost and never made it to the resupply LZ. That created a series of changes to the resupply plan. The food and supplies that came off the bird became extra for the third platoon. The second platoon would receive a separate resupply when they found an LZ suitable for a Huey to land. All we sent back with the helicopter were extra clothes that the second platoon ordered and their mail. The rest stayed with us and meant that the guys that smoked Marlboros might get a whole carton this resupply due to the additional SPs. We had extra rations, C's, LRRPs and ammo that would come in handy because the CP and third platoon were going back to the little hill where we had laagered for the past four days. I carried an entire case of C-rations in addition to my regular issue of C-rations and LRRPs. That meant my rucksack was overloaded and extra heavy form the extra C's. When we left the resupply LZ for the security of our hilltop, everyone's rucksack was a little heavier. Because I tied the whole case of C's and the box on top of my ruck, the trek up the narrow trail to the top of the hill proved quite the task. The box of C's caught on every vine that dangled anywhere near the trail, either stopping me or pulling me back to remove the entanglement. By the time I got to the top, making the last step up was impossible. I had to take my ruck off and catch my breath for about fifteen minutes before I could carry it to my location at the laager site. One squad from the third platoon dropped off at the base of the hill in the usual ambush site. Before all of us were settled in on top of the hill, the ambush squad had another VC/NVA KIA.

Captain Welsh asked me what it would take to clear a spot big enough to bring in a resupply chopper on top of the hill. I knew he had already made up his mind to stay in this location and reap the benefits of the ambush site. After I looked around, I reported to him that we had an area already large enough but there was a tree that needed to be removed to get in a chopper. Since there were woodcutters in the area already, he asked me to request axes be dropped in to us so we could cut down the problem tree.

"If we can get the axes, would it be a problem cutting the tree down by our next resupply?" he asked.

"No sir! I have used an axe to cut down trees before," I answered, remembering a time at home when I cut down a tree.

Soon a Huey was hovering over our laager site with several wood cutting instruments including a very large double edge axe. The supply sergeant from Alpha Company was onboard and tossed the bundle of equipment from the door of the helicopter to the center of the would be LZ below. We were in business!

I immediately took the axe and moved to the tree blocking our landing zone to begin the cutting. A comrade I had recently befriended came with me to lend a hand. Nick Grumbos had joined Alpha Company as the four-duce forward observer's RTO.

Nick and I had a lot in common. We were both from Illinois; he was from Chicago, about sixty miles from where I grew up in Elwood, Illinois. We both had an attraction for movies; he owned many sixteen-millimeter full-length feature films and I was movie trivia buff. Since I met him, we spent some time sparring with movie titles and actors. He would name a title and I would name the actors in the movie. It really solidified our friendship and helped us pass time when we had nothing to do.

As I walked around the tree to assess where the best position to begin cutting would be, I remember Nick asking, "Are you sure you know how to do this?"

"Sure, we'll have this tree cut down in no time. I've done this a lot of times." I assured him.

With that in mind, I set my feet, measured the distance by holding the axe up to the tree, drew the axe back and swung it toward the tree hitting it dead center as planned. The axe bounced back almost taking me off my feet because I wasn't expecting that to happen. I recovered and Nick and I moved to inspect the damage to the tree. There was none. The axe had barely made what looked like a knife slice in the bark of the tree. Nick started asking more questions, and it was apparent I had not impressed him with this first effort.

"Was that supposed to happen that way?" he asked me.

"Not really," I answered. "That kind of surprised me. This tree is tougher than I expected."

"What happens now?" Nick continued with his questions.

"We just continue chopping. It will eventually come down," I answered.

We worked all that day cutting on that tree with very little progress. The tree was only about two feet in diameter but it was the toughest tree I had ever seen. After working on it for some time, I guessed it was a teak tree from the straight grain of the wood and its hardness. We cut on that tree for two more days and finally had just an inch and a half centerpiece holding up the entire tree. I thought we could push it over; the tree thought differently. The trees I had experience with were pine and soft maple trees, nothing like this teak tree. With an axe like the one I had in my hands, I could cut big chunks out of the soft wood trees I cut down at home. I would never spend two days cutting the pine or maple trees down, even if they were double the size of the teak tree. Finally with the resupply helicopter about a half hour out, I made a desperate last ditch attempt to finish cutting the tree down. I furiously flailed away at the tiny center core causing it to splinter severely, and finally, the tree toppled to the ground. I wasn't even back up the hill to the LZ when the resupply bird came in with our next four days' supplies. I had to hurry and get the axe on the helicopter to get rid of it. I did not want to cut down any more trees in this area anyway.

We continued working the ambush site at the bottom of the hill, switching out the squads as we had done since day one. Our success rate continued to be one VC/NVA kill per day. The word came down from battalion, we were being extracted and Delta Company would replace us. We moved from our laager position on the hill back to the LZ where we were inserted. There we would link up with the second platoon and move to secure Firebase Beaver somewhere nearby high up in the mountains. We contacted second platoon to make sure they were aware of the pickup LZ location. For some reason Lieutenant Harrold had problems finding that LZ. This was the second time we were supposed to meet him there, but he still could not find his way to it. The plan to replace us with Delta Company had already begun and at this point, we could not stop it. As the helicopters brought in the squads from Delta, the third platoon would load on and fly out. It didn't take very long before it was just the CP, Captain Welsh, Borchard, me and the FO with his RTO waiting on second platoon so we could get out and back to Beaver. It became so apparent that second platoon was lost, Col. Lowery, the Rock, took his C&C bird and flew over second platoon in the direction he wanted them to fly. They were already in the same valley as we were. They just needed to head in our direction. Instead of going in the direction Lowery had flown toward us, Lt. Harrold turned the platoon in the opposite direction. The Captain waited until it was almost dark and the last helicopter came in to deliver the last of Delta Company. If we were going to make it out, we had to go on this helicopter. With some reservations, he turned over control of Alpha Company's second platoon to Delta Company's company commander.

We then got on the last helicopter out, and darkness was already upon us. The Captain was not happy with Lt. Harrold. He told me it was the responsibility of the company commander to be on the first helicopter in and the last helicopter out after all his troops were taken out. He didn't want to leave the second platoon out there, but he had no choice. We flew to Firebase Beaver to join the third platoon who had been there for some time already. By the time we arrived, it was dark and I remember we slept that night on the floor of a large bunker. I ended up getting our positions into the TOC at Uplift well after twenty one hundred hours. That is the latest I had ever reported our position that I can remember.

We spent two days on Beaver. The second day the second platoon showed up. I remember hearing Delgado as he passed by our bunker. He was livid about the fact that Lt. Harrold had them lost the whole time they were attached to Delta Company. I talked with him after he had calmed down and he told me of the helicopter incident with Col. Lowery. With Harrold's record and map reading skills, it didn't surprise me. When we left Beaver the next day, Lt. Harrold was reassigned to S-4. To everyone in the second platoon it was a long overdue change. As for me, I believe Lt. Harrold would not have survived the next trip to the field if it were with the second platoon.

When we left Beaver the next day, the first platoon joined us for another battalion excursion way up north and deep into the mountainous jungles of Vietnam.

CHAPTER 17

Straight up the Mountain

After a combat assault into a wide river valley, the whole battalion in company-sized elements was strung out following one another, moving downstream with the flow of the river. The river valley finally closed to just a swollen river running between steep sloped banks and we were forced for the most part to walk in the river along the bank. At night, we would find laager sites dotted along the riverbanks that were large enough for platoon-sized elements. The key component we were looking for in a laager site was enough level ground to accommodate a platoon. There was never enough clear area, so we would move in among the trees and clear any brush to make it comfortable for the night. Those that had hammocks were allowed to use them for sleeping when the tree size would support them. Sometimes the laager sites were used a second time by different companies depending on the progress we made during the day. Either second platoon or first platoon of Alpha Company, maybe both, was doing a bad job of policing up their laager sites. They would leave empty C-ration cans lying around throughout the laager site instead of burying them in a sump dug specifically for trash of all kinds. Captain Welsh was catching a lot of grief from the battalion executive officer, Major Lester, traveling with Bravo Company behind us. When he would pass through one of the old laager sites and see the debris scattered around, he would call the captain on my radio and chew him out for not maintaining pristine laager sites. Since Alpha was the point element, we had no one else to blame, and it bothered the captain immensely. Eventually it became such a rub on the Major, that he had us leave the column and sent us to protect the ridge above the rest of the battalion, allowing Bravo to take the point down the river.

We broke away from the column, crossing the river to our right and started following a small fast flowing stream that was feeding the large river. We only went a short distance up the stream when the point man came across a large number of punji stakes stuck in the bed of the stream planted just below the surface of the water and pointing toward the river. Their clever positioning made them very hard to see in the fast moving water. The punji stakes were intended to injure anyone using the stream for easier travel through the jungle. These particular punji stakes were sharpened bamboo about half to three quarters of an inch wide and about a foot to two feet in length, but the depth of the stream determined how much of the punji stake was exposed. Bamboo has no give so the stakes would easily penetrate a boot or calf of anyone moving among them and not looking for them. In addition, as we soon found out, the punji stakes were a protection system for the person or persons occupying the hootch that was built alongside the stream a short distance from the river.

Everyone up front approached the hootch with extreme caution. There was a small cook fire burning with food still on it. There were caged chickens and a pig near the hootch. Someone had been there very recently and fled when they heard us coming. We let the animals go and put out the fire, spreading the cooked food over the ground. A couple of squads checked out the immediate area with negative results and no further signs of the enemy.

As we followed the stream further into the jungle, we came across the most unusual thing I ever saw. The water feeding the stream was flowing out of a fissure or crack in a solid rock wall that was vertical. The only other water supply was from the monsoon rains. We checked the area and there was no way to get around the wall of rock. We were committed to use this route to get to the top of the ridge on this side of the river, and we were going to have to climb the wall. There were enough trees growing out of the wall to allow a person to step on one while holding on to another and stepping up to the next foothold. The trees grew out of the vertical precipice perpendicular to the face of the cliff but turned ninety degrees and paralleled the face. They were like a self-made ladder up the side of this mountain, sometimes only a few inches in diameter, other times more than a few inches but never anything over a foot in diameter. Because of fog in the area, we could not see how far this terrain extended up the mountain but we found out. We climbed the entire day, stepping from one tree to the next or off a tree to a narrow ledge jutting out of the side of the mountain.

We did not realize it at the time because there was no way to know how high the mountain was, but about half way up, we got a break in the climb. After taking breaks hanging on to a tree while standing on another with nothing below but the same type of trees and a straight drop of hundreds of meters, we came to a wide shelf on the side of the mountain. It was wide enough for the whole company to get onto it and actually sit down to take a rest. The largest ledge I saw prior to this one allowed only three of us to sit on it for a rest. The reason for this ledge being so wide was a large tree growing there with its roots holding enough soil to form the ledge. Other than its enormous size, this tree seemed to be growing normally; the whole trunk was reaching vertically toward the clouds that obscured the view of the top from our eyes. The sheer size of this monster tree had us all marveling. Some of us took on the task of measuring the tree. It took thirty men with both arms outstretched to reach around the circumference. The first limb we could see growing out of the trunk, we estimated to be two hundred feet above the ledge we were standing on. From there the clouds obscured the rest of the tree from our view so we could not estimate its height. We determined it was big and left it at that.

Most of us ate chow on the wide ledge figuring there would never be a better opportunity on this climb. After chow we moved to the back of the ledge where again the mountain continued its vertical stretch toward the sky still hidden from view by the clouds and fog of the monsoon rains. We continued our slow treacherous climb following the point man single file over the rain slickened young trees still growing oddly out and up from the side of the mountain. As late afternoon came upon us, there was some concern about getting off the side and on the top by twilight. Since we were strung out single file, it would take an extremely long time to get everyone to a safe location if we found the top before dark. We did not want to spend the night suspended on the side of this cliff; we did not have equipment to consider spending the night over the side instead of on top.

As some of us were mulling over the options, the point man announced," I am on the top."

That announcement caused the column to surge toward the point man's position with a little shoving to get to some level ground once again.

Then there was a desperation plea from the point man, "Hey, quit shoving. This thing isn't that wide up here!"

As more of us made it to the top, we found out what Azcona, the point man, was talking about. The mountaintop was three feet wide and then dropped straight off the other side just like the way we came up.

We turned and followed the narrow ridge into a saddle, the low area between two highpoints on the map. First platoon was still on point so as they reached the bottom of the saddle that was entirely covered with ten foot tall elephant grass, they started to flatten it to prepare it for a night laager. In the grass, the NVA had planted punji stakes. Punji stakes are sharpened bamboo cut to varying lengths and widths depending on the damage intended. In this case, the NVA were very clever in concealing the punji stakes. Bamboo, already a green color, was cut to one inch or better widths and about two feet in length, and then hidden in the elephant grass. As the first platoon flattened the elephant grass with their feet and legs, one of the punji stakes broke the skin on the front shin of Mark Maguire's leg and followed the bone up to the knee pulling the skin away from the bone causing a very painful injury. Mark was the first platoon's RTO and I knew him very well. He was one of the guys that adapted easily to the radio, knew his job, was well liked, and was a valuable asset to the first platoon. Because of the way the Vietnamese treated the punji stakes with human feces and urine, it was imperative that we get Mark medevacked out as soon as possible. No field treatment of a punji stake wound would prevent infection.

I radioed for a "Dust Off", the term for a medevac helicopter used universally throughout Vietnam. The medevac helicopters were marked with huge red crosses and would pick up wounded GIs, transporting them to the nearest field hospitals for treatment. There were some information requirements the rear needed for the dust-off. The information was normally sent in the clear, not encoded for emergency purposes. If we had to code the information for the dust-off, it would take too long and could cost the injured person his life. There was a list of questions I had to answer for the aide station in the rear, such as the name of injured, number of injured, type of injury, was it a result of contact or other, the call sign of the contact person on the ground and the type of dust-off. There were three types of dust-offs: urgent, priority, and routine. I gave Maguire's name, my call sign and the co-ordinates where the injured would be picked up: in the clear to save time. Mac, as we called him was an urgent dust-off, meaning life threatening.

The guys in the first platoon cleared the remainder of the elephant grass on the saddle carefully making sure no one else was injured. The helicopter came on station using the contact information I sent to the rear. It was raining steady and visibility was minimal. We heard the chopper long before we could see it. Finally with the helicopter in view, we threw out a smoke grenade. The pilot identified our smoke color and the helicopter landed in the narrow saddle. There was only enough area for the skids of the helicopter to touch down in the saddle, the pilot and co-pilot sitting in the front of the UH-1 Huey was looking down the side of the mountain. The tail of the aircraft extended out over the other side of the mountain. We loaded Mac aboard the dust-off bird and the pilot headed for the 67th Evacuation Hospital in Qui Nhon. When the bird left, we realized we were still on a very narrow ridge and needed to make it ready for our night position.

The rain slickened slopes off the ridge made it necessary to straddle a small tree to keep from falling or sliding off the mountain. My friend and fellow RTO Nick Grumbos slept three feet from me with a tree between our legs and a poncho over the upper half of our bodies to keep the rain off our faces. Finding guard replacements and moving to take our turn at guard was extremely treacherous. One missed step and you were over the side of the mountain. With the rain making the footing slippery, we had to watch every step and hold onto whatever was available. It was another miserable night spent in the rain soaked jungle.

The next day didn't improve our opinion even though the sun broke through the clouds. Bravo Company was on the radio asking us if we could see or hear anything of a sniper that had them pinned down on the rock covered sand bar in a bend of the river where they had spent the night. We heard nothing and told them so. The major traveling with them had been extracted the evening before off the rocky area they now used for cover.

Early in the morning just after first light, one of Bravo's troops went to take a piss outside the perimeter. A single shot rang out, killing the man instantly with a head shot. In response, one of the RTOs went to his radio, and was shot in the head. A platoon sergeant picked up the handset and was shot between the eyes. The next guy to pick up the radio was shot through the neck right at the Adam's apple. Before he was through, the sniper took the lives of eleven from Bravo Company, all with head wounds. Bravo called us because they thought he might be shooting from our side of the river. Actually, he was on the opposite side away from us and we never heard a shot. Then came the final blow to Alpha Company, they wanted us to get to Bravo Company and provide security while Bravo was extracted back to the rear. They had been devastated by the loss of so many men and needed to be relieved of field duty for the time being.

We walked the ridge toward Bravo's position and checked the map for an easy route down the steep mountain. Nobody in Alpha wanted to descend the mountain the same way as we climbed. Eventually there was a trail on top of the ridge and we began to move at a faster pace traveling on it. Suddenly the point element sounded the alarm; Azcona had found a booby trap on the trail. It was a very ingenious design with a vine and a notched stake as a triggering device. After looking it over very well, Azcona tripped the mechanism with the end of the barrel of his M-16. A sapling with two sharpened bamboo punji's swung toward the center of the trail. These were intended to strike at knee level either impaling the traveler or striking his legs to get him to bend forward. Then a large log with bamboo spikes three feet long came out of the trees above to impale the victim in the back. No one saw the second part of the booby trap; it came as a surprise when it swung out of the trees. The whole thing was intricately designed and reminded me of the booby trap Jim Hutton swung into in the John Wayne movie, "The Green Berets". It was amazing how resourceful the NVA were, making something out of nothing. If I had not seen it, I would not have believed it was possible.

We moved on, but left the trail soon after the booby trap discovery. We were just above Bravo's location and the terrain was thick jungle but not as steep as the day before. We arrived at Bravo's location in the early afternoon. I saw a friend, Virgil Reiners. I went through AIT, advance infantry training and jump school with him. He was sitting in a two-foot deep hole he had dug early that morning. As we visited, he told me of the sniper's accuracy and cautioned me about walking around with my radio.

As I surveyed the area of Bravo's laager, I was thinking someone made a very poor choice. There was nothing Bravo could use for protection, no trees or cover to hide behind. The large rocks covering the sand bar of the river bend made it difficult to dig in for any type of protection also. Virgil told me himself, the two-foot hole he dug was as deep as he could get; below that was solid rock.

We set up a perimeter and sent out a patrol into the trees on the other side of the river where we suspected the sniper fired his fatal shots. The patrol turned up nothing other than a clear view of Bravo's Laager position. Our perimeter provided the security to extract Bravo back to Uplift. I'm sure they were relieved to be out of the fix they created but we were angry for the long detour we took to get back to the river we had only left the day before. In addition, the question came up about if we would have stopped to laager in the same position had we remained as the point element instead of being diverted to the ridge. My guess is we would not have laagered on the rocky bend. The exposure was too great and cover in case of attack did not exist.

After another day or so down the river, the planners decided to move us to another area. We rode helicopters in and after making our exit from the birds; a short jump onto a rocky nob hill covered with grass, the point element found a group of hootches nestled in the thick jungle above the valley. We waited in a Taro field, a food source for the VC/NVA, until the CO descended the slope into the clump of hootches joining the point team. After searching them we destroyed the hootches and then continued our descent into the valley below. As the day pressed on, we crossed the wide shallow river which was only ankle deep. We increased the interval between each other in the event the enemy might engage us while making the river crossing. The first and third platoons laagered in shortly after crossing the river, the second platoon and CP found a spot further down the river but next to a hill just away from the river. There were some small trees scattered around for good concealment and the night passed without any incidents.

After stand to in the dim light of morning, we looked toward the river and spied four VC/NVA washing themselves in the middle of the river. The perimeter became excited and wanted to fire them up right away. Captain Welsh had a different idea. He thought we were too far away to fire them up and moving closer from our position might expose us to them before we could get close enough to engage them. The CO called upon the first platoon to move from their position further up river and engage the VC/NVA. The protests to this plan came right away from the second platoon. They wanted the opportunity to engage the enemy from our position. The loudest protest came from Sienkiewicz, the machine gunner. He wanted to show what he could do with the gun but the CO held firm to his own plan.

As we watched the first platoon move into position, they stopped when they got even with us and peered through the cane break along the river at the unsuspecting enemy soldiers. This prompted a flurry of questions from the CO.

"What are they doing? Why are they stopping there?" he asked.

"Get them on the radio. I want to know what their plans are," he said to Borchard.

The CO's plans were to have them move right up to the VC/NVA position before engaging them. The first platoon, at their present location, was no closer than we were. Before Borchard could raise them, the first platoon opened fire missing all four indigenous persons but spooking them and two of them ran in the open parallel to our position.

The CO was pissed that the first platoon fired at the VC/NVA from the position close to us. He gave Sienkiewicz the OK to fire them up. Sienkiewicz pulled the trigger on the gun and discharged a single round that was it. The rest of us were firing our M-16s but the VC/NVA escaped unscathed from both platoons.

Sienkiewicz had to explain his dilemma to the CO. He had cleaned the gun the night before which requires some disassembly. One item that is removed during the cleaning is the gas plug that controls the opening of the bolt and chambering of a new round. There is a hole in the end of the gas plug which allows the gas from the spent round to push the bolt open. If the plug is installed with the hole in the wrong position, the gun will fire once and that is all. When the gun is cleaned at night, the person cleaning it has to feel the hole to get it in the right position. Sienkiewicz left out that part of his gun cleaning procedure allowing for the misfire on the gun. After almost begging the CO to let him fire up the VC/NVA in the river, Sienkiewicz took a lot of ribbing for the missed opportunity. To his credit, Ed was one of the best M-60 machine gunners. His mistake was a common mistake made by many M-60 gunners. He never made the same mistake again either.

Because of Tet, the Vietnamese Lunar New Year, the brigade pulled units in the field close to the base camps. Alpha Company moved to the hills outside Uplift. We could see the entire base camp day and night from our perch above in the hills north and west of our home away from home.

CHAPTER 18

St. Patrick's Day Massacre

Several things happened on our next assignment in the hills outside Uplift. The first platoon went back to Uplift in order to prepare to join Charlie Company in Tuy Hoa, a coastal town in the next province south of Binh Dinh Provence where we were located. I t had long been known as a VC/NVA strong hold. First platoon was going down there to boost Charlie Company's numbers while assisting the ARVN, Army of the Republic of Vietnam, with the insurgence of VC/NVA in the area. Second platoon went back to secure Uplift, replacing Bravo Company who had some guys bitten by rats and the entire company was quarantined for twenty one days while shots were administered for rabies. The rats in Vietnam were as big as house cats and, at times, were very menacing to the US troops. Everyone in Bravo Company had to take shots for rabies. They were injected in the stomach and I am told were very painful. That left the third platoon and the CP in the mountains outside Uplift. There were nineteen of us total, not a lot for a platoon and the CP combined.

It was March and the rains were starting to diminish; monsoon season was almost over. We walked up the hills and planned to stay for several days. The tops of the hills were grass about waist high with no trees anywhere except on the downward slopes. They were not the trees we were used to like in the jungles further north. Some were scrub trees that reminded me of the apricot tree that grew in my back yard in Illinois when I was a young boy. We could see all of LZ Uplift and heard the roar of the generators that powered the base all night long. We made a dirt path out of the narrow trail we followed up to the top of the hills. The trail indicated there was some use of the hilltop before we arrived.

I found another opportunity to impress Captain Welsh on this hill. I asked him to let me find the coordinates of our location when I called them in. At first, he was skeptical about having me work up our location but he finally relinquished the task to me, providing I ran the coordinates I worked up by him before I called them in. I went off with my map, compass, and soon had our location ready to transmit to the TOC, Tactical Operations Center at Uplift. I had the captain look at them and he was OK with my work. He complimented me and told me to send them, which I did. The first night passed with no incidents.

The first morning after our arrival, we were milling about on stand-to and a rooster began to crow. The crowing came from a tree line on a separate ridgeline just to the north of where we laagered. As I looked in that direction, I noticed a curious rock formation, which appeared to be two rocks leaning against each other with a narrow opening between. It had an area large enough to allow someone to sit between the rocks. I asked the CO about going over to check it out but he seemed disinterested and said no to any venture away from our laager site.

The days at this laager site were uneventful so far and they gave me plenty of time to catch up on my letter writing. I was continuing my daily correspondence with my girlfriend plus writing the folks and continuing to write three women who sent Christmas cards through The Salvation Army and corresponded back after I sent them thank you letters. I also received letters from one of the women that worked in the cafeteria at my high school. Except for my girlfriend and parents, I would write only after receiving a letter from the other four. I liked getting mail, so it was important to me to keep in touch with everyone that wrote to me. When I returned home, I visited my high school in uniform. When Mabel, the worker who wrote to me saw me walking into the cafeteria, she screamed. Dropping the towel in her hands to the floor she came running, throwing her arms around my neck hugging me tightly. It was a nice welcome home.

After a couple days of letter writing and listening to the rooster crow, Captain Welsh gave in to my requests to check out where the sound was coming from with the stipulation that we would not go into the wood line to search. I tried to make an argument in favor of us checking the wood line, but the captain warned me very sternly, "Do not go into the wood line, I am very serious. There will be consequences if you do."

I agreed, but protested that we would not find anything without entering the wood line. The CO's decision not to let me search the wood line may have saved my life. Unknown to any of us at the time, lurking in the woods beyond the tree line was a huge VC/NVA bunker complex. We would eventually find out the bunker complex was used as a sapper training school and contained several props to simulate concertina wire. With fifty-four bunkers, the VC/NVA could shelter and muster a large enough force to launch a sapper attack on a basecamp the size of Uplift.

The next day, we broke camp and headed down the other ridgeline into the woods. Dice, a member of the third platoon only in country about one and one half months, was on point when we found the base camp. He came up through a draw on the front edge of the trees and there it was bigger than life, and much larger than nineteen of us could secure. Everyone went to ground until we determined if the bunker complex had any occupants. It appeared to have recent activity, but no one was around. We sent out OPs, the daylight lookouts, and went about searching the complex. We counted fifty-four bunkers in the huge complex. During the search of the bunkers, we found five weapons, two AK-47s, one AK-50, an updated version of the AK-47, an SKS semi-automatic sniper rifle and one Chinese forty-pound shape charge. The shape charge looked like a large bell and was filled with forty pounds of Chinese C-4. We also found a large number of maps and documents.

We called the rear to request C-4 explosives be brought in to blow the bunkers. The only helicopter available was the C&C bird; the commander's helicopter and he would not release it for an explosive run. That decision came with severe consequences for Alpha Company.

With only nineteen men, the CO made the decision we could not secure the fifty-four bunker complex safely. As we left the bunker complex, the point team found a booby trap set to protect the bunker complex from anyone approaching from the valley. It was easy to see when leaving the bunker complex because the explosive device was hidden behind a tree on the uphill side. We set up a Claymore firing device with blasting cap and blew the booby trap in place. We then took all the captured weapons, the documents we found and moved from the bunker complex to the valley floor below to find a laager site for the night that was defendable. The rifles and documents were distributed to members of the platoon that were willing to carry them. The forty-pound shape charge was a problem: it was bulky and had no handles to carry it. Sergeant Mascaro, a big burly heavy bearded, two hundred pound Italian/American from Pittsburg, PA volunteered to carry the shape charge. He could shave and five minutes afterward look like he had not been near a razor for months. It made sense to the rest of us; Mascaro was strong and had been a bouncer at a bar in Pittsburg before joining the Army. He tied it to the back of his rucksack and made it to the valley with no strain at all.

Once we reached the valley, we had a plan to link up with a recon team of thirteen men that were in the same area. The recon team would join us the next day because they did not want to compromise their ambush position since they were unable to break down the ambush and get to our position before nightfall. We would wait for recon the next morning and return to the bunker complex with C-4 brought out from the rear to blow the bunkers.

In the meantime, Nick Grumbos and I went about the task of destroying the forty-pound shape charge Mascaro brought down off the hill. Nick had some experience with explosives. He told me he got in trouble in Echo Company, which was the reason he joined us in Alpha Company. It seems a connex that was padlocked had the lock blown off and the contents were missing. They were looking at Nick because of his explosive experience I guess. Anyway we were about to use his experience to get rid of the shape charge. I had my M-16 for protection as we left the perimeter for the openness of a dry rice paddy. On our way, we passed a shell crater from a 105 howitzer round. That looked like a good spot to take cover when we blew the shape charge. From there we walked about ninety feet because the Claymore wire we were going to use to set off the charge was only one hundred feet long. We just set the shape charge on top of the ground with a small amount of C-4 explosive stuck to the side of it, stuck the blasting cap on the end of the Claymore wire in the C-4, and retired to the shell crater. Nick squeezed the firing device of the Claymore and BOOM; it went off throwing a lot of dirt about twenty-five feet into the air. We went back to survey the damage and were amazed at what we saw. There was a twelve-foot diameter hole four feet deep in the ground.

It was so perfect; it looked as if someone had dug the hole. The sides were vertical and the bottom was flat, almost level. What a blast! We ended up using the hole as a sump for all the trash from supplies we would receive.

While Nick and I were occupied with the shape charge, Captain Welsh was going through papers found in the search of the bunkers with the third platoon sergeant, SSgt. Young. He was a tough ranger but a genuine nice guy. He was a very competent leader and the men of the third platoon trusted him completely. The documents they were going over led us to believe the bunker complex was a sapper training facility. Among the documents was a map of our own base camp, LZ Uplift. We suspected it was drawn from the hills where we had recently laagered. The drawing was exact in every detail included in the map of the LZ. We wondered if there was a plan to attack the base during TET and we foiled it by being in the hills or if it was planned for a later date. We took credit for foiling the enemy's plans and left it at that.

The next morning, we watched the recon team come down the valley, walking next to the tree line. If we had not known they were coming, they could have walked right up on us. Their jungle camouflaged fatigues blended right in. We had already received the supply of C-4 from LZ Uplift and had divided it to be carried in rucksacks back up the hill to blow the bunkers.

A plan was devised to complete the demolition. One squad from Alpha Company would go with one squad from the recon team. The third platoon's squad was Sgt. Happell's squad. Dice was his point man. Happell figured Dice did not have the experience required to lead the demo team up the hill and asked me if I would walk point for him. I had been volunteering to walk some point on occasion in the past although I usually did it when we would be laagered in an area for some time and I could get away from the radio. On this occasion, I agreed to walk point for Happell and started putting on my gear.

The CO saw me and asked, "What do you think you are doing?"

"Sergeant Happell wants me to walk his point back up the hill," I replied.

"You've got a job to do here." The CO added, "Tell Happell to use his own point man!"

"Sir, he doesn't think Dice has the experience for this job on point," I said.

"I want you on the radio," the captain replied emphatically. I knew to continue to press the point would not go in my favor so I dropped the argument.

I went to Sgt. Happell to tell him I was not able to walk point for his squad. He was disappointed but Dice was standing right there and seemed willing to take on the task. A more experienced point man from recon named Mohr chimed in, "I'll walk his slack. We'll be OK."

It was set. The team of Dice and Mohr would lead Happell's squad up the hill to blow the bunkers. SSgt. Harry Young, the third platoon sergeant, went along to supervise the demolition. The demo team left our position heading for the bunker complex on the same trail we used when we left the complex the day before. Using the same trail was not an uncommon practice, but the team would be moving with extreme caution returning to the bunker complex. When they had been gone about fifteen minutes, we heard a short burst of automatic weapons fire, then silence. For the next fifteen minutes, I tried to raise SSgt Young on the radio. It was not normal to be without radio communication during any type of contact. I continued to call Young hoping I could get someone to answer the radio.

Then, Young's voice came on the radio, "We have KIAs."

I answered him with a question, "Friendly or Indigenous?"

Young's answer was short, "Friendly."

We continued the conversation on the radio with brief transmissions almost totally ignoring radio procedure. I asked, "How many and what are their names?"

Combat radio procedures allowed for names of KIAs to be broadcast over the open air waves so Young answered my question, "Dice and Mohr, I spell phonetically, Delta, India, Charlie, Echo, break, Mike, Oscar, Hotel, Romeo."

I was in disbelief. He would be spelling my name if not for Captain Welsh's intervention. I held the radio handset next to my ear but I could not say anything. My mind froze and I was not functioning to the best of my ability. I was in shock.

After that information and pause in our conversation, Young continued with his radio transmission, which brought me back to reality. He let us know he was preparing to sweep the hill on line with the people he had left. He did not tell us until later that the fifteen minutes of silence after the initial contact were spent looking for the radio operator that had bolted into the jungle when the shots were fired. Young realized that without the radio he was helpless.

As a leader, Young was one of the best. He went about getting everyone on line and started up the hill, encouraging everyone as he and the men assaulted the enemy positions. The NVA were still entrenched in the bunkers and planned to make a fight of it. As Young and the rest made their assault, the enemy fire became intense. From our position it sounded like hundreds of people shooting, all of them on automatic. As they had moved up on line, gunfire was exchanged and several more people on our side were hit. Another recon member, Kipp, went down but no one realized he had been hit. The radioman was wounded and the machine gunner was hit. Young sent the medic down the hill, out of harm's way, to set up a treatment area for the wounded. He took over the radio and prepared to help the assistant machine gunner with the M-60. In order to do that, Young and the assistant gunner had to switch places. As the assistant gunner laid his hand on the back of Young's leg to crawl over him and take the gunner's position, an NVA bullet took off the thumb on his right hand. Young sent the assistant gunner down the hill to the medic. While still carrying the radio, Young took over the machine gun, threw a two hundred round belt of M-60 ammo over his shoulder, and assaulted the hill on his own.

Then a call came in from Young," I am going to need some help up here. We might be pinned down."

Actually, he was pinned down, the return fire became so intense after his lone assault he had to go to ground and seek cover. The CO came to me and said, "OK, now you got your chance to walk point. Get me up there."

We had already started to prep for a rescue. I removed my rucksack from the radio and attached a strap to sling it over my shoulder to carry. I grabbed my bandoliers of ammo and my pistol belt with canteens of water and ammo and I was off. The CO was right behind me. I do not recall if I was over anxious or in too much of a hurry, but I picked what I thought was a short cut to the trail up the hill. As it turned out, I was hung up in a huge clump of vines I could not break through. Our FO, forward observer,

Lt. Austin, took the point from there and walked around the hedgerow I was attempting to break through and the remainder of our element was on the way to rescue Young.

About halfway up the hill, the trail split and Lt. Austin became confused about which direction to take. I took over point at that time and got us up the hill. The first people we encountered were the wounded and the medic. The doc was treating five wounded but assured us he had everything there under control so we continued up the trail.

As I came up a small rise, there in the middle of the trail lay Mohr, face down in a pool of blood. He was shot in the neck twice and the bullets had passed all the way through. Young told us later that Mohr was still alive when he got to him right after the initial contact, but he was making gurgling noises from the blood pouring into his lungs. There was nothing Young could do to save him. Next, I came upon Dice's body. He was sitting on the side of the trail leaning back against his rucksack as if he were taking a break. His eyes were open but had the blank stare that death leaves. They were like looking into a pool of water that had no bottom, the depth of eternity. At first, I did not see his wounds but as I examined him closer, I pulled his shirt open and saw the four bullet holes in his chest that could be covered with half a dollar bill. It looked as if two of the rounds that hit Dice passed through him and the rucksack full of C-4 he was carrying, then hit, and passed through Mohr. I tried to close Dice's eyes as they do in the movies but his eyelids returned to the open position. The muscles in the lids were taut and would not let them close.

We moved on a short distance, and an intense burst of automatic weapons fire sent us to ground among the scrub trees that covered the hill off the trail. We strung out in a line and the CO and I became separated. SSgt. Young and some of the others with him were slightly above us on the slope, we could not see him but we could see some of the NVA shooting at us. When the NVA would rise up to shoot at us from the bunkers they were in, Young would cut loose with the M-60 in short bursts keeping their heads down. We did not know it then, but when he did that, he was probably saving our lives. We were all pinned down, not able to move up to aide Young or move back to get off the hill.

As I lay there in the scrub trees, I felt branches falling out of the trees onto the back of my neck. I would brush them off not thinking about where they came from. A little while later, I would brush some more branches from the back of my neck.

Suddenly, the CO called out to me, "Muss, Muss, can you get to me?" He was busy talking on the company radio with Captain Bacon in the C & C chopper circling overhead.

I asked the CO, "Do you need me?"

"Yes, I need your radio," was his reply.

"OK, I'm coming," I moaned.

After that reply, I assessed my situation and felt I needed to get off my stomach before I attempted to get to the CO who was about ten yards away. I figured I could move faster if I did a sit up from my back instead of a push up from my stomach and then stand up. That would be two moves; the sit up would be one swift move and a dash to the CO. As I turned over on my back so I could do the sit up, a cold chill ran down my back. The branches that had been falling on my neck were coming from the scrub brush I was lying in. They were being cut off about one inch above my face and head by bullets being fired from the NVA. I could see the track the bullets made as they passed over my head and through the scrub brush above my feet and beyond. I did not have time to worry or rationalize about that; I quickly sat up got to my feet and made the ten to fifteen yard dash to where the CO was waiting for me. The NVA increased their rate of fire as soon as I was visible to them and the bullets whizzed all around me on the way to the CO. I handed him the radio handset as I lay down beside him seeking the shelter provided by being close to the ground. He took the handset and again spoke to Captain Bacon on the battalion radio.

"This is November," he said, that was the CO's call sign.

Then I heard Capt. Bacon's voice on the radio, "November, you and I will make all communication between us from now on your company net, over."

The CO responded, "This is November, roger that. Over."

Capt. Bacon came back with one more detail, "November, this is X-ray, Bacon's call sign. I have a gunship coming on station for your location. Someone needs to direct him on the other net when he arrives. Do you have anyone? Over."

The captain answered, "X-ray, this is November, roger on the gunship. I have a man, over."

"November, this is X-ray, roger, out."

Captain Welsh handed me the handset and gave me these directions. "Muss, we have a gunship coming on station. Can you handle directing him when he gets here?"

I answered, "Yes, Sir."

We left it at that as the CO continued to communicate with Capt. Bacon on the Company Net.

A plea from further up the hill sounded for SSgt. Young. It was from one of the men Young had assaulted the hill with after the initial contact. "Sergeant Young, come here. I need you. I'm hit."

Young responded, "How come everybody always asks for me?" Then he picked up the machine gun he was still carrying and moved to the person's location that was calling him. The bullets from the NVA chased after him as he hurried to the man's aide.

After a short while, Young spoke out, "I'm going to need some help up here."

With no hesitation the biggest guy in our company, Sergeant Mascaro, jumped to his feet as a hail of bullets brought the vegetation around him to life and ran up to help both men. All three made it back unscathed to the position where Mascaro had started. When I saw how the bushes danced behind Mascaro from the bullets being fired at him, I recalled my recent dash and wondered how any of us made moves without being killed.

The medic had been dealing with all the wounded we knew about and up until now had not requested any help. When Young and Mascaro brought their patient to him, he requested an urgent dust-off for him. He had a gunshot wound in the stomach that hit his own bandoliers of ammo and pulled a whole M-16 round from the magazines in the bandoliers inside his stomach with the AK-47 round. He also suffered two other bullet wounds in the forearm and shoulder on his left side. The urgent medevac meant the patient got the first helicopter available and the medevac chopper would pull off a lesser priority of priority or routine, to come to his rescue. I put the request through and soon a medevac was calling on the battalion net asking for me to pop smoke. I yelled for someone to "pop smoke" and I heard the familiar pop from the smoke grenade blasting cap to start the smoke burning right away, as the purple smoke billowed from the grenade canister. The medevac pilot identified the color and set the chopper on the treetops to begin lowering the jungle penetrator to extract our priority wounded. As the penetrator came down, the NVA opened up with another automatic burst of fire. We heard the AK rounds hitting as they pierced the metal skin on the helicopter. The pilot swung the bird away to prevent being shot down, abruptly and temporarily aborting the dust-off.

On the ground, Captain Welsh made the decision to increase our firepower the next time the helicopter was overhead and we passed that word around. The problem with a jungle penetrator extraction is that the helicopter has to hover in the same position while the extractor is lowered and raised while the injured are strapped to it. The whole time the aircraft is at risk of being shot down, and the men on the ground under the helicopter are also at risk if it is shot down. The medevac pilot contacted me for a situation report and asked if we wanted to call off the dust-off. I let him know our plans were to lay down an increase in firepower for his next approach. He acknowledged that and told me he was on his way in for a second attempt at picking up our wounded. Again, we heard the bullets hit the chopper as he hovered above us but this time our volley of fire was so intense, the NVA had to seek cover and we were able to extract the guy with the stomach wound. After that, the CO and the dust-off pilot figured it was too risky to try for any of our other wounded.

Once the medevac was complete, the gunship Captain Bacon had requested, a Cobra type helicopter, came on station over the battalion net using my call sign. "November Mike, this is Peacemaker. Over"

I answered, "Roger, Peacemaker. This is November Mike. Over."

"November Mike, this is Peacemaker. Is the person giving me direction at your location? Over."

"Roger, Peacemaker, that person is me. Over."

The pilot then gave me a series of instructions that I needed to follow explicitly. I would pop smoke or have someone pop smoke and watch where the smoke broke out of the tree cover above our location. The Cobra pilot would identify the color of the smoke, and I would tell him how far, and what direction we were from where the smoke cleared the trees. He would then unleash the rockets he was carrying in front of our position to try and break the contact. I remember the words he spoke on the first run in: "OK, get your heads down. Here I come."

The first time the rockets hit scared everybody; they hit twenty-five or thirty meters away from us but might as well have been in our back pocket. They were closer to us than we were used to having them but the rifle fire from the NVA let up a bit immediately after the rockets exploded. We repeated the whole scenario again for the second rocket run. On that run, the Cobra pilot brought the rockets even closer to our position. The whole time the pilot and I were talking on the radio, I was giving our location and he was identifying smoke color and asking me for an adjustment to where I wanted the next rockets. I was too busy to notice the NVA fire had let up so much the rest of the guys were making a hasty exit off the hill. I was preparing for the pilot's next run and still had not noticed they had left me behind. Luckily, for me, Borchard missed me in the group and came back for me. He called out to me, "Muss, come on. We're leaving," as I stood up to follow Borchard down the hill, the last rocket hit about fifteen feet from me just up the hill and slightly behind a tree. I hustled to get with Borchard and we both hurried to link up with the rest that were hastily moving down the hill. The group took turns carrying the litters with our dead as we moved back to the laager site in the valley.

The command group back at Uplift organized a Phu gas drop for the bunkers on the hill. Phu gas was a mixture of oil and gasoline in fifty-five gallon drums. The drums would be dropped from a Chinook helicopter. The drop would spread the drums out, blanketing the ground. Gunships then made a pass over the area firing M-60 tracer rounds into the drums to set off the gas and oil mixture. The Phu gas was supposed to pull all the oxygen out of the air in the area where the drums were dropped.

When we got back to our laager site, I called for a dust-off for the rest of the wounded we could not get out with the jungle penetrator while we were on the hill. Everyone else just wanted to relax after the tension from being pinned down on the hill for three hours. Captain Welsh had other ideas for us; he told everyone to clean their weapons and asked SSgt. Young and SSgt. Adams, the recon leader, for a head count. SSgt. Adams came back to the CO with one man missing.

The CO said, "Take another head count." The result was the same: recon was missing one man.

"OK, put your gear back on. We have to go back up there," the CO added.

We had to wait for a short time for the Phu gas fires to die down. That also gave us a chance to get the rest of the wounded medevacked back to Uplift. We had a total of seven wounded. One we got out on the hill and six left after we returned to the valley laager site. Since the medevac helicopters did not pick up bodies, the C & C, Command and Control bird brought in a resupply of ammo and picked up Dice's and Mohr's remains.

After distributing the new ammo and reloading magazines, we were now free to return to the hill to look for the one man missing from recon. Knowing there were enemy troops on the hill in bunkers, we went back using extreme caution. The fact that Phu gas was dropped would aide us somewhat. We did not expect it to eliminate the entire enemy and it didn't. We immediately came under fire when we reached the area in which the Phu gas was dropped. The difference this time was we had eliminated some of our cover with the Phu gas and we did not have any wounded to deal with. It was a firefight with close bullet exchanges from both sides. We found ourselves in the same position as before. We could not move up and we could not retreat to safety. We just kept shooting back and forth trying to gain an advantage.

Nick Grumbos and I were lying next to the trail when two recon team members came up to us from our left. They cautioned us not to move to the left because there was VC/NVA over there. Shortly after that, the recon leader, SSgt. Harry Adams came up to us and told us to work our way around to the left to see if we could flank the enemy. We told him there was no way we were going that way. I told him, "Just before you got here, two of your men came from that direction and told us not to go over there." Nick and I stayed where we were on the trail.

After about four hours of being pinned down, SSgt. Young belted out, "There is only one way we are going to take this hill, and that is to stand up and take it. On the count of three, get to your feet and move up the hill firing as you go. If you see anything or come to a bunker, yell stop and we will do what we need to progress. If it is a bunker, throw a grenade in it before you walk up on it. Now, one, two, three, let's go." We all stood up and started shooting. The volume of fire was deafening. After a short time someone yelled, "Stop." He had found the missing man from recon, Kipp. He was lying right in front of the bunker from which he was shot. We took a short break to try to determine what had happened to him. We could not see any wounds in his body. As we turned him over to check his front, it was easy to see rigor martis had set in. His body was frozen in the position he fell. His M-16 was across his chest, his finger still on the trigger. Someone noticed a small amount of dried blood in his right nostril. The bullet that killed him went in his nostril into his head. There was no exit wound so it was very hard to see the entry wound.

We continued on with our assault of the hill after finding Kipp's body. This time we had no gunships, so we did it all on our own with help from Captain Welsh and SSgt. Young. The assault was complete after being pinned down for an additional four hours. We built another litter to transport Kipp's body back to the valley laager site. The remaining twenty-two of us in the final assault were exhausted after seven hours of intense fighting and the two trips to the laager site. We had put in a full day. No one was wounded or killed in the second assault of the hill. Battalion elected to reward us by removing Alpha Company from the field. Finally, two days after the battle on St. Patrick's Day we were extracted back to Uplift. Except for the small respites on the fire support bases, we had been in the field one hundred thirty eight days without a break.

SSgt. Harry Young was put in for a Congressional Medal of Honor for his actions on St. Patrick's Day. All of us on that hill were in agreement. He saved our lives that day. He certainly proved he had no regard for his own life while he protected ours as he charged the hill on his own with the machine gun. His CMH was reduced to a Distinguished Service Cross at the company level by Captain Welsh. His reason, he said was, Young is still alive and they will not award a CMH unless you die while earning it. From there it was reduced to a Silver Star by battalion. We did not learn the reasoning behind that reduction or the next when Brigade reduced the award to a Bronze Star with a V device for Valor. SSgt. Young deserved the CMH but was finally awarded the Bronze Star w/V at a ceremony held at Uplift more than a month after the event.

CHAPTER 19

Return to Uplift/My Birthday

Finally, we returned to LZ Uplift. All of us were tired from the recent battle experiences on St. Patrick's Day and the length of time we had spent in the field. The battalion figured we deserved a rest; we knew we deserved a rest. Everyone experienced a lot of stress when the company suffered close combat battle losses. As we reflected back on the close combat situation, the reality starts to set in and we felt fortunate to be back at Uplift. I could say safe at Uplift but no one was ever safe anywhere in Vietnam; the base camps were always vulnerable to attacks from mortars, rockets or sappers because they were stationary. The maps we found of LZ Uplift in the bunker complex confirmed that the VC/NVA were always watching and planning attacks on firebases and base camps.

A day or two after we got back to Uplift, the battalion held a memorial ceremony for Dice, Mohr and Kipp at the white chapel on the hill next to the first battalion theater. Participation or attendance was not a requirement, but I attended the service. I figured I owed Dice that much. The Chaplain began the ceremony, reflecting on the lives of the men being honored. Captain Welsh, who had studied for the priesthood, spoke about each individual and read from the Bible. When these memorials were presented, they usually had a pair of boots with an M-16 and camouflaged helmet for each of the deceased troops, the M-16 standing inverted with a bayonet and the helmet placed on the top over the butt end of the rifle. It is a very solemn and fitting ceremony to the fallen soldiers.

We had been away so long we almost did not recognize our own base camp. Some changes took place that we needed to get used to seeing. An old bunker was transformed into a library with mostly paperback books but it was a step in the right direction. We still did not have a PX, Post Exchange, but a Vietnamese run laundry and tailor shop was now open that sold things like cigarette lighters, baseball caps, and other necessities. The tailor shop would make a drive on rag with the herd patch and your name on it. The drive on rag was a triangular shaped neck scarf made from black cotton material. The guys that wore them usually had their name embroidered in white thread with the company and battalion and a Herd patch sewed on it. They were worn around the neck like the cowboy neck scarves in the movies. Of course, everything that was sold in the little shop gave the Vietnamese running it more business. The cigarette lighters could be engraved there. The tailor would embroider your name with jump wings and the Herd patch on the baseball caps. Of all the items, the drive on rags were probably most popular and the most expensive running about five dollars on the average depending on how much needlework was done. Each rag was customized for the individual requesting its creation. Some of them were really fancy or had clever sayings or nicknames on them. One guy in second platoon had "Jungle Pimp" on his drive on rag.

The new Battalion Surgeon, Captain Coleman, had started construction on a new aide station. The Doc and his medics were moving to an abandoned building with high sandbagged walls right next to the theater for the Third Battalion, which was also outside our sleeping barracks while we were on stand down at Uplift. The theater was an outdoor theater with no seats and the projection booth was a little building about the size of a broom closet. It was just big enough for the projector and a chair for the projectionist. None of the rustic accommodations kept the crowds from going to the movies; they were always popular no matter what was playing. As I remember, we never knew what the movie was ahead of time; we showed up and watched whatever was playing. Once the movie started, no one wanted it stopped or interrupted for any reason. If that happened the individual that stopped it, even if it was the projectionist, took a pelting of beer and soda cans from the crowd. One of the movies we saw on this stand down was a comedy western "They Call Me Trinity" with Terrence Hill. That movie played on the night of my twenty-first birthday, March 24, 1970. I remember that because I did not celebrate by getting drunk. I wanted to remember my twenty-first birthday and everything that happened. I was only going to turn twenty-one once. There was a new movie every night but sometimes guard duty took precedence and we missed that night at the movies. Once a movie played, it was not shown again so if we missed a show, we had to hear about it from someone who saw it.

The steakhouse was still a popular spot and we visited it for lunch many times. A steak and a plate of beans was still only a dollar fifty and usually beat what was being served in the mess hall. We got back into our routine of playing bid whist when there were no details. I learned the card game when I arrived at Uplift, but have forgotten how to play. The variation of Whist is not in any card game book. Borchard is the only person I know that remembers how to play bid whist.

It was good to sit down at the steakhouse with Colon and Delgado, have a cold beer or soda and reminisce about the good times in second platoon. Mangilardi, Squad leader in second platoon had gone back to the states in February, another change we had to get used to. He was a good leader and made Staff Sergeant before he left for the states. That was a compliment and recognition of his experience. Not many NCOs from NCO school in the states were able to accomplish a promotion to Staff Sergeant without reenlisting.

We were enjoying our time in the rear to the fullest. The word came down from battalion that our time at Uplift would be extended because of all the time we had spent in the field. Some of the guys got overnight passes and visited the nearby air base at Phu Cat. I was lucky enough to be one of them.

When we visited the base at Phu Cat there was always a problem with finding security for our weapons. We were not allowed to leave Uplift without a weapon, but at the air base, we were not allowed to take weapons into the NCO Club, the place most frequented by visiting troops. The NCO Club had a cafeteria for breakfast and afternoon chow. For the evening meal, they converted the cafeteria to a full service restaurant with waiters for the tables. The airmen worked as waiters making one dollar fifty cents an hour, and we could get a steak and baked potato for two fifty. After the restaurant closed, there would be entertainment on the stage that shared the room with the restaurant. We always left one guy outside guarding our weapons while we ate and watched the entertainment. Eventually we would spell the guy outside so he could eat or watch the show. Colon worked the problem and finally found one of the armors on the airbase that would check our weapons and keep them secure until we left the base. But there were complications with securing the weapons that way. First, Colon's friend had to be in the barracks when we checked the weapons in and when we checked the weapons out. The Air Force barracks housed their sleeping quarters, armory and their orderly room in the same building, making it easy to contact Colon's friend. We signed the weapons in by serial number and owner, and then we were free to enter any area without having to secure our own weapons. To everyone that used that service it seemed legitimate but it was actually illegal as hell. Everyone leaving a weapon or storing a weapon could be court martialed for that offense. We did not know that at the time so we used the service in ignorance and were happy with the outcome. If Colon's friend did not happen to be in when we showed up, we went back to the old method of security for our own weapons.

An overnight stay at the air base meant we had to find a place to stay. There was a hotel on base but it cost money to stay there. I think it was two bucks a night but I am not sure of the cost. Because of an unusual find, I never had to stay in the hotel. We were at the swimming pool during the day just taking a dip in the pool, a regulation in ground Olympic sized swimming pool. We had to go to the PX first to purchase the required swimming trunks. It's funny how used to things people get; there were hardly any Air Force guys in the pool. They had access to it all the time, but for us it was a novelty. We had never seen a swimming pool in Vietnam except for this one and could not figure out why it was almost empty. After our swim, we discovered a group of abandoned barracks next to the swimming pool. There were boards over the door but we decided to check it out anyway. We pried the bottom board off the door and ducked inside the building. As we checked the place out we discovered there was running water in the showers and the latrine. All the fixtures were still there also. There were bunk beds on both floors and they had thick mattresses on them. They were dusty but very comfortable compared to the cots we were used to sleeping on at Uplift. Somebody flipped the light switch and the lights went on. Not all the bulbs lit up but there were enough to see at night so we left it that way. At that moment we decided this barracks would be the 173rd barracks at Phu Cat Air Base. We spent a very quiet night there after the floorshow at the NCO Club.

The show at the NCO Club was another plus for our overnight stay. The Air Force was used to a show every night. Either a local Air Force group would play or a USO show would come in and perform. I know they had very good local talent, because I saw one of the Air Force country bands play one night to a packed house in the showroom at the club. This night they had a Philippine Group hired by the USO performing on stage. The group was quite large with several brass horns, guitars, drums, and female dancers. I remember how we thought we were hearing a professional group perform because they sounded just like the real persons when they sang. If we closed our eyes when they sang, "Someday We'll be Together" by Dianna Ross and the Supremes, we would swear it was the Supremes on stage performing. They also did the theme from "The Good, the Bad and the Ugly" and it was the same way, it sounded like Hugo Montenegro was performing it on stage. The women were nice eye candy and when they danced they were very scantily dressed, no nudity but a lot of skin was showing. When the women were on stage, the Air Force guys were out of control up around the stage pushing, shoving, and taking pictures. I think they scared the women a bit; they acted as if they had never seen a woman in a bikini before. After the show, we went to tell the performers how much we enjoyed the show and found out no one in the performing group spoke English. They sounded so good because they listened to the original performers on records and then mimicked the sounds they heard which came out exactly like they heard it on the records. It worked perfectly for them. We thought they were excellent and told them so even though they never understood a word we said.

We went back to Uplift completely refreshed from our mini R & R to Phu Cat Air Base. It was the last day of March and Borchard and I drew bunker guard that night with two other guys. Alpha Company's bunker was on the west end of the perimeter looking out toward 506 valley. There was also a village out that way and behind the village was what we referred to as sniper hill because as trucks left Uplift on Highway One, they received sniper fire on occasion from that hill as they passed. We reported to the bunker after the guard duty formation and familiarized ourselves with the adjacent bunkers. The bunker to the left of ours had the radio for contact with the OD, Officer of the Day, on duty for that day. We had nothing but M-16s and a half of a galvanized culvert sitting on top of our bunker. It was there to protect the fifty-caliber machine gun that used to be on top of our bunker. The bunker to our right had an M-60 machine gun and a pit that was dug for a twin forty millimeter "Duster" track which was no longer on our basecamp. The "Duster" was like a small tank and the twin guns operated like pom pom guns, one barrel firing, then the other. The gunner used to break rounds out of the six round magazines and it would make the "Duster" sound like it was playing a tune. Those people were really clever and the "Duster" sounded good playing tunes.

Borchard and I had the second guard on our bunker which started sometime after midnight. We switched places with the other two guys on the bunker and took over the top, lying down under the half culvert. Shortly after we moved to the top of the bunker, we heard a distant thump, which sounded like it came from sniper hill. The next sound we heard was a mortar round cutting the air right over top of our bunker, then the explosion on the other side of Uplift. Bill and I started straining our eyes to see if we could see where the round came from. Then there was a second thump. This time I caught the flash off the tube the VC was firing from. It was about half way down the end of sniper hill where the slope leveled off for a short distance. I pointed it out to Borchard and we called over to the bunker on our left as we saw another flash off the tube.

"Hey, call the OD and tell him we are being mortared and we see the flashes off the tube," I yelled.

"The radio doesn't work, it needs a battery and we don't have any," they answered.

More rounds were coming in and the explosions were getting closer to us as they walked the rounds through the middle of Uplift. Bill and I were counting the entire time, keeping track of how many rounds we were being hit with. After trying for the radio, we turned our attention to the bunker to the right with the M-60 machine gun. We figured the distance would be at the far reaches of maximum effective range on the M-60 but we knew the mortar tube was well beyond the range on our M-16s.

"Hey, see if you can hit the nob about half way down on the north side of sniper hill." We yelled. "We will try and direct your fire right on them"

"There is something wrong with the M-60; we think the gas plug is missing. It won't fire a round," they answered back.

All we could do was count the rounds and wait for the OD to show up so we could report to him. As we counted the seventeenth round fired, it hit just behind our bunker. Shrapnel off the exploding round came past Borchard's and my feet and made big holes in the half culvert right over our heads. We hastily slid over the front of the bunker and climbed into the front firing port to the safety of the sandbagged bunker. No additional rounds came in after that seventeenth round. We were discussing the fact that our bunker was probably used as the sighting mark since it looked like all the rounds walked right up to it in a straight line from where the first one hit and the last one hit just behind us. The OD showed up and asked if we saw anything.

"We saw where they were firing the mortars from and we counted all the rounds." We reported.

"How many rounds did you count?" the OD, Captain Jackson asked.

"Seventeen," Borchard and I declared simultaneously.

"You couldn't have seen or heard them then; we only received fifteen rounds total," the OD corrected us.

"We are certain, Sir. It was seventeen rounds," we assured him.

"You may have thought you saw and counted the rounds but you are wrong on the count. It was only fifteen," the OD told us again and then he left.

The next morning at the guard duty formation, Captain Jackson apologized to us because after sunup, they found two duds that hit Uplift but did not go off. If we would have had a radio and machine gun that worked, we might have been able to inflict some damage on the enemy location and could have prevented some of the injuries and damage at Uplift. Borchard and I were disappointed we could not fire back at the VC.

Right after the guard formation, we found out Alpha Company was going out to the field. Our long rest at LZ Uplift was over. We also found out that while mortars fell on us at Uplift, the first platoon working in Tuy Hoa with Charlie Company and the ARVNs had some bad luck. They had two killed and several wounded after the ARVNs they were working with walked away from the ambush they had set up, and a group of NVA walked in on them and fired them up at close range. There were questions after the fact as to whether the ARVNs were ARVNs or VC/NVA. I don't think that question ever got answered.

At about 13:30 that afternoon, second and third platoons were combat assaulted back to the hills and jungle forests to seek out the VC/NVA. After the experience the night before, I think all of us were glad to be back in the field away from Uplift.

CHAPTER 20

Hill 466

Shortly after returning to the field, Captain Welsh left for R & R, a week of rest and relaxation away from Vietnam. The captain chose Hawaii for his R & R although there were other places like Japan, Taiwan, and Australia. Lt. Chapla, now Alpha Company XO, executive officer, took over the command of the two platoons remaining in Alpha. The first platoon was still assigned to Charlie Company and working in Tuy Hoa. We were working a line of mountains that were heavily forested north of Uplift. The mornings started every day with heavy fog, making visibility and movement difficult. We were following an old trail along the top of the ridgeline. The trail was wide and at one time in the past had been well used. It was almost a gravel trail, small pebbles embedded in the clay path covered the entire width of the trail. We were on the hunt for a spot to bring in resupply choppers. We had been in the field for three days and on the fourth day we were always resupplied.

Early in the morning on 4 April, Sergeant Satterfield the four-duce mortar forward observer got the idea that he wanted to check out a trail that intersected the one we had been following. The four-duce mortars were the Army's M-2, 4.2-inch diameter mortar located in the rear area back at LZ Uplift. The forward observer traveled with a line company along with his RTO and set up fire missions for the mortars to defend the company if attacked. Satterfield recruited Nick Grumbos, his RTO, and me to go along with him on a small patrol to check out the trail. The morning fog had not lifted yet and visibility was only a few feet. Shortly after leaving

152

our night laager, the trail started a downward trend into a saddle. A saddle was a low point between two hills or mountains just like the saddle on a horse; the seat is the low point between the horn and the cantle. Once the trail began ascending the next hill, Sgt. Satterfield got an uneasy feeling about continuing the patrol with the fog as thick as it was and the uphill trend. We had moved about four hundred meters away from our laager and made no discoveries, so we turned back. Sgt. Satterfield reported to Lt. Chapla who seemed satisfied with the outcome of our adventure but decided he would wait for the fog to lift and send another patrol to investigate the next hilltop.

On our map, the hill we were about to scout was numbered 466. That meant it was four hundred sixty six meters above the valley floor. The fog lifted and a patrol left to scout the hill using the same trail Satterfield, Grumbos, and I had used earlier that morning. A second platoon squad leader, Sergeant Marcus Davis took his squad with Colon at the point and set off for the crest of Hill 466. On the way to the top of the hill, the trail split. Sgt. Davis made the decision to split his squad, half going with Colon, and the other half continuing with Davis. They had not gotten out of each other's sight when Davis set off a booby trap, mortally wounding himself and slightly wounding Colon. Lt. Chapla organized the rest of the company and we went to the site of the incident. Davis had succumbed to the wounds he received from the blast and Colon was wrestling around in some kind of pain, but we found no wounds on him.

I called for a dust-off, medevac helicopter, and though it is not normal for a medevac to remove any bodies, we were able to extract Davis' remains with Colon on the dust-off. Once the medevac chopper took off, we all moved to the top of hill 466 and discovered it had been an ARVN mini firebase at one time. There was a good LZ right on the crest of the hill with a circle of old foxholes that had been completely or half-filled with dirt and tree branches to eliminate their effectiveness as a fighting position. We established a perimeter for the night with the second platoon pushing out past the circle of old foxholes. The third platoon pushed past our laager site following the trail that continued down the other side of the hill. They moved about three to four hundred meters past our laager and established their own perimeter. Lt Chapla established his laager spot in a group of small scrub trees just off the trail from which we accessed the top of the hill. As I started to set up my area, the lieutenant asked if I would move off the top of the hill just down from his position. The area he pointed toward was very steep in comparison to the area where he was set up. I did not argue with him, even though I was the only one singled out to move down the hill. I started down the steep slope covered with the same scrub trees and a few larger trees. Because the slope was so steep, I was only ten feet out but thirty feet down when I asked, "Is this far enough, Sir?"

"No," he replied. "You need to go a little farther."

After going another ten feet I asked, "Is this OK, Sir?"

"Just a little bit farther," he answered.

"Wow, Sir, are you sure you want me to go farther?" I asked.

"Just a bit farther," he repeated.

Once I went another ten feet he said, "That is far enough."

I was so far removed from the perimeter, I was starting to feel as if I was the listening post at this laager site. A listening post is an early warning position, usually two or three people sent out at night beyond the perimeter for early detection of the enemy should they decide to attack a laager site. With a bit more grumbling on my part, I started to string my hammock in the trees. I tied one end of the hammock only six inches above the ground to the base of a tree. The other end, where my feet would be, I had to reach over my head to tie the rope to the tree. Someone came down the sharp incline with a Claymore mine and I grabbed a trip flare out of my ruck as we went together to set them up. I ran the trip wire across an area. Then we moved about twenty feet back up the steep incline and set up the Claymore, aiming it at the middle of the trip wire. A Claymore mine has a cord one hundred feet long with a blasting cap attached. The blasting cap screwed into the top of the Claymore mine. The other end of the wire plugs into a firing device that generates a volt and a half, enough to set off the electric blasting cap. With a hundred feet of wire, the Claymore was about thirty to thirty-five feet from where my hammock was tied in the trees. Normally that distance would not have been enough to protect me from the sixty-foot back blast the Claymore delivers. If it had not been for the steepness of the slope, I would have to move back up the hill. I set up the guard position next to where the lieutenant was sleeping. That meant all the radios were there: the company radio, the battalion radio. The FO's radio was next to where he was sleeping. The Claymore-firing device was placed next to the radios for easy access.

By the time darkness had set in, I had the guard list put together and notified every one of their time slots. Lt. Chapla had first guard, followed by me and then Sgt. Satterfield. We had two guard posts that night, one on either side of the perimeter and both next to the trail so the time slots for guard were rather long. We were on guard one and one half hours starting at 20:00 hours or 8:00 P.M. With the heavy weather, clouds and fog, it made for a very dark night. After my guard, I returned to my hammock and propped my rifle against the tree next to my head. I went to sleep but I was never a heavy sleeper even when I was back in the world at home. At some point, I was awakened by someone walking out in front of my position. I reached for my rifle and laid it across my lap moving the safety to the fire position. I made sure I was looking with my right eye closed so if the trip flare went off I could sight my rifle with the proper eye. The steps were very distinct and moved cautiously in my direction. I did not know what time it was but I assumed Satterfield was still on guard. There was no way to confirm who was at the radios and the firing device for the Claymore.

Suddenly the trip flare went off throwing a bright flickering light out to my immediate front. I hastily rolled out of my hammock to a prone position facing away from the perimeter above me. I saw nothing but I yelled, "Satterfield, blow that Claymore!" When nothing happened I yelled again, "Satterfield, blow that Claymore!"

When there was again no response, I scrambled up the hill with my M-16 in hand. When I reached the guard post area, I grabbed the clacker, the Claymore firing device with the safety wire in place and mashed the handle right through the safety wire, instantly setting off the Claymore ant-personnel mine. KA BOOM! A massive explosion carried across the whole perimeter setting off a fearsome hail of bullets from small arms fire all over the perimeter. The third platoon was awakened by the explosion and grazing fire from our position. They thought they had come under attack. They held their fire because none of their trip flares had gone off. Finally, the call of "cease fire," went out around our perimeter and all was quiet. After explaining to LT Chapla what I had heard and what the reason for blowing the Claymore. He told me, "OK, now you need to go check the kill zone to see if there is a body count."

At that point, I tried to change my story saying, "I think it was an animal or a monkey that set off the trip flare, Sir." The third platoon had reported seeing three monkeys holding hands crossing the trail in front of them before they moved into their laager below us.

It did not work, the lieutenant told me, "Muss, you still need to check it out."

"Sir, can't it wait until morning?" I pleaded.

"No, you need to check it out now," he replied.

A couple of the guys from second platoon went with me as we probed the blast area in total darkness. Actually, we were feeling for a body or carcass because we could not see anything. It was too dark to see but our search satisfied the lieutenant. There was nothing in the kill zone of the Claymore mine. Whatever or whoever tripped the flare got away clean.

The next day was resupply day and the third platoon rejoined us for a hot meal sent out from the mess hall at Uplift on the first chopper along with mail. As we ate, we enjoyed the written company of loved ones and the news supplied by the "Stars and Stripes", the newspaper the Army published for GIs. It usually contained a myriad of interesting stories. I was sitting next to my friend from Illinois, Specialist Nick Grumbos, Sergeant Satterfield's RTO. He asked me to read an interesting article he found in one of the "Stars and Stripes" newspapers. I read the article about a GI that had been wounded, losing both of his legs from a land mine while in Vietnam. He wrote his parents, who were not aware of his situation, telling them his tour was ending and he was coming home. He also told them he had met a good friend and was bringing him home with him. His friend had no family but had been wounded and had no legs. He wanted to know if it was OK with his parents to bring his friend home. When his parents wrote back and told him they thought it was a nice gesture but they did not want to be burdened by someone without any legs. The guy killed himself because the friend he had described was actually himself and he lost hope of making something of himself because he did not want to burden his parents.

Nick said to me, "What would you do in that situation?"

"I don't know, but I wouldn't kill myself," I answered.

Nick responded, "If I lost both my legs today, I know I could make it. I wouldn't kill myself."

We talked a bit more about the article then I went on about my business, breaking down the SPs and sorting out cigarettes for the smokers in the company, leaving Nick sitting there reading the newspapers.

The resupply was distributed; everyone got their cigarette supply and candy from the SPs and meals from C-rations and LRRPs. Chow was over and as we started the cleanup, Nick and another guy named Whitfield discovered a suspicious object sticking out of the ground where Nick and I had talked about the newspaper article. On closer inspection, we determined it could be the top or nose of a 105 howitzer round. We had to hold off the last chopper in to our LZ, coming to pick up the Marmite Cans for the hot chow until we blew the booby trap. Everyone cleared the area and Nick set a C-4 charge on it and blew it in place. It was some sort of explosive round buried where it could easily be detonated. It was a narrow escape for anyone that ate chow that day. We were lucky to find it before someone set it off.

Lt. Chapla asked me to find another site for the radios used on guard duty. It seems the changing of guard every hour and a half disturbed his sleep. He did not mind being woken for important things, but changing the guard was not one of them. I complied with his request and went to the other side of the perimeter to find a likely spot. I had to cross the LZ and walk through a small row of scrub trees to get to where Nick had put up a small shelter made from a poncho. He had also constructed a small bench out of cut trees and lashed them together with vines. A foxhole, almost filled with branches and dirt, was about thirty feet from Nick's location right in the middle of the trail. I stepped into the foxhole and sat down on the edge inside the perimeter. I was considering this spot for the guard position. After I thought about it, I figured the radios would have too much exposure right in the middle of the trail. I went to Nick and asked him if I could use his bench for the guard position. He let me know he was OK with that and we then began to talk about nothing in general.

Suddenly Lt. Austin, our artillery FO spoke up, "Grumbos, you need to get to work cleaning out that foxhole. It needs to be done before dark."

I did not know what was going on but I questioned the lieutenant's order. "Sir, why do you want to have these guys clean out that foxhole?"

"Well, it is for protection in case there is more contact tonight like we had last night," the lieutenant explained.

"Sir, we did not have any contact last night, that was just an animal. Besides even if someone shit in that foxhole I would get in it if we had contact," I answered.

"Sergeant Musson, you take care of your side of the perimeter and I will take care of mine," he chided.

I snapped to attention and acknowledged his command by saluting him, something I was not supposed to do in the field. Acknowledging rank by saluting could get an officer killed by identifying him as a leader. I turned to Nick and said to him, "I'll talk to you later." I tapped him on the arm and walked over the rise between the scrub trees toward the LZ.

I was only seconds away from where I left Nick and had covered no more than fifty feet when I heard a terrific explosion. I jumped to the ground and covered my head thinking it was incoming mortar rounds. Then I heard the blood curdling screams in the direction I had just come from. No more rounds had come in to our location so I quickly got to my feet and started running for my radio at Lt. Chapla's location. As I ran, I passed Lt. Chapla running toward the location of the explosion. We said nothing to each other as we passed on the run.

I reached the radio's location and grabbed my handset. I knew we had some seriously wounded people. I called into the handset," Dust-off, Dust-off, this is Papa Mike. Over."

A familiar voice I recognized as the TOC radio operator named Pirc answered my call immediately, "Papa Mike, this is dust-off. What do you have? Over."

"This is Papa Mike, I have wounded and I need a dust-off ASAP," I answered skipping the information I was supposed to supply for a dust-off yet observing correct radio procedure.

"Papa Mike, this is dust-off. How many casualties do you have and what are their names? Over." Pirc asked me trying to help direct me to the dust-off checklist.

"I don't know," was my reply.

"Papa Mike, this is dust-off. What is your location? Over." Pirc again tried to get information.

"I don't know," I replied again.

I think he could tell I was very excited and a little rattled. He went on, "OK, relax and take a deep breath. You have to give me some information or I can't help you. Give me something."

I took a deep breath to calm my nerves and I went to a short deep thought. I asked Pirc, "Do you still have the coordinates of our resupply?"

"Yes," he replied.

"That is where we are," I said.

"OK, the dust-off is twenty minutes out," he said and our conversation was over.

I left the radio and went back to where the explosion had taken place. I saw Nick Grumbos lying on his back right next to the foxhole in the middle of the trail that I had checked for the guard post. I stood in that hole, Nick was lying where I sat on the edge of the hole. Everyone was running around but it seemed no one was attending to Nick. As I got up to him, I could see both of his legs were missing below the knees but he was not bleeding at all. His face looked chalky white; I could tell he was going into shock. I asked if anyone had given him any morphine. Someone answered, "We can't find the morphine. It's not in Doc's bag." That is when I found out Doc Ozuna, our current top doc had also been wounded. Shrapnel from the round that took off Nick's legs had hit Doc, taking off his chin just below the lower lip and severed his left arm right under the armpit. The only thing holding it on was the triceps muscle on the top of his shoulder. There were several people tending to Doc and looking for the morphine he had. My attention went back to Nick. He was lying on his back with his legs up and bent at the knees. His left foot was missing just above the ankle and all the skin, muscle and meat was missing all the way up to his knee, leaving the leg bone exposed. His right leg was off right below the knee. I asked someone nearby to get a towel to put over his legs so he could not see them, hoping to protect him from going into shock.

I knelt beside Nick and started to talk to him while the others looked for a towel for his legs and the morphine in Doc's bag. I said to him, "You are going to be alright, the dust-off is on the way." There was no response but I could tell he was digesting what I said. I also knew if he saw his legs he would definitely go into shock; he was already close. Then I asked him, "Is there anything I can do for you?"

He looked up at me and answered, "Yeah, take my boots off. They're too tight."

At that point, I lost control of my emotions, almost bursting into tears right in front of him. I got up and got away from him until I regained my composure. I then went back and started directing some of the guys to make a stretcher for Nick so we could get him to the helicopter when it came in. I ended up giving them instructions on how to make a stretcher out of a poncho. We learned that in basic training but no one remembered but me. I told them to cut two long poles, lay the poncho on the ground. Lay the two poles in the center of the poncho spaced far enough apart to allow a person to fit between, and then fold each side of the poncho over the poles. When the injured party is laid on top, his weight won't let the sides slip and a litter is created to allow the injured person to be moved. It worked just like the instructor in basic training said it would.

I had seen Lt. Chapla run over here but I did not see him now. I found out he was on the radio filling in the information I didn't know when I called for the dust-off. I was rattled and not thinking straight but I knew we had serious injuries and needed the dust-off as soon as we could get it. I found out the lieutenant had called the information in when Pirc told me he had it when I tried to call it in.

We made a thorough search and still could not find the morphine in Doc's bag. We dumped the entire contents on the ground but still no morphine. Because Doc could not talk, we called for the third platoon to send their medic, Doc Mooneyham, to our location. We knew he would have a supply of morphine. For Doc Ozuna's injuries, we covered his chin with the largest field-dressing bandage we could find and tied it on top of his head. For his arm, we jammed another large field bandage under his arm and tied the bandage around him thereby tying his arm to him. Because of his head wound, we were not allowed to give him morphine. Someone remembered seeing Doc trying to untangle a trip wire, raising his arm over his head in the process. That made it clear to us that the shrapnel took off his chin, and then severed his arm.

I went back to get my radio and prepare for the dust-off chopper to come on station. Satterfield went down the trail to escort Doc Mooneyham to our location. When he arrived, Nick got his shot of morphine. Lt.

RUN THROUGH THE JUNGLE

Chapla was supervising the care and movement of the wounded. The helicopter came on station asking for smoke to identify our location.

"Papa Mike, this is Dust-off one on your net. Pop smoke. Over," the pilot said.

"Dust-off one this is Papa Mike, smoke is out. Over," I answered.

"Roger, Papa Mike this is Dust-off One, I have yellow smoke. Over," the pilot said as he circled our location.

"Dust-off one, this is Papa Mike. Roger on the yellow smoke," I verified.

"Papa Mike, this is Dust-off one. Can you tell me the nature of your contact? Over," the pilot asked.

"Dust-off one, this is Papa Mike, negative on the contact, this was a booby trap. Over," I informed the pilot.

"Roger, Papa Mike. Understand it was a booby trap, so we won't be setting down. Over," the pilot told me. He was thinking if there were any more booby traps, the static electricity from the prop would set them off.

"Roger, Dust-off one," I acknowledged.

They walked Doc Ozuna to the helicopter and boosted him up into it while the pilot hovered four feet above the LZ. When it came to loading Nick, it was a bit more cumbersome. His back was scraping against the floor of the dust-off helicopter and they could not get him loaded onto the helicopter.

Satterfield looked at me and yelled so I could hear him, "Tell him to set it down." He indicated to the pilot by waving his arms in a typical downward motion used to direct helicopter landings.

The pilot was shaking his head and talking to me on the radio, "We are not sitting down. We don't want to chance setting off any more booby traps that might be in the area."

I looked at Satterfield and said, "He says he won't set down."

Satterfield grabbed the M-79 grenade launcher from the guy standing next to him, loaded an explosive round in full view of the pilot and told me, "Tell him I said to set it down." Then he pointed the grenade launcher at the pilot's head.

As I transmitted, "He says to set it down." The skids on the chopper touched the LZ. By the look on the pilot's face, I would not have had to say anything. It was clear he understood Satterfield's universal language.

Nick was loaded on the dust-off and as the pilot lifted off, I thought about the prophetic statement Nick had made earlier in the day, "If I lost both of my legs today, I know I could make it….." and tears welled up in my eyes again.

Before we escorted Doc Mooneyham back to the third platoon, he explained that the new battalion surgeon, Doc Coleman had changed the location where the medics carried the morphine. They put it in an inside pocket in their jungle fatigue pants. It was required because some medics were having trouble accounting for the vials of morphine in their medical bags. We did not search Doc Ozuna because none of us knew the morphine location was changed. We thought it was still in the medical bag. Medics are wounded in combat, but who knew ours would be wounded in a place where he could not tell us where the morphine vials were located.

The next day, Lt Chapla told everyone we were moving off the hill. We packed up and were moving toward third platoon right after morning chow, about 08:00. Satterfield was up near the point element, carrying his own radio. The lieutenant was back about mid column and this time, for some reason, I was behind him and the company radio operator was behind me. Borchard was on R & R and I don't remember who was carrying his radio that day. The word came back to us that the point element found another booby trap so we sat down on the trail where we were to take five. I sat down and was leaning against my rucksack with my legs slightly spread and my knees up. A call came in for the CO, Lt. Chapla on the company net. I reached back to hand him the handset from the company radio but it only extended to my head. The lieutenant stood up and stepped between my legs, then leaned over next to my right ear and took the call. As he withdrew his foot from between my legs, he dragged some leaves and sticks away from a round metal object. I finished brushing the leaves away and discovered it was the top or nose of a 105 howitzer round.

I pointed to it and said, "Sir, look at this."

He bent forward again to look at what I was pointing at and said, "Are you shitting me?"

It was obvious that we were still at risk and the trail had already produced two more booby traps. Lt. Chapla told everyone to get on their hands and knees and brush everything off the trail to return to the top of the hill.

"Mark anything that looks suspicious," he told us. "Once you get to where the guy next to you has cleaned the trail, then you can get up and walk."

I brushed the trail clean where I had been sitting, leaving only a triangle of sticks marking the top of the 105. As I walked up the now cleared trail, some guys behind me had marked two more spots. As I passed the marked spots, neither looked menacing but the lieutenant did not want to take chances. He told me once we were back at the top of the hill he wanted me to call for a demolition team to take care of the places we marked. I complied with his request and once again, a helicopter was landing on the LZ at the top of Hill 466.

The four members of the demo team got off the chopper and went right to work. The leader of the team was a staff sergeant. He was asking questions to help the team locate any booby traps we may have overlooked. I told him I was interested in the third marked spot down the trail.

"When we get to the third spot," he said," I will let you know."

They used an instrument that appeared to be a metal detector, sweeping it over the ground. As they came to each of the marked spots, they returned to our location at the top of the hill and would prepare their explosives. Then they would return to blow the marked area in place. When they reached the third spot, the staff sergeant said to me, "So this is the spot you are interested in huh?"

"Yeah, this is the one, Sarge," I said.

This time Lt. Chapla went with them, he was so interested in finding out what the thing was. The demo team let the lieutenant set off the explosive device on what we thought was a 105 round. We were right. The two previous marks had proved to be nothing, but this one was a huge explosion and sounded like we just fired a 105 howitzer. I remember watching as a large black smoke ring rose above the trees spinning as it rose higher in the air before dissipating.

The staff sergeant came to the top of the hill and looked at me saying, "Yeah, that one was a good one alright. It was good thing you were concerned."

The total of all the booby traps we found was ten. The last one we found was after the demo team had gone back to the rear. Satterfield found it near the first one he had found earlier in the day. He injured his shoulder taking cover after rigging an explosive device on it and we had to get a medevac helicopter in for him. The booby trap was set up differently than the others we had found that were all buried in the ground. We think that is why the demo team never found it. We found out later that when the firebase was dismantled by the ARVN artillery unit, they lost a sling load of 105 rounds on the hill and recovered all but ten. We could always count on our Vietnamese allies to help us out.

Third platoon still out in front of us found a trail that intersected the one we were following. For safety the point man, Michael Clickner paralleled the trail on a patrol to check it out. They found nothing suspicious so the decision was made to take the trail back to the third platoon's location. He set off another booby trap, knocking him unconscious. When the medic was checking him, he could find no wounds but he appeared to be bleeding from his pores. That made us think it was a concussion booby trap. We called a dust-off and got him to the hospital. He died three days later from internal bleeding that the doctors could not stop. They found out the booby trap he set off was made from ground glass that cut him every time they moved him for exploratory surgery to see if they could stop the bleeding.

That night the CP and the second platoon laagered in a bunch of trees far away from hill 466. Between the big trees, there were a bunch of scrub trees and the typical jungle vegetation. I took my hammock and strung it up and again. I was out away from the perimeter farther away than I felt comfortable. Sometime in the middle of the night, I heard the brush breaking like there was somebody out there. I laid my rifle across my lap and took the safety off. All of a sudden, there were screams from a large cat and a wild disturbance in the brush. Borden, Lt. Austin's RTO was on guard and he started to call for me.

His voice was louder than a whisper, "Sergeant Musson, are you OK?"

The commotion got wilder and louder, but I did not answer Borden.

Again, Borden asked, "Sergeant Musson, Sergeant Musson, are you OK?"

I did not answer again feeling the animals were too close to me and I did not want to talk above their ruckus to answer Borden. Then I heard Borden go over to Lt. Austin and wake him. The lieutenant must have been sleeping soundly because I heard him come awake with a start, as if he were surprised.

"Lt. Austin, Lt. Austin, wake up Sir," Borden commanded.

"Ah, huh, what is going on?" Austin asked.

Borden answered him, "Sir, something is out there and I think it's got Sergeant Musson."

I had to smile when I heard that conversation but I called out, "Hey", to scare the animals away and then I said, "I'm OK out here."

The next morning nobody said anything about the incident and we moved out of the area of Hill 466. We were all glad to be done with it and the problems it brought us.

I never saw or heard from Nick Grumbos after the incident on Hill 466 until I got home on 4 October 1970, He had called my parents the night before on 3 October 1970 when I got back to the states. I don't know how he knew because I extended and we never discussed the dates either of us DEROSd. When my parents told him I would be home the next night, he insisted they have me call him no matter what time of night it was. I called him at 23:00 hours or 11:00 o'clock on 4 October. He was home on convalescing leave from Ft. Carson, Colorado. Leaving on the fifth, he wanted me to come to his house and have dinner with his family.

I asked him, "What time shall I come over?"

He said, "Come early."

I was sitting in his living room the next day at 09:30 and watched him walk around the foot of his bed on his knees before he was dressed. When he got dressed, he walked out on his artificial legs and shook my hand. I was amazed at what I saw. He drove me to the store on an errand for his mother and later to the airport to pick up his ticket back to Colorado. I was nervous both times because I did not know if he could drive a car with his new legs. When we pulled up in front of the airline terminal at O'Hare Airport, he stopped the car curbside, locked it and we went into the terminal. I asked if he was sure he wanted to park there in the tow away zone and he just shrugged his shoulders and kept walking.

Once inside as we approached the escalator to go upstairs, I noticed some hesitation on his part. I asked him if something was wrong.

"I have never been on one of these, " he said, "Can you stand behind me in case I fall?"

"Sure," I answered.

When we returned after he purchased his ticket, he asked me to stand in front of him on the down escalator. Naturally, I complied. To my amazement, his car was still parked at the curb where we left it when we arrived. In the forty-four years I have known him those are the only two times that he ever asked for help. He remains a good friend today. We talk and see each other frequently. He still owns a wide variety of video and CD movies.

CHAPTER 21

Sappers at Firebase Tape

Once we were finished in the area of Hill 466, we moved further north into mountains more rugged with thick forests of towering trees. Captain Welsh returned from his R&R and was once again at the helm of Alpha Company. He was extremely disappointed to learn the fate of Davis, Colon, Grumbos, Ozuna and Clickner. As a result, we got some new people to replace them and made a couple of changes within the CP, the command position in Alpha Company. Borchard became the Como chief in the CP and carried the code machine, the Green Machine as we called it. A new guy took Borchard's place as company radio operator; Specialist Fourth Class Donald Bowles accepted the job when offered it by Captain Welsh. That broke the order that was customary within the company about CP jobs and Borchard and I had to field many questions from the guys in the other platoons that thought they might be in line for the job. Normally the selection process was sort of the way I got the battalion radio job, someone recommended me. The only thing we could tell them was that it was the CO's decision and we had no say so in the matter.

Working high in the mountainous jungle, the monsoon rains and fog played havoc with our resupply days. It was tough finding an LZ to bring in resupply choppers, even tougher to find a LZ on a day clear enough for the pilots to be flying. We had gone several days without a resupply because the fog had us socked in. If we heard a chopper go over, it was high above us in order to stay out of the duck soup we were maneuvering in and around.

The forests were thick in the region we were searching for the NVA. The seventy-five to one hundred foot tall trees blocked off the light reaching the jungle floor. With the heavy fog and damp air, it did not matter much since there was not any light to speak of anyway. At night, the jungle would eerily give up some secrets that were strange phenomena. The trails and jungle floor would glow in the dark from leaves that had fallen off the trees and began to decay. When walking around, our feet and legs appeared to be shadows on the ground covered with the decaying leaves. It was a strange light show that would illuminate faces and hands in the darkness.

The NVA used the triple canopy jungle to their advantage; they could operate under the trees undetected by US observation planes. The US came up with a plan to eliminate the thick cover and expose the NVA maneuvers; it was called Agent Orange. Agent Orange, when sprayed on the jungle, defoliated everything. Green jungle plants of all kinds became dead or dying with no exceptions. It only took two to three days for green foliage to join the decaying leaves on the jungle floor. Several times, we passed through or laagered in areas that had been defoliated. Once we passed through an area that had recently been sprayed with Agent Orange. The leaves on all the trees and plants looked like they had been in an overnight freeze, soft and limp. Two days later when we came back through the area, there were no leaves on any trees or plants. They were lying on the ground dried and brown. They crunched like potato chips when we walked on them and we could not help but walk on them, as they were three to five inches deep all over.

We were on our sixth day after our last resupply. That is already two days late for our normal resupply. Everyone was hungry and searching their rucksack for any kind of canned or freeze-dried food. We laagered on a high ridge that night in the midst of huge trees and, if not for the fog, would have been a nice overlook of the deep valleys between the ridges. During the daylight hours, the fog was so thick visibility was down to about fifty feet. Once the cooler night air came in, the visibility improved so much we could see Firebase Tape, which was three ridges over from us. Nonetheless, we were not in a position to receive resupply nor did we have a good location with an LZ to receive choppers.

About 01:00 hours or one o'clock in the morning, Firebase Tape came under attack from sappers. Sappers were the NVA version of demolition commandos with special training to stealthily penetrate the defensive perimeters of US bases undetected and blow up bunkers or artillery with satchel charges. From our position, it looked as if they were celebrating July 4. At our location, the perimeter guard got everybody up and awake as the battle increased on Tape. We watched as tracers of both colors, green for them, red for us, ricocheted off rocks and the ground like a fireworks display gone wrong. The tracers were bullets dipped in colored phosphorus that would light up at night when fired from weapons. We were able to tell where our rounds were hitting so we could adjust fire if needed. When loaded, the magazines containing tracers were loaded with every fourth round being a tracer.

The command back at LZ Uplift contacted us on the battalion net and asked if we could go to the aide of the troops on Tape to prevent them from being overrun. I remember Captain Welsh discussing the request with the platoon leaders. I think everyone, including Captain Welsh found the request laughable since we were three ridges away in two thousand meter high mountains at one in the morning with no way to be transported over there except by foot. I delivered the message exactly like Captain Welsh told me.

I radioed the rear, "This is Papa Mike. Please be advised, Papa says that is a negative on the request from this location."

They acknowledged my transmission but somehow I thought they were disappointed in the answer. More than likely they were looking at our straight line distance which was a half mile at the most. We could see the attack clearly but getting there to help that night was impossible. There was a mad scramble by the rear to get men and equipment evacuated from the firebase. Gunships were circling overhead. The battle on the firebase continued for most of the night. We could not tell from our position who was winning the battle or if at the end of the night we might be on our way to try to recapture the firebase from the enemy's hands. Flares illuminated the beleaguered firebase all night. We had more light that night than we had seen in the previous five days during the daytime. We could even see the huge rock next to the helicopter pad that had the 173rd patch painted on it.

They evacuated all the big guns, ammunition, and equipment on the firebase before they took the troops off in any chopper that would risk flying into the firebase that night. We saw several medevac choppers extract wounded troops also. We watched the entire battle and evacuation all night long, helpless to go to their aide. Once all troops were evacuated and accounted for, the gunships worked over the firebase with their mini guns. "Puff the Magic Dragon" was on call but because of our proximity to the target, they would not allow them to work over the firebase. Puff was a C-47 prop airplane with a mini gun in the left rear door, capable of putting a round covering every three square inches in the size of a football field in about one minute.

At first light, the next morning we were up and moving in the direction of the now fully abandoned Firebase Tape. We moved swiftly but were not running down the side of the steep mountain on which we had just spent a sleepless night. We stepped over a small stream about a foot wide at the bottom of the mountain and began the ascent up the next ridge, which was equally as steep as the one we just came down. Our pace was slowed by the steep climb to the top of this second ridge. Here the steep slope gave way to a gentler downward slope covered in the tall grass that was usually found in higher elevations. Suddenly the point element spotted movement up in front of the column. Captain Welsh dropped his rucksack and moved forward just as the point opened fire on the individual they had seen. When the CO took off, I went with him, rucksack and radio intact. We joined Taylor, the second platoon's point man, and his slack man Stiltner in the chase. Since the three of them had dropped their rucks and were now running downhill to try to catch up with the VC/NVA they were chasing, I could only follow their trail through the tall grass. Because of the extra weight, I was trailing them by about fifty feet. My rucksack was still close to seventy or eighty pounds; the only thing I was missing was ten pounds of food. I saw them disappear behind a huge boulder down the slope in front of us. When I rounded the boulder, there they were, stopped by a tangle of brush and vines all in a bunch.

As I stopped my forward progress, both Taylor and Stiltner looked at me as if I was a solution to a problem. Then I heard Stiltner say as he looked at Taylor, "What do you think?"

I had no idea what he was talking about but it obviously made sense to Taylor because he answered, "I don't know. Let's give it a try."

Nothing else was communicated between the two men before they grabbed me by the seat of my pants and on each shoulder and threw me head first into the brush and vines, making a hole for them to pass through. On the way through, the men, including the CO stepped on my ass as all of them jumped uninhibited through the hole. We learned that maneuver in Infantry School. It was used to cross barbed wire after one guy would throw himself onto the barbed wire collapsing it, and the remainder of the element would step on his ass as they ran across the barbed wire. It worked for entangled vines too.

By the time I freed myself from the vines, the two point men and the CO were long gone. Luckily, for me they were still leaving a trail that was easy to follow in the brush and now in the ten-foot high elephant grass. The slope started leveling out to a flat plain covered with elephant grass. As I entered the level area, gunfire buzzed overhead from two directions. Although they say the AK has a clear distinct sound, I could not tell which shots were ours and which were theirs. I had to find which way they had gone and link up with them for my safety.

I called out, "Hey, where are you guys?"

Someone answered, "We are over here."

"Where is over here?" I asked, as I heard more automatic weapons fire.

I was afraid to move, thinking I would go in the wrong direction so I stayed there until Stiltner came for me. The VC/NVA slipped away in the tall elephant grass. By the time we made it back to where we had left the rest of the company, darkness was creeping in so we spent the night there in the grass on the gentle slope. When some of the guys put out their Claymore mines around the perimeter, they found some terraced gardens of onions growing. We figured these were planted by the VC/NVA who had attacked the firebase and we had chased. Since we were seven days without resupply, the guys that found the onions picked them and ate them, at least temporarily satisfying their hunger.

As we moved from the grass-covered slopes back to the tree covered mountains, the climbing became more difficult and slowed our progress once again. Captain Welsh remained committed to getting to the overrun firebase as soon as we could. It took us all the next day to reach Firebase Tape or what was left of it. Someone did a good job of cleaning it up. Not everything was removed by the US troops that left in the middle of the night. In the days that it took us to get there, some things must have been removed by the VC/NVA. Cold weather was moving in and so was the night, so we did not get a chance to check over everything we wanted. The wind, or the "hawk" as we called it, picked up and it started to feel bitter cold sitting on top of the hill in the former firebase.

I got word that some of the guys were fixing a meal out of anything they could find that was eatable. They were referring to it as a mulligan stew. To get an invite to eat, all I had to do was contribute something to the meal. Thinking I had nothing to eat, the guy organizing the meal told me they had nothing to cook it in and asked if I had a canteen cup. Normally, I did not cook anything in my canteen cup but I was so hungry, I gladly offered it to the group for a bite of their stew. They also pressed me for a canned contribution that I was sure I did not have. However, when I went through my rucksack, I found a severely dented can of beef with potatoes and gravy, a heavily greasy meal that I was surprised to find it in my ruck. I would have thrown it out long before if I had realized I was carrying it. But to this group, it might as well have been a prime rib dinner. When I showed it to them, they were ecstatic. Here is the list of contributions to the mulligan stew:

One can of beef with spiced sauce
One can of beef with potatoes and gravy
1 bunch of fresh onions, thanks to the VC
½ inch of ketchup from the bottom of a bottle of ketchup
One can of beef slices
Celery salt
Onion salt
Hot sauce
One canteen cup

We all sat in a circle and passed the canteen cup full of stew. Each one of us was allowed one spoon full of stew as we continued to pass the canteen cup around until it was gone. It was not a lot of chow but it was hot and tasted good on the chilly night. When we finished, Captain Welsh produced a number ten can of pineapple chunks left over from our last hot meal on resupply eight days ago. He had been carrying the can, hidden in his rucksack, all that time. His only stipulation was that everyone who wanted some pineapple got some. We were happy to comply and regretted not offering some of the stew to the captain. He said he probably would not have accepted our offer anyway, but I think he was just making us feel better about leaving him out. That night at least some of us went to sleep with some food in our stomachs, and we were grateful for that. There were no incidents with security on the perimeter that night. We were all anxiously awaiting the overdue resupply that was coming the next day.

With the helicopters bringing in resupply later, the CO wanted to get started with our mission of being sent to the firebase in the first place. We were supposed to search for any equipment or material that might be useful that was left behind when they evacuated the firebase three days ago. In addition, command at Uplift was interested in body count or blood trails. Since all US troops were accounted for, we were only searching for signs of VC/NVA that may have been left behind. We found nothing but spent ammunition cartridges. The US or the sappers that attacked the firebase removed everything else.

We spent one more night on the mountaintop that used to be a mini firebase, and then we moved on into the thicker mountain forests in the area. All our leads went cold and the command group back at Uplift asked us to get to an LZ because they had a hot spot they wanted to move us to. Luckily, we happened upon a B-52 bomb strike right in the middle of the thick forest. We had several bomb craters to choose from for an extraction. These bomb craters were huge, made by one thousand pound bombs dropped from thirty thousand feet above. The trees were pushed into a pile of sticks on the edge of the bomb crater. The crater itself would allow three UH-1 Huey helicopters to land on the top edge of the crater, setting one skid on the piled up trees. That was the only side we could load from because the crater fell away so fast on the other side of the Huey. There were no trees, brush or any vegetation in the crater at all, just yellow orange clay and a pool of water in the bottom, twelve feet in diameter and two feet deep. I shaved in the ice-cold pool before the helicopters arrived to pick us up.

When the Hueys showed up, the pilots had to hover at the top of the trees and drop straight down onto the edge of the creator. After we loaded on the Hueys, the pilots would go straight up until they were clear of the trees and then take off over the trees. They repeated those maneuvers until they extracted the entire company.

CHAPTER 22

R & R

From the high jungle mountains, the battalion planners took us to the low lands somewhere near My Lai. We worked this area several times before but never without contact. It was always a trouble spot and a VC stronghold. We were expecting trouble from day one. The CO split the company into platoon-sized elements. The CP was traveling with third platoon.

The second platoon finally got a new lieutenant. Ryan was from Boston and had the typical accent that went with being from Boston. He was short and stocky but a genuinely nice guy and he was good for the second platoon. I remember once making some Army instant coffee because I was out of hot chocolate. Lt. Ryan asked why I was using that coffee and offered me some new instant coffee his mother sent from the States. It was called, "Tasters Choice". He told me it tasted like fresh brewed coffee and it did. He saved me from having to drink the bitter Army instant coffee.

Colon made a full recovery from his wounds earlier in the month and was back teaching and walking point. When we got together, Colon and I talked about the extensions we had applied for. We were expecting confirmation on them any day. The Army offered anyone in Vietnam with one hundred fifty days or less left on their enlistment an early out. In other words, the Army would drop the last hundred and fifty days off your term of service if you left Vietnam with fewer than one hundred fifty days. It was a good deal so I went for it. Colon put in for his extension about the same time and we were both waiting on the decision from the Army.

The company was together shortly for resupply and Colon and I found out our extensions were accepted. In order for me to go home early, I had to extend almost a month. I had exactly one hundred forty nine days left in the Army when my tour was over in Vietnam. I did that on purpose because I had been in the Army long enough to realize there was fine print on all their deals and there was no way they could tell me I had to have fewer than one hundred fifty days to be eligible for early out. After resupply, we went our separate ways again.

The CP and the third platoon were located on a small hill covered with brush and scrub trees while the second platoon worked the low area covered with palm trees and the thick brush that was prevalent in and around villages and along the trails running throughout the area. Colon was teaching a new candidate in second platoon how to walk point. He was following the new point man acting as his slack man. The point man went through a trip wire, actually, a vine tied to a hand grenade stuffed inside a C ration can with the pin pulled. Once the grenade leaves the can, the handle flies off and starts the fuse on the grenade. The guy on point never felt the trip vine and Colon was back far enough he did not see it either. He walked on top of the grenade just as it went off. He sustained lower leg and groin wounds and some fragments hit him in the chest. The point man was hit in the back and legs.

We heard the blast from our location and the call for a dust-off came in from second platoon. As usual, I called everything in to the rear in the clear but I was shocked when I heard Colon's name on the call to me on the radio. After all the information was sent to the aide station in the rear, they told me there would be a twenty minute delay for the dust-off while gunships came on station because the injuries were a result of contact. That was procedure and nothing I could do would change it. Lt. Ryan pressed for the arrival of the dust-off. Colon was in bad shape, he needed assistance now! Doc Espinoza, second platoon medic, one of our best medics, was vigorously working on him just to keep him alive.

The dust-off helicopter arrived with gunships in tow. Second platoon had one ambulatory and one critical injury to load, but because of the tree height, the chopper was unable to set down. They walked the point man, who was the ambulatory injury, up to and lifted him on the chopper. Because they were working on Colon, they could not load him right away and he succumbed to his wounds. The pilot took off with his one injured passenger.

After the dust-off was gone a few minutes, I got a call from Lt. Ryan on the radio. "Is it possible to get the dust-off back? We got a heartbeat and he is breathing again."

Before I could answer, the pilot came on the air, "We'll be right there. Turning around now."

Then Lt. Ryan came back with, "What about the gunships?"

"To hell with the gunships. We won't need them," the pilot answered.

They obviously did not need me either. I just monitored the conversation between the lieutenant and the dust-off pilot. I was pleased by the dedication of the pilot. All the dust-off pilots seemed to have that trait.

As the pilot approached the LZ, Lt. Ryan came back on the radio. "I don't know if we will be able to lift him onto the helicopter. The medic is giving him mouth to mouth."

As the pilot answered, "Understand, I am setting down," without hesitation, he cut the tops of the small trees off with the rotor on the helicopter that had prevented him from setting down before.

As I watched and monitored the radio, the rotor spit the treetops into the surrounding brush and the chopper was on the ground. Once they loaded Colon on the chopper, the pilot again headed for the hospital in the rear.

Lt. Ryan came on the radio one more time, "Thanks for what you did for us."

The pilot answered knowing the compliment was directed at him, "Think nothing of it. It's all part of my job. Glad I could be of service."

Later, we learned that Raphael Colon died on the way to the hospital of wounds he received on 17 April 70. Despite the heroic efforts of the medic Espinosa and the daredevil pilot, he could not be saved. The day he found out his extension had been approved, the war was over for him. Those of us that knew him best tried not to dwell on his passing. But there was more agony coming.

The practice then was for the Army to send an escort home with the deceased. Delgado had petitioned to be that escort, but his request was denied. He knew too many details of Colon's death and the Army did not want the family to know the details so intimately. It was better if a stranger went as the escort and the family learned the details from the documents prepared by the Army. I felt sorry for Delgado; he deserved the honor of escorting our friend home. He struggled over not being able to do that for a long time afterward.

Shortly after Colon's death, the first platoon returned from Tuy Hoa and we joined them at "Sky Soldier Beach" for a short, in country R & R. The 173rd was thrown out of so many in country recreational spots, Sky Soldier Beach was created just for the 173rd. We carried our reputation of being tough fighters to the extreme limit of most recreation areas, sometimes causing trouble with staff over nothing. However, we could not be thrown off our own beach.

The beach was remarkably set up! There were motor boats for water skiing in the clear aqua colored water of the South China Sea. Volleyball nets and other beach games were available if we wanted. A crew was permanently assigned to maintain the beach and the perimeter bunkers were manned by the companies visiting the beach so the rotation schedule was covered by all four battalions of the 173rd Airborne.

I waited in line for the water skiing. There were so many guys waiting, the driver of the boat put a limit on how many times a skier could fall on the attempt to get up on the skis. One drawback was the boats were fitted with speed props designed for fast speeds, not the power props needed for water skiing. Some of the guys had no skiing experience so they were allowed three attempts to get up. If they did not make it by the third try, they had to pass the skis to the next person in line. Because of sharks, the skier could not have any open wounds. Once the skier was up, he had to give up the skis after his first fall. Usually the skier's first attempt to cross where the waves were breaking caused him to fall so the line was moving right along. I was in line behind Bowles, who had never skied before. He failed at his third attempt so I swam to take the skis from him. I had plenty of experience skiing behind my uncle's boat in Lake Mattoon back in Illinois. I was not worried until Bowles told me when he fell on his last attempt something huge and black swam right underneath him when he was gathering the skis.

I put the skis on as fast as I could and was waving for the boat to come and bring the ski rope. The driver lined up the rope so the handle was coming toward me from behind me. As it passed by me, I grabbed it and waved for the driver to push the throttle on the boat so I could get out of the water. Even with the speed prop, I popped right up and was skiing for the first time in the ocean. The driver took me out where the waves were breaking and I made it through with no problems. The driver realized I had experience, so he tried various ways to dump me. He would double back on the wake the boat made as we crossed the breaking waves. I had a real incentive to stay on the skis so I rode out all the challenges. He finally dumped me when he crossed over the breaking waves, then doubled back so there were all kinds of different moving waves in the water. I went down and immediately started looking below me and waving for the boat to come and pick me up. I was too far out to swim for shore. The boat finally arrived to pick me up. I tossed the skis in and climbed over the side. I could not get out of the water fast enough. I did not see anything, just the thought Bowles put in my head about something in the water terrified me. I was done for the day after that water skiing incident.

We were resupplied at the beach and afterward headed back to the An Lao Valley Mountains and jungles. I was not out there long because I had put in for R & R and I returned to LZ Uplift to get my orders. I wanted to go to Hawaii or Australia, but my older brother was in the Air Force and stationed in Japan so I went there to see him, his wife and new son. I figured it would be like going home almost.

The Army called R & R a week even though it was only six days; by the time travel was figured in it was actually a lot longer. SSgt. Harry Young, the Ranger and platoon sergeant in third platoon, and David "Flash" Rhodes from first platoon were leaving for R & R in Hawaii at the same time. Once we had our orders, we were free to leave Uplift and make our way to Cam Ranh Bay where all the R & R flights departed Vietnam.

A transit barracks located at Cam Ranh housed us until our flights left Vietnam for the R & R destinations we chose. We had a couple days layover so we went swimming at the beach at Cam Ranh. It was a pre R & R treat and we enjoyed it immensely. We also got a chance to attend a show at the Naval NCO Club after SSgt. Young could not talk the doorman at the Army NCO Club to let me and Rhodes in to that club. I was only an E-4 and the NCO club was E-5 and above. We saw a better show at the Naval NCO Club where E-4 was considered an NCO and we were pleased Young's persuasive powers were a little lacking. The band up first was from Australia and had a topless dancer performing while the band was playing. I will never forget her name, Saffron. One of the songs she danced to, "Waltzing Matilda," was an unofficial Australian National Anthem. I liked the song so much, I searched for years to find a version that sounded like the one I heard that night. The next group of performers was the troop we saw perform at Phu Cat Air Force Base, the Philippines group that sounded good but spoke no English. When we talked to them after their performance, they acted glad to see us but we could tell they did not understand a word we said.

After the short respite at Cam Ranh, I was headed for Japan to see my brother and his wife. He was stationed at a base on one of the southern islands in a city called Sasebo. I did not have a clue how I was going to get there. The plane for R&R to Japan was going to Yakota Air Force Base outside of Tokyo.

The plane landed at Yakota and we deplaned into a hanger for processing. The Army did not do anything without paperwork. I was pleasantly surprised when the sergeant in charge asked, "Is there anyone in this group that is visiting relatives in Japan?" I raised my hand along with two others in the group.

Then the sergeant said, "OK, fall out over here and sign out. You do not have to do any paperwork. As soon as you sign out, you are free to go. Just be back here by 1800 hours on the tenth of May." I signed out and headed on foot for the flight desk in the terminal at Yakota Air Base. It was in the next building, but when I got there, the flight director told me there were no flights leaving for Sasebo until the next morning at 0800. I had a conversation with him to find out what I could do in the meantime. The flight director recommended staying in the base hotel for the night.

"Just tell the cab driver outside the terminal. They all know where it is. The cabbie will take you there," he said.

I thought I did that but wound up in a Japanese hotel off base. I was not sure the hostess understood what I was saying but somehow a room was prepared for me and a fee was charged which was much more than the two dollars American I would have paid at the base hotel for one night. As I settled in, I knew there was a problem with the bed. A Japanese hotel bed is five foot square and has a comforter on top with no blanket. I am six foot three so no matter which way I tried to sleep on the short bed, my feet stuck out. The weather in Japan was damp and cool in May so my night was very uncomfortable to say the least.

The next day, when I awoke, it looked to me as if I was in an alley somewhere in a suburb of Tokyo. I was up in plenty of time to make the eight o'clock flight at the air base but I did not know if I could communicate that to the hotel hostess. Luckily, for me, she was the person from the night before and she seemed like she understood when I asked her to get me a cab. One showed up in front of the paper door of the hotel anyway a short time after I made the request. I told the driver I wanted to go to the terminal at the airbase but I think he already knew that and somehow I arrived at my destination. The cab rides were 2500 yen each way, including the tip, and the hotel was another 3200 yen, which was about twenty-five dollars total for the one night. At that rate, I was on a luxurious vacation I could not afford.

The jet I rode in to Sasebo was chartered by the Air Force so it cost me nothing to fly into the little one runway airport on the base. It was pouring down rain when we landed and I remember running to the TAC Shop, the only building on the airstrip and I was soaked to the bone when I got there. I do not know why they called it the TAC Shop but it was the size of two Photo Mat drive up buildings put together. Including me and the guy behind the desk, the building was already out of capacity. The other passengers that got off at Sasebo had cars waiting for them and were long gone by the time my brother showed up to take me to his home on the air base. The guy in the TAC Shop knew who my brother was and contacted him somewhere on the base. He was expecting me the day before and when I did not show up, he figured I changed my mind about spending my R & R with him and his family.

The highlight of my stay at my brother's house was waking up with my eight-month-old nephew, Steve. I slept in the same room with him and when he awoke, I would move him to my bed laying him on my chest and letting him play. He was happy with that and his mom and dad got some extra rest. When they would get up to make breakfast, Steve and I would get up too. I soon found out there was not much going on at the airbase so I walked around trying to find some extracurricular activity. I found the base BX, Base Exchange, the equivalent to the Army's PX. There were bars just outside the gate of the base living quarters, but I was not sure how to exit the gate since I was visiting or if I did go out, if I could get back in. I passed on the bar visits to eliminate any of the red tape. I purchased a few trinkets at the BX to send home. One was a jade bracelet and necklace I sent to my girlfriend. Other than that I spent time writing to my folks and girlfriend in the comfort of a real home for a change.

One of the days, my brother took off work and we went south to the coast of the island where there was a big naval base. I was looking to buy some china for a wedding gift for my girlfriend's brother. He was always my best friend and I missed being the best man in his wedding because I went into the Army. As it happened, the town also had a china factory where countless sets of china were made for sale all over the world as well as in the huge PX on the naval base. I found a twelve-place set of china for my friend's wedding present and it only cost me ninety-eight bucks. It was such a good deal I bought my mom and dad a set and a set for me as a wedding present to myself. I spent fifty bucks on my mom and dad's set and seventy-nine dollars on mine. They were all twelve place sets and shipping for all three was forty dollars. When I got back to the States, I found a set exactly the same as mine for sale in a jewelry store in downtown Joliet, Illinois for forty-five dollars a place setting. They were a great deal in Japan and I am glad I did not pass them up.

Before I left Vietnam, Lt. Chapla had given me some money to buy him a 35mm camera and accessories while I was in Japan. He gave me a list of all the things he was looking for and I found most of them at the naval PX. It was such a good deal I was going to have money left to give back to Lt. Chapla when I got back to Vietnam.

I found out a lot about driving in Japan on the trip to the naval PX. The roads were narrow and most of the time the drivers stayed in their lanes except they were opposite of the US. Most of the cars in Japan had steering wheels on the right side of the vehicle and the cars drove on the left lane. As we were traveling to the naval PX, a car moved out around to pass another as they both approached our vehicle. I was sitting in the middle of the back seat looking over the front seat. I could see that we did not have enough room for the car to successfully pass the other car and get back in his lane. My brother moved over toward the side of the road in his lane, the guy being passed moved over to the side of the road in his lane and the guy passing him stayed in the middle of the road. No one touched the brakes; we just passed three abreast at full speed. It did not affect my brother in any way. He said it was standard practice in Japan, but I had to lie down in the back seat. I had seen enough for one day.

One of the nights on my R & R, my brother took the whole family and me out for dinner at the base NCO Club. I got two surprises there that night. I saw what the Air Force did with the AKs we would trade them for steaks. One was hanging in the main entry to the NCO Club. It was in a glass-covered frame and looked very official. There was a brass plate in the bottom of the framed glass but I do not remember what it said.

The other happened as we sat down to order dinner. The waiter came over to me with a note from a very good-looking woman seated all alone in the restaurant. The note said, "After dinner, please join me for a night cap. I would like to get to know you." I was actually considering joining her but my brother took me out of the room and explained to me that his wife was aware of what had happened and she was not happy about it. It seems the young woman was married to an airman that was TDY, on temporary duty somewhere, and while he was gone, she had a habit of picking up airmen and taking them home with her. I would have been just another of many before me. I thought it was better for me with a girlfriend at home if I turned down the opportunity. When we got back to the table, I sent the waiter over to her table with my regrets.

The day before the visit with my brother was over; he took me to the TAC Shop to make arrangements for a flight back to Yakota Airbase. The same guy was manning the TAC but he told us the charter flight was full and I would have to make other arrangements on a commercial flight out of Sasebo Airport. Again, I was lucky; I got a seat on the only flight out of Sasebo for Tokyo on Nippon Airlines, a Japanese airline. The flight left very early in the morning, which was better for me because I had to get transportation back to Yakota the following day to go back to Vietnam. Since I was flying a Japanese airline there was no discount or military standby rate. I had to pay full fare, which was ninety dollars American or 32,400 yen in Japanese currency. I was handling a lot of Japanese yen on my trip. If I remember correctly I told everyone when I got back to Uplift I was a millionaire in Japan because I converted US dollars to over one million yen while I was in Japan. Of course, not all of it was my money but it made for a good story to tell the guys.

My brother gave me a ride to the airport to catch my flight to Tokyo and again it was raining steadily when we arrived. I thanked him for his hospitality, we said our good byes, and I got on the plane for Tokyo. All of the directions given by the flight attendants were in Japanese, so I was operating off memory while watching them go through the motions for the floatation devices and the oxygen masks. The rain had stopped by the time we landed in Tokyo. I grabbed my bag and headed for the line of cabs out in front of the very busy Tokyo Airport.

Because of my experience with a Japanese hotel, when I got to the cabstand I was asking each cab that approached me in the line of cabs to take me to an American hotel. They were all shaking their heads, because they did not speak English. I remembered passing a book display in the center of the airport on my way out to the cabstand so I went back to see if they had an English to Japanese dictionary. I found one and went back to the cabstand. On the way, I was paging through the dictionary trying to find the word for hotel. It was hoteru, pronounced almost the same with a ru on the end and I could not figure out why the cabbies did not understand the word hotel. At last, I got a cab driver that told me, "No have American hoteru, have International hoteru."

"That is good enough. Take me there, "I told the cabbie. I threw my bag in the back seat and we left the airport.

We drove up to the International Hotel in Tokyo. It was a tall building on top of a small round hill. The cab driver pulled in and dropped me off right in front of the door. I paid him and he drove off. I walked inside through the revolving door and up to the front desk, which ran the length of the lobby. One of the many desk clerks turned and said, "May I help you sir?"

I answered, "Yes I would like a room for one night."

Then the answer I never expected, "I'm sorry sir there are no rooms available. We are sold out."

When I looked at the hotel from the outside, I figured there was no way they could be sold out. There must have been five thousand rooms in the International Hotel. I regretted letting my cab go. I was alone in Tokyo without a room for the night and I did not know where I was. I walked to the end of the drive of the International Hotel, turned up the street to the next corner and then I walked about two blocks toward what looked to me was the city. As I walked I passed many Japanese women in short skirts or miniskirts and see through blouses with no bras. The view on the streets of Tokyo was good! I approached a busy intersection and I stopped to get my bearings. I looked down the street and I saw a sign that was perfect for me. The sign said, "Tourist Information", exactly what I needed. I walked to the building where the sign was mounted and went inside. The young girl working there indicated to me she could not speak or understand English. Somehow, I was able to convince her to get the older gentleman out of the back room who did understand English but did not speak it well.

I told the old gentleman I was looking for an American style hotel for the night. He started making calls and finally found a hotel that had a room available until four o'clock in the morning but I would have to be out of the room by three in order for them to clean it for the four o'clock arrival. There was nothing else I could do but take that room and get a few hours' sleep. The old gent wrote the name on a piece of paper and gave it to me. The hotel I was looking for was the San Bancho Hotel in downtown Tokyo.

I went outside, but when I could not raise a cab, I went back into the Tourist Information shop and asked if they could call a cab for me. Once again, the older gent phoned for a cab and walked outside to help me with directing the driver to my destination, the San Bancho Hotel. I do not know what the old gent told the cab driver but I went on a forty-five minute tour of Tokyo and from the time, I left the tourist shop I had no clue where I was.

Eventually, the cab pulled up in front of the San Bancho hotel. I paid for the costly ride to the hotel, with the tip, that one cab ride cost me twenty thousand yen or fifty-five dollars in American currency. The desk clerk had been notified by the Tourist Shop and was waiting for me. I signed in took the room key and went to the eighth floor where the room was located. In the hall was a woman I can only describe as a room monitor, because when I started to put the key in the door she moved between me and the door and opened it, handing the key back when we entered the room. She moved swiftly to the bed where she turned down the covers. I was pleased to see the bed was a regular sized bed and I tipped her a token amount for her service but I did not recognize the custom of the room monitor. As she backed toward the door to make her exit, she bowed politely and I reciprocated with a bow of my own. Again, she bowed and I returned the bow. The woman kept bowing and backing toward the door and when she would bow, I would return her bow with my own. Finally, she bowed very quickly, turned her back on me and ran through the door closing it quickly behind her. I did not realize a custom of the Japanese was to get in the final bow. Sometimes when I think about it, we could have been there a long time bowing to one another if she had not gone for the door when she did.

Now that I was alone in the room, I went into the bathroom to check the shape of the toilet. Japanese toilets were long, narrow and only two inches off the floor. There was no seat on them because you squatted over them to do your business. My only experience with that style of toilet was from the night I spent in the Japanese hotel outside Yakota. The toilet in this room was more the conventional type I was used to. I was glad about that as the Japanese style was not a comfortable experience.

While I was settling in, I inquired about making an overseas phone call. I wanted to call my girlfriend and my folks in that order. I was trying to calculate the time back home but I was never sure of the time the call went through. My girlfriend was at school in Carbondale, Illinois and stayed with her brother and sister-in-law. Her brother was also attending school at Southern Illinois University, They lived in a trailer somewhere near campus. My timing was off on the call to Carbondale for my girlfriend because her brother answered the phone and told me she was not at home. Her brother and I had a nice chat and I told him to let her know I missed her and that I was doing OK. After I hung up, I immediately called my folks and talked to them. We talked about my visit with my brother and they wanted to know about my nephew. I was calling collect and I know the call was expensive so we did not talk long. I knew when I hung up, my mother cried because she did when my brother called when he was in Vietnam. I left the room after that to go to downtown Tokyo.

I asked the desk clerk to call a cab for me to go to the Ginza, the downtown Tokyo hot spot. He told me I did not need a cab. I could walk to the Ginza, only three blocks down the street. He took me outside and pointed the way to the Ginza because I wanted to be sure I did not get lost. While we were out there, I noticed the hotel was right across the street from the Imperial Palace. The sidewalk he had pointed out to me to take to the Ginza paralleled the moat around the Imperial Palace. Above the stonewall on the other side of the moat, I could see one side of the Palace. I had a very scenic view just outside my hotel.

I started walking the three blocks to the Ginza and just as I reached the third block, I looked down the street and saw a familiar sign; it said "Tourist Information". I felt robbed. I was only five blocks from the hotel when I left the tourist shop in a cab that took me on a wild goose chase for fifty-five dollars. If I would have had more time I might have gotten even but it was too late to do anything. I chalked it up to one of life's experiences.

The Ginza was a brightly lit street full of shops and department stores that covered both sides of the street. There was a McDonald's Hamburger shop so I stopped and ate a hamburger. The space for shops and stores in Japan was limited. The McDonalds had a golden arch but instead of coming out from the back like in the states, the arch went over the top of the storefront, parallel to the street. Orders were taken from a walk up window and handed out from another. There were no places to sit down or go inside; it all happened on the street outside. On the other side of the street was a Dunkin Donut Shop. That shop was four stories high. The donut order happened on the first floor and there were spiral stairs leading up to two tables on each of the other three floors. I went into a department store, bought some souvenirs, and sent them home. After shopping in the Ginza, I went back to the hotel and had a steak dinner in the hotel restaurant.

After I ate dinner and before I went up to the room, I talked with the desk clerk about securing a cab ride to Yakota Air Force Base. He assured me he would have no problem finding someone to take me to the airbase, so I went up to the room to get some rest.

The desk clerk woke me at our agreed time, 0300 hours. It was forty or fifty miles to Yakota Air Force Base. I wanted to make sure I arrived on time for my flight back to Vietnam. I was supposed to check in at 0600 for the flight that left at 0800. When I got to the lobby of the hotel, the desk clerk told me he was having a problem finding a cab. It seemed none of the drivers wanted to travel that far from Tokyo. A last attempt turned up a young driver willing to take on the task but he told the clerk he was not familiar with the route. If he got lost, he was willing to ask directions and was willing to take on the trek for thirty thousand yen or a little over eighty dollars. I was in a pinch, but I had to take his offer. We headed for Yakota. The driver missed a turn and stopped for directions only once. I was on time and happy he got me there on time. I did not tip him because he agreed to the lump sum price before we left Tokyo.

I got back to Cam Ranh Bay and laid over there for the night. I learned that the day I left for Tokyo, Cam Ranh Bay was rocketed by the enemy. It was one of two attacks the NVA attempted on the base while I was in Vietnam. The second time was the night I returned from Tokyo. Just my luck I guess.

View of Cha Rang Valley Jungle School early September 1969.

L-R_ Unknown and Cliff Root at Cha Rang Valley. Root and Musson
attended airborne training and Jungle School together. Root was assigned
to Charlie Company 3rd Battalion 503rd Infantry LZ Uplift 1969-70.

View of Highway 1 South of LZ Uplift.

Aerial view of LZ Uplift 1969.

Author sitting in front of the 3rd Bat. Movie screen shortly after being assigned to A Company. (Note no watch on his left arm)

Another view of the movie screen showing the speaker used for movies.

Author standing in front of the future aide station after working a detail in late September. The small building in background is the projection booth for movies. (Notice the watch on Musson' s arm)

Ed Sienkiewicz holding his M-60 machine gun.

Borchard taking pictures of Sienkiewicz and Musson
practicing with M-60 machine gun.

View of A Company formation in front orderly room (far left bldg.) on the
company street. Colon is in the center holding rifle looking at the camera.

L-R_ 1st Lt. John Chapla, Capt. Patrick Welsh, Sgt. Alandino Robles

L-R_ Sergeants Aguilar, Colon (KIA), and Davis (KIA) on
the company street in front of the orderly room.

Author sitting in the Steakhouse at LZ Uplift with his favorite beverage.

View of the entry doors of A Company stand down barracks.

Specialist 4 Nick Grumbos four-duce FO's RTO
outside the mess hall at LZ Uplift.

Author outside mess hall at LZ Uplift.

L-R_ Spec. 4 N. Grumbos, unknown behind Nick, FO Sgt. Billy Satterfield,
Lt. Tim Austin artillery FO ready on the helicopter pad for upcoming CA.

UH-1 Huey in flight/ A Company makes a CA

Author standing on a rock with PRC-25 radio on his shoulder and Long John antenna to establish communication with the rear area.

L-R Grumbos, Borchard, Lt. Austin and Musson in the hills outside Uplift just a few days before March 17, 1970.

Resupply in 506 Valley on March 17, 1970

Author and Capt. Welsh cleaning weapons after
1st action on March 17, 1970

L-R_ Spec. Cal Sunderland, SSgt. Harry Young, Capt. Patrick Welsh, Doc
Lonnie Mooneyham after Young's Bronze Star w/V decoration ceremony at
LZ Uplift. Mountains in the distance behind the group are in 506 Valley.

Borchard, Grumbos, and Musson on resupply day.

Capt. Patrick Welsh with 2nd platoon leader Lt. Ryan
and 3rd platoon leader Lt. Mott on resupply day.

Author with Capt. Welsh in bush. Notice the long
john radio antennas in front of Musson.

RTO Musson with Capt. Welsh deep in the jungle. Capt. Welsh's favorite photo he called it "Mutt and Jeff".

Author makes water run to refill canteens deep in the jungle.

Author finishes a rough climb in extreme heat carrying 100
lb. rucksack with full load of gear, radio and ammo.

A USO Show in the 1st Battalion theater August 1970

L-R_ Sienkiewicz, Lemon, Bright, Singleton, Borchard, and first name Lanny sitting on the back porch of the supply room on Author's last day at uplift.

Musson and Hendricks giving the short timers sign on the last morning at Uplift. Hendricks is wearing my watch.

Picture of Bailey. This Ronson lighter never failed me
and still works today.

Photo of souvenir homemade Chi Com Captured on August 28, 1970.

CHAPTER 23

Hollywood Visits Alpha Company

Arriving back at Uplift after R & R, we were too late to join the company in the field. The First Sergeant told us the company was scheduled for resupply the next day so SSgt. Young, Flash, and I were on our own until then. We took in the movie that was playing that night and got another good night's sleep before we had to go back to the field. The ten days we had been gone seemed like an eternity.

The next morning, I met Young for breakfast. He started talking to me about going on the NCO side of the mess hall. I was not receptive to his suggestion because I knew I could get in trouble if someone recognized I was not an NCO. The difference in the EM enlisted man's side and the NCO side was real eggs made to order on the NCO side. The EM side had powdered eggs. It was easy to tell the difference; the powdered eggs were green. Young finally talked me into going for breakfast on the NCO side of the mess hall, but I was nervous the whole time I was in there.

I ordered a three-egg omelet, which until that day I did not know existed in Vietnam. After we got our food, we took a seat along the aisle in the middle of the room. I sat against the wall and looked out over the whole room. When I looked up once, I noticed Alpha Company's First Sergeant Soto looking right at me. He did not say a word; he just finished his breakfast and left the mess hall. I told Young we dodged a bullet and left it at that.

Later that morning First Sergeant Soto saw me and came over to me to let me know, we would be going out to the company in the field that afternoon so he wanted us to be ready to travel. We would ride in the chopper with the resupply items. Then he surprised me by saying, "By the way, I see congratulations are in order."

I did not understand what he was getting at so I answered, "Congratulations for what, Top?"

"On your promotion," he answered and smiled.

"Oh that, Sergeant Young said no one would mind and I believed him," I explained.

I got his drift, it was just his way of saying he noticed. He did not tell me not to eat there again but his look led me to believe that is what he was suggesting. Eventually I was promoted to sergeant but I don't remember eating on the NCO side of the mess hall again. If I did eat there after I made sergeant, it was not as memorable as the first time anyway.

Young, Flash and I got notification we were going to be transported out to the company. We went to the helicopter pad to wait on the chopper taking us to the field. They put a hold on us going out as there were a lot of resupply articles going and they did not have room for us. We sat on our rucksacks on the tarmac and waited for another chopper.

The mess hall sent a truck with hot chow down to the pad. The next chopper in took all the melamine cans containing the hot food and told us there was no room for us. "Sit tight. We will be back." That is the way we spent most of the day until late afternoon when a chopper came in with a strange group of people on board. No one in the rear had let us know that famed Hollywood legend Johnny Grant and two starlets were visiting the company in the field. The group had spent the entire day at the resupply location, sharing hot chow and lots of conversation with Alpha Company. When they got off the helicopter, we did not have time to talk with them. They were greeted by someone from Battalion with handshakes and smiles, but not a word or how do you do for us. The pilots were motioning for us to get on the bird. It was late in the day and the pilots were working overtime. We got on the chopper and soon we were stepping off at the resupply LZ for the company.

The troops were still buzzing about the visitors that had just spent the day with them so our arrival was insignificant. I talked to Borchard who was carrying my radio while I was on R & R, about the big topic of the day. While they were visiting, one of the girls had to pee. That was a big challenge for a couple of the guys. Normally when any GI had to pee, they went out of the perimeter letting someone near them know they were going and they went behind a tree. With a starlet, it becomes a whole different matter. Two GIs had to go with her to stand guard. They walked her far enough from the perimeter so no one could see her when she dropped her pants. In the jungles of Vietnam that would not have to be a great distance. There were plenty of bushes to hide one's derriere while peeing. I am sure the starlet felt strange walking into the jungle with two strangers to take a pee. Borchard was one of the lucky ones picked to guard her while she peed. One of the guys has to be in front of her, the other behind her. They had to swear not to look while she was peeing so their backs were turned. When she finished, and had regained her composure, she let the two guards know. They in turn had to make sure the spot was covered and the toilet paper was buried leaving no evidence for the enemy. I often wondered if the young starlet knew it was such an ordeal just to take a pee.

After all the hubbub of the Johnny Grant tour settled down and our days returned somewhat back to our normal routine. The temperatures were getting up there because we were moving into the hot season. We were working on one side of a mountain range and needed to get to the other side. There was a trail that lead through a cut between the mountains and came out on the other side. It was a perfect ambush site and Captain Welsh expressed concern over the use of the trail without some protection. On his suggestion, we employed a method used to protect the main body of the moving element as they traveled through the draw. This protective method was called clover leafing. It required two small elements to turn perpendicular to the direction of travel and go thirty to fifty meters and then turn parallel to the direction of travel and move fifty meters in front of the main body on the trail. When the two small patrols met on the trail, the main body would travel the fifty meters to their position. It was a good way to avert an ambush but it was brutally slow for making progress. It was better to be safe than sorry so we continued with the cloverleaf method through the mountains.

When we arrived on the other side, the mountains gave way to rice fields. We spotted an island of palm trees in the distance and decided to go for them using the path on the dike walls until we had to get our feet wet, crossing the last rice field to the palm grove. Once we arrived and got settled for what possibly could be our night laager, a call came over my radio from Lt. Col. Lowery. He was flying in the area and happened to see our column crossing the rice paddy. As he spoke to the captain, I heard him say, "I am going to fly in the direction I want you to move. You have got to make the other side of the mountains before nightfall." With that being said, he flew directly over us and through the cut we had just used to get to this side of the mountains. I remember the threats from some of the guys hoping he would fly back over so they could get a shot at his helicopter. Col. Lowery had a way with pissing off the troops, but I think for the most part, shooting him down was just idle talk.

We all put our rucksacks back on and started to reverse our steps, this time without the cloverleaf maneuver. Captain Welsh figured since we had just traveled through the area the likelihood of an ambush was nonexistent and if we were to make it back to the other side of the mountains before dark, we would have to do it without the time consuming extra protection of the cloverleaf.

On our return trip through the mountains, we picked up three VC following our trail. As we came around the end of a finger sticking out into the rice paddies, Captain Welsh wanted to move off the trail while sending a squad from third platoon to continue along the path. Sergeant Waki and his squad continued to follow the trail and the rest of the company stepped off the trail into the rice paddy and moved to a higher finger on the other side of the paddy. Once back on dry land, Waki radioed our position to tell us his squad had found a small bunker complex up the hill from us and was setting up an ambush on the trail. Before Waki could finish his transmission, the OP at his position opened up on the three VC that had been following us. They turned and ran back down the trail toward our position and Waki hastily sent that message to us on the radio. Just as we got the word from Waki, one and only one of the VC burst out into the rice paddy. Everyone began to fire their weapons in the direction of the rice paddy. The CO was standing next to Bowles when Bowles started shooting, injuring the captain's ears. The captain was not firing and asked Bowles, "What are you shooting at?"

Bowles answered, "I don't know. I was shooting because everybody else was."

I was not firing my weapon either. I was on the radio trying to get information from Waki and missed the VC run into the rice paddy. The two other VC continued running down the trail and stopped on the opposite side of the rice paddy from our position. I did not see them until one of the M-79 grenadiers put a white phosphorus round right behind them and exposed them as silhouettes against the white smoke. Then I began to fire at them as long as they were standing in front of the white smoke. When they disappeared into the heavy brush around the trail, we sent a squad to see if anyone could claim a body count.

SFC Ramsey, the new platoon leader in the third platoon told Captain Welsh he saw the third VC in the rice paddies go down but he never saw him resurface. He asked me to go with him to see if we could recover a body or capture a VC prisoner. As we moved into the rice paddy with water about thigh high on me, we separated until we were twenty feet apart. From the area where SFC Ramsey saw the VC fall, we started to sweep our feet trying to make contact with the VC if he was under water. Next to the dike wall, the grass was tall and drooped over into the paddy. We again probed up under the tall grass with our legs and had closed the gap between us to about five feet.

Suddenly from under the long grass, the VC popped up startling both SFC Ramsey and me. We saw right away that the VC was carrying a rifle. I stepped toward the VC reaching for the weapon in his hands. When I did, SFC Ramsey fired a single shot on either side of the VC, narrowly missing my chest with the first shot. Though I was startled by the shots, I continued to reach and captured the VC's weapon. He put up his hands and we were able to capture him with no struggle. The rifle he was carrying was an SKS, a Russian designed semi-automatic rifle used by VC/NVA snipers in Vietnam. This particular SKS was manufactured in China, which would make it a little less desirable for collectors. When I checked, there was a round in the chamber. He had a chance to shoot both SFC Ramsey and me but did not take it. He chose, instead, to surrender. The other two VC got away unscathed. We looked but found no traces of them. We sent the captured VC back to Uplift for interrogation along with the SKS tagged for Alpha Company.

Soon after that incident, we traveled back through the cut in the mountains and once again to the elevated palm grove on the other side. We moved from there a short distance to a blacktop road and were picked up by trucks and transported back to Uplift. That was a first for us. Trucks had never been used to transport the whole company to or from an area of operation before. It was something that would become a more popular mode of transportation for the remainder of my tour. If there was a road available, they would truck us to our area of operation.

At the head of the truck column a Sherman tank was traveling on the blacktop road. It did not have to slow down for holes in the road. The tracks rolled right over them without any jostling of the people on board. The trucks we were riding in had to slow down because some of the holes were so deep, anyone riding in the back of the truck would have been thrown out of the vehicle. The Sherman tank would run top end at fifty-five miles an hour so they were so far ahead of us, there was almost no value to them leading us for protection. If the truck convoy was attacked the tank crew, being so far ahead, would not even hear the gunshots.

When we got back to Uplift, we found out the battalion had some celebrities visit two days before we got back. Ron Ely of TV's Tarzan fame was at Uplift along with actress Susan Oliver. The only way I can describe her is, a good-looking blonde actress with many TV guest appearances. She pretty much ran the circuit on all the TV series in the 60s and 70s. Some of the guys that had rear jobs at Uplift were talking about how the brass in the rear made the four hole latrine behind Alpha Company's Orderly Room off limits to everyone but Susan Oliver. We really did not have facilities for women and I could understand why she might have to have a latrine of her own while she was at Uplift.

The guys were also talking about the lone GI that was using the latrine on the street that led to the mess hall when they walked Ron Ely and Susan Oliver by. Not realizing he was taking care of business, they pointed in his direction, and he just smiled and waved to them. The latrines were different sizes and had wood siding half the way up, then screen wire up to the roof. Anyone sitting in there was in full view. The story was funny and we all got a good laugh out of the tale. No one would fess up to being the person in the latrine though.

LZ Uplift was still buzzing about the recent visit from the Hollywood celebrities. I know there were other celebrities that visited Vietnam, but I do not remember any more visiting Uplift during my tour. I missed both opportunities to see Hollywood visit. My luck at work again.

CHAPTER 24

Dangerous Animals Out in the Boonies

As we traveled in the dense jungles of Southeast Asia searching for the VC/NVA, we encountered many things that were unusual and I would be remiss if I failed to mention them. Any infantryman that spent time in the jungle will recall the "fuk-u" lizard, a small green lizard resembling an iguana. Most of the ones I saw were about six inches long but we did encounter one about three feet long on an excursion through the mountainous jungle. He had a deeper voice and we heard his fuk-u a long distance away from where we saw him. The big lizard was sitting on a huge rock as we passed by and he was more of a dark brown color than the others. I do not know if they would bite because I never tried to pick one up. I never heard of anyone bitten by one either. It was just strange to hear the very clear call from the fuk-u lizard. We would have a good laugh about the lizard's strange call at times when the reptile came up in our conversations. Those of us that saw the three-foot lizard would marvel at the size and deep voice in some of those conversations.

Another strange creature was the "reup bird." Instead of chirping, the sound he made was "Reup, reup." Of course that reminded everyone of reenlistment in the Army because that was the term we used; reup for reenlistment. The bird was a tiny finch or canary-like bird with very little coloring except brown. I remember he was a fast mover and was constantly tipping his head as he hopped along the ground or a tree branch.

Of course, everyone has heard of the famous snakes in Vietnam. The most famous of all was the bright green Bamboo Viper or "old step and a half" as the men who encountered it referred to it. That name was given the snake because the story goes if you were bitten, after you took a step and a half you were dead. Actually, there was a two-hour time limit on getting treatment before there was any danger but if no treatment happened within the two hours, you could be dead. I never heard of anyone who was bitten by the snake. I saw two Bamboo Vipers on my tour in Vietnam: one I killed when it dropped from a stand of bamboo onto the black soil in which the rigid grass was growing. The snake was easy to see on the ground, it was a bright almost florescent green against the dark black soil. I killed it with my Bowie knife, severing its head from its body. The second one I saw, a guy with me killed it as it was slithering away from us.

The other famous snake in Vietnam was the Cobra. I can think of only one time when the company may have encountered a Cobra. We were traveling in a dense jungle area and were moving silently, meaning there was no talking so all communication was whispered or by hand signals. The column was stopped for a break and the word traveled by whisper down the line. I was sitting next to our new Battalion Commander, Colonel Clark, who was traveling with us at the time. He received the word from his RTO in front of him, and then turned to deliver the message to me, "Watch out for the snake." I gave him a puzzled look and he just shrugged his shoulders. When I turned my head to tell the guy behind me, I saw the snake. The snake was moving parallel to our column about fifteen feet away. It was about fifteen to eighteen feet long and four to six inches in diameter. It was slate gray in color and that is what makes me think it may have been a Cobra. There were no patterns on the snake that we could see. I never looked to see if there was a design behind its head. I figured a snake that big needed to be left alone. I bumped the Colonel on the arm to get his attention and pointed to the snake. He just raised his eyebrows in amazement and we left it at that.

Scorpions were another menace found in the lowlands and the dryer regions. Unlike what the movies show, a scorpion sting is not as deadly as portrayed. One sting will not kill anyone unless they are allergic to bee stings. I had people who were stung tell me a scorpion sting was like a sever wasp sting. It supposedly hurts a lot and does swell. The treatment is Benadryl, which the medics had in their aide bags. I saw scorpions myself close up and was fortunate enough not to be stung. I learned that scorpions like to travel in pairs, and usually if we saw one there was another close by. I remember sitting on some stacked flat rocks one time near a tiger cub carcass when two scorpions came out from under the rocks. I jumped up and crushed them both with the soles of my boots. Another time one of the RTOs in the CP jumped up suddenly early one morning. It was the dry season and we had laagered on top of a low bluff overlooking a well-used trail hoping to engage some enemy traffic. Sometime during the night, the two scorpions that stung the RTO had crawled into his bedroll. The guy wanted to stay in the field but our medic dusted him off because he received multiple stings and the medic wanted to be sure he did not have a reaction to them. The medic gave him a shot of Benadryl while we waited for the dust-off helicopter to arrive. We were close to LZ Uplift so it was not long before we popped smoke for the helicopter to identify and our scorpion casualty was on the bird and headed for a cold beer at the steakhouse at Uplift.

Leeches were a nuisance in the wet season or sometimes traveling in the deep lowland streams and swamps a squirt of insect repellent or a lit cigarette would make them drop off if they attached themselves to us. Once they were off, the area they attached to may bleed for a while longer because of the anti-coagulant there system injects into its quarry. The anticoagulant also causes the area to itch which sometimes is the only way we discovered a leech was on us.

Monkeys and apes were common all over Vietnam. Small monkeys in the mountains stayed mostly in the trees so they could piss on you at night. Several times on my tour when we would encounter a bunch of monkeys, I would be awakened by one of the little bastards relieving himself on me. I am sure it happened to others in the company also. First thing one morning, a guy named Aldrich went to get something out of his rucksack. He opened the flap, reached in the ruck, and a monkey bit him. He went wild and started shooting into the trees trying to kill the monkeys. All he did was stir them up so they were pissing all over everybody. Finally, one of the platoon sergeants took his rifle away and calmed him down. It was a melee for a while and had everyone ducking for cover and looking for VC. No one announces, "I am just shooting at the monkeys," so some of the guys further from the fracas thought we might be under attack. They took up defensive positions until we passed the word about the monkey biting Aldrich.

Rock apes were about the size of a chimpanzee and resembled a chimp but they had very long sharp canine teeth and part of their defense was to show them. Sometimes guys assigned to the rear areas would capture them and keep them for pets. They were not good pets because they were never friendly. Someone always abused them when they were in captivity. They were a perfect example of monkey see, monkey do. There were stories of guys picking up a rock and holding it to their ear while the rock ape watched; then they would pull the pin on a grenade and throw it to the ape. He would hold it up to his ear and of course, when the grenade went off, the ape's head did too. It was a cruel trick and the Army eventually banned keeping the apes in captivity because of the tricks. There was also a problem with the apes biting soldiers, subsequent infections or perhaps rabies if the apes were not inoculated.

I was on guard one night out in the field when over the battalion radio I monitored an attack by rock apes on another unit. The apes were clubbing the GIs in the perimeter, arousing some of them out of a sound sleep. As the GIs awakened, they began to shoot at the attacking apes. Some of the shots went across the perimeter making the GIs on the other side believe they were being overrun. Consequently, they fired back, wounding some of their own men on the other side of the perimeter. At the time, it seemed so surreal, almost hard to believe but it happened. Luckily, no one on our side was killed in the confusion.

One night Sienkiewicz set up on the edge of the perimeter with his M-60 machine gun. It was not the best laager site I had ever been in because there was tall elephant grass all around and visibility was only as far as the guys either cut or pushed down the grass. Sienkiewicz did neither of those; he just set up the gun. Just before dark, Sienkiewicz heard someone breaking through the grass. He went to the gun and asked for permission to fire from his squad leader but was told to wait until he had a target. All of a sudden, a huge orangutan sprang out of the grass both arms held above his head and screaming at the top of his lungs. Sienkiewicz fired the gun sweeping the grass in front of his position with machine gun bullets. When he checked for a body count, there was none, no blood trails either. He made everybody swear to keep his secret. He did not want his reputation on the machine gun damaged by an orangutan.

Razorback hogs were prevalent in some areas of Vietnam. I mentioned earlier the incident back in November of 1969 when we encountered a bunch of the wild hogs. In addition, another hog was more domesticated and raised by the villagers. We called it the pot-bellied pig because its belly almost dragged the ground when it was rooting around in the village. Sometimes we would find them fenced in a village, other times they would be wandering around loose. We assumed they were used as a food source; consequently if we found some of these hogs in an abandoned village we would destroy them so they were not a food source for the VC/NVA. The ugly pigs became another casualty of the war.

Water buffalo seemed to dominate the lowland areas that were planted in rice. The buffalo served as a means to pull the plow through the fields when the Vietnamese prepared for planting. When we saw them, with the handler or farmer, they seemed to be docile enough but there were cases where the buffalo could turn on a group of soldiers and try to run them down. The buffalo had a very big set of horns and if he pawed the ground and lowered his head, it was time to move out and get a safer distance away from him. Their skulls were so thick, they were hard to bring down with an M-16. It was better to take their legs out from under them if they charged.

Elephants were another huge mammal to watch for in the lowland areas. We would find signs of them when we were in areas with tall elephant grass. Borchard used to tell a story when the company was down at Phan Thiet before I joined the company. Second platoon was laagered in among some palm trees and banana trees. Borchard was awakened by a trip flare going off. It was set off by a herd of elephants. When Borchard opened his eyes, all he could see was elephant asses. He was so scared; his voice broke when he proclaimed, "C-C-C-Claymore!" He would then say they were lucky because the Claymore going off scared the elephants and they all stampeded out through the trees in the direction they had been facing. "If they had come our way, they would have trampled all of us," Borchard added.

Another encounter we had with elephants was a time in November or December 1969 when we were moving through some ten-foot tall elephant grass. We happened upon an elephant trail that was going in our direction so we started following the elephant's path. When the elephants move through elephant grass, it is completely flattened to a trail about six feet wide. It was smooth sailing following in their footsteps. Another reason to follow elephants was the NVA used the elephants as a means to transport supplies and heavy weapons. We continued to follow the elephant trail until the point man came up a rise and the trail made a sharp right turn away from the direction we were traveling, In addition, there was a steaming pile of elephant dung on top of the rise. In the eighty-five degree temperatures, with a steaming pile of dung that looked like a stack of bowling balls, we were too close to the elephants for our safety. We started cutting the elephant grass, going our own way again.

While researching some information and subject matter for this book, I called a friend who was the first platoon sergeant in Alpha Company. His name is Thomas Kaulukukui and he lives in Hawaii. Everyone calls him SSgt. K. I was trying to figure out when the first platoon came back from Tuy Hoa and I knew he would have the date. While I was speaking with him, I mentioned I had written about the first platoon, but I did not include his name anywhere in the text. I was apologizing for the omission when he said he would send me something he wrote for his family. I have included the article SSgt. K sent to me which takes place sometime after Christmas but before New Year 1969.

Tall Grass by Thomas K. Kaulukukui, Jr.
Former Staff SSgt (E-6)
1st Plt, A Co., 3/502d Inf.
173rd Airborne Brigade
Vietnam, 1969-70

At the end of December 1969, while near the base of a mountain, we entered a large field covered with 8-10 foot high elephant grass. The grass was mostly dry, and we trampled a narrow trail through it as we wound towards the hill we would have to climb to reach our objective.

When we moved as a platoon, the lineup was as follows. Sgt. Harlan Spencer's squad usually led the way because the point man, Pasquale Pino, was the most experienced and skilled point man in the platoon. The other squads followed in the order dictated by the armaments they carried, so that the platoon could best strategically respond as needed. Usually, there was an M-60 machine gun in the first and last squads. The squad leaders, who at the time of this story were sergeants Spencer, Jeff Zettle and Paul Ramer, traveled near the middle of their respective squads. The platoon leader, Ed McIntyre, was usually located between the first and second squads so he could lead the front and middle of the platoon in case of attack or defense. I, as platoon sergeant, usually traveled between the second and third squads so I could provide leadership to the back and middle of the platoon. Sometimes, to ensure that no one was lost or left behind, I walked last in line, in the position we called "drag."

On that afternoon, I was walking drag as the platoon wound its way through the thick, tall grass in the stifling, humid heat of our area of operations. We were moving towards a ridgeline that would be our path to a hill we had to climb. It was so hot that we walked for 20 minutes and rested for 15 minutes, then repeated the sequence. In the front of the column, men took turns holding their rifles in both hands above their heads, then toppling forward like felled trees to crush the thick grass in front of them to flatten six feet more of matted trail. In the rear of the formation, we walked and waited and walked and waited, then rested so that we could repeat this drill over and over. It would take us more than two hours to emerge from the grass.

Each time we stopped to rest, I moved back down the trail a few meters, turned my back on the men who I had been following, and sat quietly guarding our back trail as the rear guard; the infantry calls it the "OP", i.e., observation post, a technical term for a sentry. For the first hour and a half, I neither saw nor heard anything at all that caused me any concern. All of us sat quietly with no talking. Those who communicated did so by sign language. However, the next time we stopped, I thought I heard the faint rustle in the grass about 15 feet away from me. I tensed and peered intently into the grass, but though I looked and listened hard, I neither saw nor heard anything again. I wondered if I was imagining things.

We moved on again for several minutes. Then, we stopped again to rest. I again backtracked to guard our rear. A few minutes later, I once again heard a soft rustle in the grass. This time it was about 10 feet away. It sounded to me like there a small animal like a rodent that was following us. I considered the possibility that an enemy Montagnard scout, a native Vietnamese, was tracking us but eventually dismissed this possibility because no human being could possible move through that thick grass without making considerably more noise.

I moved nearer to the next man in line, pointed behind us, and signaled for him to listen. He did, but neither of us heard anything because the noise had stopped. He lifted his chin and eyebrows at me as a questioning "What?" gesture, and in reply, I shrugged at him, answering, "I don't know." Nevertheless, the rustling in the grass, which occurred twice during this rest stop, definitely made me nervous because I now knew that it was not my imagination. Though I was also concerned because I did not know how long we had been followed, the slight noise told me if an animal was following us, it was probably a small, curious animal, or a tiny scavenger.

I was relieved when the platoon arose and began to move again. My head constantly swiveled around to check behind me, and I was now walking close behind the man nearest to me. I was relieved to see that the line of soldiers in front of me had begun to emerge from the tall grass into the low scrub brush that marked the beginning of the ridgeline. We were now leaving the grass and beginning to enter the jungle quickly to climb the hill. The knot in my stomach dissolved because now I could see all around me. I exhaled a sigh of relief.

I turned around to take one last look at the grassy plain that now stretched below me. The edge of the grass was now 20 meters behind me, and I could clearly see the narrow empty trail marking our exit from the grass. Then, moving across my line of sight and as silent as a shadow, a tiger emerged from the grass on one side of the trail, glided across the trail, and disappeared in the grass on the other side. I could clearly see the tiger's black-striped orange coat, contrasted against the dry grass. In that instant, I knew what the rustling in the grass had been. At some point in our trek, the human hunter had become the hunted. I was on patrol, but it was I who had become the prey. When I saw the tiger that had been hunting me, my heart began to pound, the hair rose on the back of my neck, and sweat popped out on my forehead. I turned and caught up to the man in front of me, and together we moved quickly up the hill into the jungle. I spent a sleepless but quiet night in the dark jungle, but when the sun rose the next morning, it was a new day, the first day of the rest of my life.

I will always remember the experience of being stalked by a tiger, in the tall grass, but for many reasons. I learned several lessons. I realized then, as I had not really known before, that the land was not ours, but that it really belonged to the animals that inhabited it. I realized how wild the land was, and how tame we humans are by comparison. I learned that an animal as large as a tiger has evolved so that it moves with amazing stealth when it stalks its prey. In addition, I learned that no matter how intelligent, prepared, well armed and vigilant I was, to a wild animal like a tiger I was potentially merely a morsel. It is a humbling reminder we are not as important as we sometimes think we are. In a different context, we are merely *lunch*.

Thomas K. Kaulukukui, Jr.

Drinking water in Vietnam was sometimes a big problem and in short supply and other times were plentiful. It depended on the time of year or the season. Vietnam had two seasons Hot, wet, hot, and dry, although in the mountains it could get very cold at times. When we were in monsoon season, the rainy season, we had plenty of water. We used the mountain streams for our water supply; they were cold and clear and tasted good. Many times the water would be running over solid rock and was crystal clear. In the lowlands and during the dry season, we stuck mostly to using the purified water sent out on resupply in huge rubber water blister bags. There were a few occasions when we would find a clear running stream in the lowlands and fill our canteens from it. Usually I would use iodine tablets in the water from the lowland streams. I felt safer when I did because plenty of guys got hepatitis from unpurified water. I did not want to be one of them.

Even though I carried a lot of extra weight with the radio, I also carried ten quarts of water at all times. We ate a lot of LRRPs, the freeze-dried meals that required hot water to mix them up to make them eatable. Ten quarts of water weighs twenty pounds but I was never without water and I shared water at times when guys we were traveling with ran out. The guys always appreciated it and I did not want to see anyone go thirsty. Kool Aide used to make one-quart packages pre-mixed with sugar. My mom used to send them to me in a care package. I would mix the cool mountain water with a package of my favorite flavor, grape Kool Aide in a one-quart canteen. What a cool, special treat that was!

On a resupply once during the hot season in the lowlands, a full water blister bag rolled out of the helicopter, leaving us short on water. Some of the guys did not get any so they were filling up canteens from a shallow stream that looked clear. I still had water so when they asked if I was filling up my canteens I told them, "No." When we went to leave the resupply site, we moved up the stream and saw a buffalo cow pie right in the middle of the stream about twenty feet from where the canteens were filled earlier. Everybody that filled a canteen from that stream was dumping it out as we move away from the site. I laughed a bit because they were remarking how much of a fool I was for not filling my empty canteens. In the lowlands when we got water from a stream or river, I always made sure the water was running clear and I used the iodine tablets the Army furnished to purify water. Most guys did not use them because they did not like the after taste the tablets left in the water. I did not mind the after taste at all. I figured it was better than a bout with hepatitis.

CHAPTER 25

Night Ambush Outside Uplift

One night back at LZ Uplift, Captain Welsh sent for me to come to the orderly room. He needed to talk with me, he said because some of the people in Alpha Company felt the guys in the CP got too much preferential treatment. When the company was in the rear area at Uplift, we would sometimes have to send out patrols or night ambushes leaving the wire at Uplift after dark to avoid detection from the enemy. He told me the people complaining felt the CP should have to provide some of the manpower on the night ambushes. He asked me if I would volunteer to go on the ambush leaving Uplift that night, making sure the emphasis was on volunteer." I do not want to tell you that you have to go, but I would appreciate it," he told me.

I answered," I am OK with going on ambush."

"I want you to go as radio operator," the captain told me.

I should have checked who was leading the patrol. When I found out the sergeant in charge of the ambush was a guy that had initiated a Congressional investigation of Alpha Company, I wanted to change my mind. It appeared his father was friends with a congressman from his state and he wrote to his daddy fabricating some tale about how he was forced to do something against his will. In a Congressional inquiry, members of the U.S. military may ask members of Congress for help in matters involving the service member. A member of Congress then forwards the request, called a Congressional inquiry, to the appropriate federal agency or department; in this case, it was Alpha Company. The company was exonerated and no charges were brought against any members of Alpha Company. The sergeant had been "ghosting" in the rear because he felt his life was in danger in the field with the company. Ghosting was a term the GIs used for someone who was "getting over" or doing nothing. This sergeant had been doing nothing since the Congressional was announced. Once that was over, the company told him, he was returning to the field and this ambush was his first introduction back to the field. If I would have known he was leading us, I might have declined to go on the ambush.

We left Uplift through the wire on the north side of the perimeter at 20:00 hours. Just north of where we went through the wire is the ARVN firebase or the South Vietnamese Army firebase. I think they had both mortars and artillery on that firebase. Because of the proximity of the ARVN firebase to our exit point in the wire, the ARVNs had to be notified of anyone leaving Uplift to the north so there are no mistakes or friendly fire incidents. We were only passing through the area between Uplift and the ARVN base. Our objective was supposed to be on top of the mountains outside Uplift where we had worked before in March. On our way, we had to cross an old railroad bed just down from the ARVN base camp. That area was heavily booby trapped and sometimes served as a thoroughfare for enemy activity around Uplift's perimeter. After we went through that area, we encountered some tall elephant grass that continued as the incline uphill increased. Eventually the incline was almost straight up and began to get hard to navigate. The weather was hot and humid and everyone had to take a turn at the front leading the way through the tall grass. We were only half way up the mountain and it was approaching 02:00 hours in the morning. I was convinced we were not going to make our objective before daybreak and expressed a desire to return to level ground and call in our location to the TOC, Tactical Operations Center, at Uplift. The sergeant disagreed with my assessment and wanted to continue trying to make our way to the top. I implored him just to look at us; we were soaked through our clothes with sweat from cutting our way through the elephant grass in ninety degree plus temperatures and nearing exhaustion from trying to scale the mountain to our objective. He insisted we go on. It was a reflection on his integrity and he was not going to give up.

Finally, I told him, "I am done in sergeant, I can't go any farther."

Several of the other guys that had been up on the point with me agreed. We were all too exhausted to go on any further.

"What do you suggest then?" the sergeant asked me.

"I think we ought to move back to level ground, set out our Claymores and laager for the night," I answered.

"If we do that, I want you to call in our location at the coordinates on top of the mountain," The sergeant told me.

"I can't do that," I told the sergeant.

"What do you mean you can't do that? I am ordering you to call in our location on the top of the mountain," the sergeant admonished.

"I mean I won't do that, sergeant!" I told him.

"You will do it, or I will recommend you for a Court Martial when we get back to Uplift tomorrow," the sergeant exclaimed.

"Recommend me for Court Martial on what grounds, Sergeant?" I asked.

"Disobeying a direct order for one, Specialist Musson," he said, as he looked me directly in the eyes.

"If you think you can give me a direct order to call in a false location and make it a Court Martial offense, you do what you got to do sergeant," I told him as I returned his glare.

"Are you going to call in our location like I told you or not?" the sergeant asked. "I am only going to give you the co-ordinates for on top of the mountain."

"I don't need your co-ordinates sergeant. I have my own map and compass and can work up our location myself. But be assured it won't be on top of the mountain," I told him.

By then, another sergeant, Sgt. Mike Tiutczenko, who was new to Alpha Company became involved. He was the new Como chief for Alpha Company and would start traveling with the CP when we left Uplift and returned to the field. This was his first ambush and I am sure by the conversation so far, he was having a hard time believing us, but he took my side of the disagreement and I was happy about that.

I had to explain to the sergeant in charge that to call in a false location would jeopardize everyone in the ambush. If at some point during the night one of the guard positions on the ARVN camp or LZ Uplift detected movement while we were changing guards at our position, they might fire us up. With our position identified on top of the mountain, there would be no reason not to fire up movement so close to the perimeter of two base camps. I am not sure I convinced him but he dropped the conversation for the remainder of the night. He then told me to be prepared for court martial proceedings when we returned to Uplift. I was not worried at all about a court martial on terms, as he had described. I figured that if the fool wanted to bring me up on those charges, even the Army would get a good laugh at him. The night passed as expected, very uneventful. Our location had everything to do with that. As an ambush, we were ineffective. I never questioned that in the discussions I had with the sergeant in charge. I understood his point about it making him look bad, but it was not as if we did not try to reach our objective. It was impossible to reach that objective by the route we chose. I did not care about who looked bad. I was concerned with the safety of all the ambush members including the sergeant.

The next day, after our return to Uplift, the sergeant pursued the court martial but I think he was convinced by Captain Welsh not to pursue the proceedings any further because it had no foundation and would be dismissed if it went to trial. The captain asked me about the incident and after I explained my side of the story, the captain asked, "What was he thinking?"

We never found out what his thinking was because he was transferred out of the company, out of the Airborne to another unit. I guess the battalion figured they had had enough of his trumped up charges and let him go. I do not know if Captain Welsh was involved with the transfer, but I suspect he contributed to it in some way. The captain was a fair man and often sided with the troops. In this case, I am sure he was looking out for all of us and eliminating a potential problem for him. He expected NCOs in the company to make good decisions and, based on my experience with him, I am not sure the sergeant was capable of making any good decisions.

The first night back at Uplift, my accusers and complainers silenced, I found an empty cot in the group of old engineer buildings in the center of Uplift to settle in for the night. There was one there for Sgt. Tiutczenko also, which gave us a chance to get acquainted. Mike was very intelligent, could speak fluent Russian and had a million questions about the job he was taking. He had the MOS, Military Occupation and qualifications for the job, He just wanted all the verbal information he could get on it before we moved back to the field.

Early the next morning we were all awakened by a 122 mm rocket screaming in right over our sleeping quarters. The screaming rocket and its explosion were so loud everyone became gripped in fear. It was hard to figure where to go to escape any more rockets. I hesitated in the door to our hootch only long enough to see there were no ground attacks and no more rockets. I then dashed from the door on our hootch to the library on LZ Uplift, which used to be a security bunker for the engineers when they were located at LZ Uplift. I took a head first dive through the sunken door passageway and onto the concrete floor of the library. I skinned my elbows pretty badly but did not notice them at the time because of the excitement and adrenalin I had flowing. Once we realized there were no more rockets we returned to our night quarters to learn the incoming rocket took out the largest building other than the mess hall on Uplift. The building was living quarters for several of the cooks and others that had permanent residence at LZ Uplift. Three US soldiers were killed and ten wounded because of the rocket attack. All of the KIAs and wounded were in the building when the rocket hit. One of the KIAs was from Alpha Company as well as one of the wounded. All the activity treating the wounded and bagging the KIAs was taking place just outside our building in the open area used for movies for Third Battalion so we hung out at the orderly room until the area was clear. I remember Captain Welsh coming to the orderly room and asking me if I knew the first name of the guy from Alpha Company that was wounded in the rocket attack. When he gave me his last name, Smith, I gave the CO his first name, Curtis. I also remember seeing the medics bagging the corpses of the KIAs. When they moved Tommy Clayton, the Alpha Company KIA from a stretcher to a body bag, his left leg remained on the stretcher and had to be put in the bag separately before they zipped it closed.

The brass at Uplift somehow discovered there was a pot party going on in the building the night before it was hit by the rocket. They sent around a team of officers and NCOs to search the remaining buildings for stashes of pot. The team confiscated two duffle bags full of pot all together. They decided the building that took the hit in the rocket attack would make a good bon fire to burn up the pot that was collected. They set the building remains on fire and threw the two duffle bags into the flames, then walked away.

Alpha Company's third platoon leader, Lt. Jensen was OD, and on duty that night. The OD, Officer of the Day was the officer that all the guards on duty reported to if there were problems. He had other responsibilities but that night he discovered a bunch of potheads standing around that building fire in the smoke it was giving off, getting high on the marijuana that was burning. Lt. Jensen ran everyone off and stayed at the burn site to make sure no one returned. I remember seeing him coming toward the orderly room the next morning. He looked as if his feet were not touching the ground and his movements were as if he was traveling in slow motion. When he arrived at the orderly room, he said to Top and me, "WOW man, I can understand now why those guys smoke pot. That shit is great!"

As I left the orderly room chuckling to myself, I heard Top tell him, "Come with me lieutenant. You need to sleep this off and no one else needs to know about it." Top took him to the screened in porch on the back of the orderly room where there was a cot for him to relax and sleep it off. Nobody saw him for the rest of the day.

CHAPTER 26

A Very Important Kill

At the end of May, we began experiencing interference on our radio nets throughout the third battalion. Word came down from command to report any communication problems so they could get a fix on where the problems originated. Several times when I was calling in our laager positions, I would get someone talking in Vietnamese. This caused a break in the communication to the base camp and unwanted delays in getting the information to the rear areas. Often I would have to send the same transmission several times in order to get it through to the TOC so the person there could understand my message. There were times when we laagered for the night that I would spend time getting all the information transmitted back to the rear when the other guys were sleeping. Often I would be up with the perimeter guard sending in locations on the battalion radio. He was enjoying the company; I was losing precious sleep. The problems with the jamming of our radio net just prolonged the time I had to spend awake and did not help my attitude due to the extra loss of sleep.

Captain Welsh came to wake me for guard on one occasion during this time. He told me the next day that he had trouble getting me awake for guard duty. I was arguing with the captain, as he would ask, "Are you going to get up for guard?"

"What's it to you?" I would reply.

"I'll tell you what it is to me, private," he responded jokingly. If there was anyone who understood the time I spent on the radio, it was Captain Welsh. He realized my dedication to my job.

That must have brought me out of my deep sleep because I came awake and had no recollection of our conversation. The next day when we talked about it, the CO let me know he was using the term "private" loosely during our conversation. I told him I understood. He did have a sense of humor and I understood that also. He was reminding me as my friend, not the company commander that he was in charge.

All of the RTOs in the battalion were reporting interference, so all of the companies in the field were searching for the source. Command intelligence in the rear at Uplift was narrowing down the locations for the company in the field to search. Alpha Company returned to Uplift from the field for our normal three-day rotation in the rear. Bravo Company was selected to take the area where intelligence thought the radio jamming was coming from. For the three days we were in the rear at Uplift, Bravo Company turned up nothing and reported no contact in the area where command thought for sure we would find the radio jamming station. When we went back to the field, they took us in a Chinook helicopter into the area Bravo was working and Bravo secured the LZ for us. One platoon of Alpha would get off the Chinook and one platoon of Bravo would get on effectively rotating Bravo to the rear for their three-day stand down.

With the entire company on the ground, we split into platoon sized elements and proceeded to scour the AO for signs of the VC/NVA or any radio jamming sites. The CP went with third platoon and had moved only a couple hundred meters from our LZ when the point element spotted two VC/NVA moving in our direction. They fired them up, wounding one of the two and began chasing them. The area was grassy with some trees along a stream just over the hill from where we engaged the two VC/NVA. There were obvious signs of a well-used trail along the stream leading up into the thicker forested trees. There were plenty of rocks and boulders to hide behind on the way up the slope. The point element identified a slight blood trail but did not want to persue the two enemy soldiers up the hill. Evening was fast approaching, which was a disadvantage for anyone moving uphill knowing there were enemy up there somewhere.

Instead, the squad under direction from Sgt. Trego elected to set up an ambush along the trail and hope there were others coming back in to the area later. The rest of the platoon along with the CP continued across the stream climbing the hills on the other side into the heavily forested trees.

As we settled into the laager site, we began to question why Bravo had not found anything while they were in this area searching. The trail we found was fairly obvious and we encountered two VC/NVA within the first twenty minutes we had boots on the ground. We questioned if they had done any searching at all. It was well known that Bravo was the favored company in the third battalion, and always seeming to draw the comfortable assignments or reap rewards for someone else's efforts. Bravo got credit for the hospital Alpha had found near the coast when Bravo was securing the beach and we were working their AO for them. It seemed that Alpha was quick to be inserted in this AO when Bravo could not come up with any activity. Bravo also had an in with the command at Uplift, Captain Bacon, the operations officer at Uplift who used to be Bravo's Company Commander.

As the first night in our new AO got underway, the squad at the ambush site alerted us of movement to their front. The hour was about 0100 and a trip flare went off in the kill zone of the ambush. Claymores went off and the squad filled the ambush with automatic weapons fire and tossed some grenades in for good measure. After everything quieted down they reported to us that they were positive they had wounded someone because they heard moaning from the ambush area. They were holding their position because they could also hear someone talking in the ambush site. In order to keep from exposing their position any further to the enemy, the squad would throw grenades in the direction the talking was coming from. This chatter and grenade throwing went on the rest of the night with neither side gaining any foreseeable advantage.

Just before first light the squad at the ambush site reported that they identified where the talking was coming from and the CO suggested they fire up that area. As they did, they also fired up the now visible body that had been the moaner throughout the night. At daybreak they swept the ambush site for confirmation of KIAs reporting two, the moaner and another killed in the initial blast from the Claymore. They also reported a NVA WIA that looked to be of some importance. He was carrying a new AK-47 with a fiberglass stock and bluing still on the barrel of the weapon, indicating the rifle was new. He also was clad in a new uniform that Trego could not readily identify as one he had seen before.

I was standing next to Captain Welsh as he was talking with Trego on the radio. As he began to instruct Trego about the wounded NVA, he said. "I want that man alive!" but it was too late, in mid-sentence a single shot rang out from the direction of the ambush site.

Trego came on to the radio and exclaimed, "He moved."

The CO followed with, "We will be right there." Then he directed us to saddle up, we were going down there. He was upset with Trego because he wanted the wounded NVA soldier alive. When we arrived at the ambush site, he had even more reason for being upset.

Trego had gone through the satchel the soldier was carrying and found his orders. This was not just any NVA soldier with orders. This was a NVA Navy Admiral with fresh orders typed out on bonded onionskin paper. We had a very important prisoner if Trego had let him live. Captain Welsh was pissed now and began to question Trego's decision and questioned him about his "He moved" comment. Trego really did not have an explanation for what he did; he could only apologize to the CO.

I talked with Sgt. Trego after the incident. He told me the CO asked if the Admiral appeared to be trying to get away when he was shot and Trego told the CO yes. He told me he just put the muzzle of his M-16 up to the Admiral and pulled the trigger. He executed the Admiral and had no remorse. What a mistake.

The guys going through the satchel turned up another surprise. It was a small tablet with handwritten letters on it. The letters were in groups of three and there were several rows of them on the pages with Vietnamese writing.

Captain Welsh showed them to me asking, "Do you recognize any of these?"

"Yes, they are our current CAT Codes," I answered.

"Get that in a message for the rear but send it on the green machine," he told me.

"Yes sir!" I answered.

"Let them know about the Navy Admiral and there will be more to follow," he commanded.

"Yes sir." I answered again and set about getting the green machine ready to transmit the message the CO had given me for the command at Uplift. On the green machine the message could be sent just like talking on the phone. The machine scrambles the message so it could not be understood if intercepted by someone else on our radio net.

While I was prepping to send the message, more information about the Admiral surfaced. We were starting to put together the whole story on his existence inland in Vietnam. His orders told us he was put ashore just off the coast near where our AO was. The group he was traveling with had a generator used to generate power to jam radios. The generator was a typical Marine style generator. The person generating the power sits on a bicycle seat and cranks out the power with hand cranks. It was a common generator used during WW II by the Marines and the Army. It was considered a relic in today's modern electronics.

We figured out that the guy who was moaning all night was carrying the generator and the Admiral stayed with him trying to talk him into getting up and going with him to get away. Evidently, the moaner was too scared or wounded so badly he would not risk leaving. Both the admiral and the wounded moaner made the mistake of staying until daybreak when Trego and his squad finished them off.

We did get some good news from the capture of the AK-47 the NVA Navy Admiral was carrying. For some time the command had put out the word they were looking for a good AK-47 to present to General Creighton Abrams, the commander of all the troops in South Vietnam. He replaced General Westmoreland as commander and was scheduled to go home soon bringing in someone else to relieve him. Alpha Company had attempted to submit a candidate weapon twice before and both were rejected by Major Lester, third battalion's executive officer. If one of the companies got a candidate, he would fly out to look at it and would make the determination on the spot. I remember him telling me, "This one is not good enough." for the two we submitted before we captured the Admiral's AK.

When I called for the NVA Admiral's weapon, I remember Major Lester getting off his chopper and walking up to me saying, "So you think you have a good one?"

"No sir. I have the best one!" I answered with confidence as I presented the AK-47 with fiberglass stock and bluing still on the barrel to him.

"You are right, this is the one. No question about it. Congratulations!" the Major exclaimed.

Capturing that Ak-47 was one of the highlights for Alpha Company, but visualize what a live North Vietnamese Naval Admiral could have meant to all the US forces in Vietnam. The possibilities were endless and the information he could have provided was priceless.

When all the buzzing about killing a North Vietnamese Admiral died down, we were instructed to return to the LZ where we had been inserted. The command in the rear was going to bring Bravo Company back in to find the radio jamming station. I guess Alpha had gotten too much recognition and Bravo Company wanted some of the glory. We were certain the trail along the stream led to the jamming station and that is where Bravo Company picked up the search once they were fully inserted in the AO.

We had only been back at Uplift a short while when the word came in that Bravo Company was in contact. Because we now occupied the rear area at Uplift, we were the reaction force that would respond to help Bravo Company if necessary. For the time being we were not restricted and were free to move around Uplift normally but all of Alpha was aware we could be called to respond at a moment's notice.

I remember walking to the steakhouse and watching the dust-off helicopters land at the aide station as we passed by on our way to enjoy a steak. Bodies were piled on the floor of the helicopter with arms and legs dangling out the door. The bodies looked lifeless and the medics were running to retrieve them inside the aide station.

When we returned to the company area passing by the aide station one more time, we saw the green body bags stacked outside the aide station on blood soaked stretchers. There were ten total body bags and the helicopters were still arriving at the front of the aide station. Bravo Company had paid a hell of a price to be popular or get recognition. One of the casualties was an unpopular new lieutenant in Bravo. There were rumors circulating that he would not survive the first firefight he was in and by coincidence he did not. Several of Bravo's troops had threatened to kill him. Ironically he was shot in the back. We do not know if the gunshot was from his own platoon as he led them up the hill toward the VC/NVA or from the enemy as he retreated down the hill while in contact. Even though the threats were common knowledge, there was no investigation into the incident because of the number of casualties Bravo suffered that day. All of us in Alpha

Company considered ourselves lucky; we dodged another catastrophe that day. We remained on call the rest of the day but never had to leave Uplift to help Bravo Company. Bravo was able to overcome the enemy contact and capture the radio-jamming site without help from Alpha.

CHAPTER 27

Balls of Fire in the Hills Outside English

The first of June, we were working the lowlands in a valley over the mountains not far from LZ English, the home of the second and fourth battalions of the 173rd Airborne. Captain Welsh received an urgent call from the command in the rear at LZ Uplift. They wanted us to get to the top of the mountains where we could see LZ English. Some intelligence led the brass in the rear to think there was eminent danger from an attack on English and they wanted us to be in a better position to support English if an attack happened. The mountains or hills were covered with some low trees similar to young willow trees easily bent but not easily broken. It was ideal for making our way to the top of the mountain. We did not have to cut brush, we just walked over the trees or around them as we traveled single file up the hill. It was tough going but not as tough as it would have been if we cut the trees down to make a path up the hill. When we arrived at the top, we discovered a well-used trail running along the entire ridgeline.

We were trying to figure out what we were going to do from this point on when I got another call for Captain Welsh on the radio. He took the handset and listened intently to what was coming from the command back at Uplift. When he was done, he commented, "Why are these lifers always fucking with me?" Then he told a small group of us that we had twenty minutes to get him back to the valley floor. Command was sending a helicopter for him and he had twenty minutes to get to an LZ. After taking about two hours to climb to the top of the ridge we were standing on, getting back down in twenty minutes seemed impossible. We started running downhill with the captain in the lead. He was determined to make it to the valley floor no matter how much the six of us traveling with him told him to slow down and let one of us point out for our trek to the valley. He refused to stop and continued to lead us downhill like a man possessed. To our surprise, we made it to the valley with time to spare, the helicopter showed up about five minutes after we called in our position. The temperature was soaring over a hundred degrees and we were exhausted from our run down the hill. There was a stream in the valley and the captain instructed us to wait at the LZ for him to return from Uplift.

As we waited on the elevated bank of the stream for the COs return, a rifle shot rang out from nowhere and the round hit about three feet from me. I dived into the shallow ravine cut by the stream along with the five other guys with me. We peered out from our new position to see if we could see where the shot came from or if any movement could be detected in the direction of the rifle shot. We remained in the ravine in the shade until the CO returned later in the day. We experienced no more sniper fire and figured it was an isolated incident. We admitted to Captain Welsh that we did not send anyone in the direction of the gunshot to do any searching. We figured with such a small force, we would only invite trouble and possibly bite off more than we could chew. If there were more than a single sniper lurking in the area, we would all be at risk and endanger our lives if we went looking.

After all the explaining was over, we started back up the mountain for the second time in one day. We were using the non-cut trail we went up the first time. This time it was a little easier to navigate but the temperature was a lot higher than the first time we went up. Now we were climbing in well over one hundred degree temperatures.

When we got back to the top of the hill, we began to cut a LZ on the top of the ridge with the rest of the company. The next day we would be resupplied from our present location. The trees were an inch in diameter and easy to cut using the machetes carried by several people in the company. The guys cutting the trees were chopping them off as close to the ground as they could so no one walking through the LZ would trip on the stubble. We dragged the cut trees off the LZ and piled them in numerous places around the LZ making sure not to interfere with fields of fire or visibility down the slope of the hill. We did not finish the cutting of our resupply LZ until the following morning.

As we were finishing the final clearing of the brush and scrub trees, a rapid volley of automatic weapons fire rang out in the valley below. A recon team who was unknown to us in the hills across the valley had sent a couple of team members down to the stream on a water patrol. They encountered two VC/NVA cleaning up in the stream about fifty meters from their position in the stream. Both The VC/NVA and the recon members spotted one another at the same time and engaged each other simultaneously. One of the recon members was hit in the exchange and according to their procedures, the team required immediate extraction.

We were in a position to watch all the action, and I was monitoring the conversations on the radio. Captain Welsh wanted to offer our assistance, but with contact involved and a wounded US soldier, I could not break in to let the recon team know we were available to help. The recon team and the VC/NVA were still engaged in an intense firefight in the valley below.

The recon team was asking for a dust-off as well as extraction helicopters but because of the contact both would require gunship escorts. As luck would have it, our new battalion commander Colonel Clark was just passing overhead in the C & C bird, on his way to a meeting at LZ English that morning. He was also listening on the radio to the events happening with recon. The colonel offered to fly cover for the recon team until the gunships came on station. Of course, no one involved in a firefight would turn down help from a helicopter with two machine guns. In that case, it would not make a difference who was on the chopper.

As the colonel's helicopter dived to make the first pass to cover the recon team on the ground, the chopper received some intense fire from the VC/NVA ground forces fighting with recon. We learned shortly after the helicopter turned away and headed back toward LZ Uplift that they had casualties on board. Colonel Clark was wounded, taking two rounds in the chest from the VC/NVA shooting into the helicopter from the ground. He never made it back to Uplift alive.

Because of the colonel's death, our resupply was delayed until later in the afternoon. We had plenty of time to clean up the LZ and make sure we had plenty of room for the aircraft to land. The weather was still hot and humid for the dry season and we were all sweating profusely from our clean up task when the first chopper landed. There was nothing special about the resupply; it was typical rations, ammunition, SPs and mail. We also got a few articles of clothing to replace ripped or torn fatigues through normal wear and tear. We also received a coded message to have the captain go green which meant we had to set up the green machine with the radio to receive a scrambled message. After we had the radio and green machine ready, the captain called in and received the details of Colonel Clark's death so he could officially release it to the company. Colonel Clark commanded the battalion for only one month but when his name was mentioned, it was always with the respect he deserved.

After that message, I broke down the radio and started going through my resupply chow, dividing the C-ration units and LRRPs so I was carrying only the chow I liked. I was swapping some fruit with Cal Sunderland or Sunny as we called him. He was the replacement the rear had sent out for Nick Grumbos. Sunny was a very friendly, likable guy from California and we got along well. He was a good fit for the CP and was very knowledgeable about the four duce mortars and artillery. There was a little bit of urgency to finish the chow because there was a severe thunderstorm coming down the valley toward our location and it looked as though we were going to get wet. There was a lot of sharp lightning coming with the storm, which was strange because we did not see lightning during the rainstorms in the monsoon season; a summer storm was unusual during the hot dry season. The difficulty about the storms in Vietnam was we had no place to go for shelter. We had to deal with each storm wherever we were. This time there were no tall trees to protect us from the rain torrents as we were on a mountaintop in the open.

Sunny and I were about fifty feet from the LZ where we received resupply. He was swapping peaches that he did not like for my applesauce that I did not like. The three-foot wide trail that ran along the top of the ridge was between us. As I handed him the applesauce and he handed me the peaches, a sharp flash of lightning hit the center of the LZ above us. The wind picked up with strong gusts making us cover our eyes to protect them from flying debris. Eerily there was no rain with the storm. When the lightning hit, there was a great deal of static electricity in the air. Sunny and I both felt the electricity in the air all over our bodies as we tingled from the static. We had just finished the fruit exchange when a ball of fire,

237

three feet in diameter came rolling down the trail between us. It passed by us and we continued to watch as it followed the trail through the "S" curve in the saddle below us and on over the next hill out of site. When it went between us, I watched as Sunny's red, slightly curly hair was standing straight on end and he told me after the incident my hair was straight up also. He and I declared not to tell anyone what we saw and we did not tell anyone in the company that day. When I returned home and told the story, I described the ball of fire that rolled between us as if a tumbleweed was on fire and rolling down the trail. I also read an article in a magazine questioning if ball lightning exists. I am here to tell you it does exist because I am convinced that the ball of fire was ball lightning. Sunny and I asked ourselves many times wondering what would have happened if the ball of fire would have touched our arms as we passed the fruit cans. The fact that the fireball followed the curves in the trail still astounds me today.

We continued our guard on LZ English for a short time after our resupply with no more incidents or distractions. The weather continued to be extremely hot and dry with temperatures exceeding one hundred twenty degrees daily. Because of the extreme temperatures, we tried to stay near water during the day and moved to a new laager site during the night when the temperature cooled off to one hundred six degrees. During one of the rest stops near a stream in the shade, Captain Welsh came to talk with me. He started out by saying, "Muss, I have a problem and it concerns you."

I asked, "What did I do that concerns you?"

"It's a dilemma and I need your help," he said.

"Well sir, what can I do to help?" I asked.

"My problem is I want to promote you but I do not have anyone to replace you on the radio," he said.

"Sir, that's not a problem. You can promote me and I will still carry your radio," I replied.

"I was hoping you would see it that way. I think you deserve to be a sergeant but I cannot promote you and have you carry the radio. I need you to volunteer to continue to carry the radio until I can find a replacement for you," he told me.

"Consider it done, sir," I said. I was looking forward to making sergeant; it was my goal when I came into the Army. I wanted to make sergeant before I got out. It appeared as if it would happen soon.

The next resupply, I had to go back to Uplift for the E-5 review board. No one became a sergeant in the Army without two things that had to happen. There had to be a slot or opening for sergeant in the company. Each company only had so many allocations for every grade above E-5 or sergeant. The other thing was each candidate had to go before a review board and pass the review in order to make the rank of E-5. The review board consists of officers and senior NCOs in the battalion and they ask the candidate a myriad of questions a NCO should and must know if he is to gain the rank of NCO.

When the chopper I rode back to Uplift in landed on the tarmac, I saw the Command Sergeant Major, Sergeant Major Teague, the highest-ranking NCO in the battalion walking by the helicopter pad. When he saw me get off the bird, he stopped by the entrance and waited for me to come to him. For some reason he acted as if he knew me personally and he asked, "What are you doing back here?"

"I came back for the E-5 board Sergeant Major," I answered.

He looked me up and down, and then said as he pointed, "Those boots need some polish." Then he walked away.

I was irritated, he just saw me get off a helicopter coming in from the field and I know he knew we did not polish our boots in the field. The only time I ever polished my boots was to get a pass from our first sergeant and then I would only polish the toes. They never looked at the heels of your boots so polishing them was a waste of time. I knew I would have to polish my boots for the E-5 board, but it pissed me off that he made the comment after seeing me get off the helicopter.

Years later when I saw him at a reunion, I figured I would remind him about the incident and as I reminded him of the story, I mentioned to him about watching me get off the helicopter right out of the field and telling me to polish my boots.

Then I learned a lesson about old senior NCOs and especially Sergeant Major Teague because he asked one question. "Did you make E-5?"

I answered, "Yes, I did."

"See, the polish worked, didn't it?" he said as he deliberately grinned at me.

He got me again! I found out you never get one up on the old senior NCOs. They have been in the Army too long and have all the answers. We both got a good laugh out of our chat.

As I left the Sergeant Major standing at the entrance to the helicopter pad, I caught a glimpse of Alpha Company's First Sergeant standing leaning against the doorframe on the front of the orderly room. I headed for his location at a brisk walk. Suddenly there was a huge explosion behind the orderly room and I dropped to my stomach in the middle of the company street where I began to low crawl toward the first sergeant. He was still standing in the front door but was now laughing histerically at my crawling prowess in the middle of the street. The Fourth Infantry had moved a couple of their 105 howitzer batteries to Uplift. One was located behind our orderly room. They had received a fire mission just as I was walking up the company street. When a battery has a fire mission, they fire all four guns at the same time causing a horrific explosion sound. I was a victim of circumstance that day, and the first sergeant got a good laugh.

I remained at LZ Uplift for several days studying for the E-5 board and getting a new uniform washed starched and pressed with all the proper badges and awards sewn on it at the local Vietnamese laundry located on Uplift. All the companies used the laundry to wash the uniforms the troops turned in on stand down in exchange for freshly washed uniforms. The supply sergeant would have some new uniforms from guys coming from stateside. The first thing we had to do was turn over all uniforms except the one we were wearing to the supply sergeant. I talked the supply sergeant out of a new pair of boots; my old ones were not suitable for polish and would not pass inspection. The new boots were looking good even though I had to wear them everywhere until the E-5 board convened.

I passed the E-5 board test, even though I was a little disadvantaged. Lieutenant Ed McIntyre, the former first platoon leader in Alpha Company and now a member of battalion S1 at Uplift was on the board. He knew my background as a radio operator and Como chief and he asked a question that normally would not come up in the test for E-5. He asked me, "Are you familiar with the term green machine?"

I answered, "Yes, sir."

Then he said, "Would you briefly tell the board what a green machine is and what function it performs."

"Yes, sir. The green machine is an encoder decoder that attaches to the PRC-25 radio by a short cable and allows messages to be sent in the clear,

240

scrambling the message as it is transmitted and unscrambling the message at the receivers end through another green machine."

"Thank you Specialist Musson. That was a very good, brief and concise description of a green machine," the lieutenant said.

That was the only question Lieutenant McIntyre asked me but I knew by the grin on his face he knew my answer was impromptu and not rehearsed. It was something I never studied for on the test. When I talked to Lt. McIntyre years later about his question, he told me he knew I was familiar with the intricate workings of the green machine and he thought the board would benefit from my knowledge. Even after getting a good grade on the question, I would be the first to admit, I was not as confident as the lieutenant about the question.

CHAPTER 28

Unbearable Temperatures/Hump to 506 Valley

I never returned to the company after the E-5 board. They joined me at Uplift for our typical three-day stand down rest in the rear area. The temperatures continued to soar up in the one hundred twenties during the day. For the entire month of June 1970, the average temperature twenty-four hours a day was one hundred eighteen degrees, ranging from one hundred twenty six degrees during the day to one hundred six degrees at night. The temperature never dropped below one hundred degrees the whole month. The three days we spent at Uplift pulling details and guard duty were torture. There was no relief from the heat to be found anywhere.

We drew rations and ammo at the back of the supply room as usual when we were on stand down. The porch on the back made a good staging area to pick up the C-rations, LRRPs and ammo for our rucksacks. Our rucksacks had to be ready to go if we were called to help someone in contact. Not only were we on stand down, but we were the battalion reaction force for anyone in trouble for those three days also.

After the three torturous days went by, we got word we were going to work in 506 Valley west of Uplift. The valley got its name from an old highway numbered 506 that had overgrown and was little more than a wide path running the length of the valley and connecting the sparsely inhabited villages in the valley. Electronic devices planted in the valley by the US Army to detect enemy movements informed the command in the rear at Uplift that enemy movement had increased up and down the valley recently. The electronic devices would alert the rear of the movement and then they would send mortar rounds out to saturate that area with high explosives. We were going out to see if we could surprise some of the enemy moving in the valley with ambushes. Because of the elevated temperatures, we left Uplift under the cover of darkness on foot walking the five kilometers to the 506 Valley at night when the temperature went down. That in itself was dangerous because Charlie, the VC/NVA owned the night everywhere in Vietnam. That was typically when they did all of their moving. The US troops, with the exception of recon, only did night moves occasionally for our own safety. We went out through the wire leaving Uplift around 20:00 hours. Our movement was slow and calculated. No one wanted to walk into an ambush so we took our time getting to 506 Valley.

We reached the valley at 03:00 hours and set up a perimeter to laager in until daylight. Between the hours of 03:00 and 05:00 hours, the temperatures dropped so much all our gear was soaking wet from the dew that formed in the early morning hours. At 05:00 hours, we sent out a patrol to find a shady spot with water to run patrols out of into the valley. Platoons decided for themselves how they wanted to patrol. Some broke up into squad-sized elements, others stayed in platoon-sized elements. The CP group traveled with an element of the second platoon. Almost immediately, reports of enemy movement started to flood into the company radio. Borchard was back operating the company net while Bowels was on R & R. I do not think Borchard was happy about that but he did not complain. For me it was a pleasant change to have him back with the CP again.

Bowles and I did not get along very well. Any time I tried to help him with understanding radio procedures, he took it personally and would never follow any of my directions. He never asked me a question if he did not understand something about the radio. He did not understand any radio slang, such as the word used for a trail was thong and everyone on the radio understood that term meant trail. Bowles would refer to a trail as dong and no one understood what he was talking about.

Other things he did irritated me but I continued to try to help him and give him instructions on the radio when he needed them. One of the things that irritated me was he never monitored the radio when we stopped or were laagered for the night. Sometimes I would hear his call sign from across the perimeter and run to answer the radio myself. He would look at me and say, "What?" Clueless as to what had just happened. I think the only mistake Captain Welsh made was making Bowels the company RTO. As time went by, I am sure he realized his mistake and I may have influenced some of his displeasure with Bowels because the captain saw Bowles' resistance to my help.

As the calls on the radio came in to the CP identifying contact in the valley, we shared in some of the VC/NVA contact also. Our point team from the second platoon came around a clump of trees one morning and saw two VC/NVA carrying a comrade who had been wounded in one of the mortar barrages from Uplift. Seeing us, the two uninjured VC/NVA dropped the litter they were carrying and ran for the protection of the trees. The point element chased the two VC/NVA but was unable to find them and eventually gave up searching for them. We settled for capturing the wounded VC/NVA on the litter. We called for a helicopter to come and pick him up for treatment and interrogation. We found the enemy could be more cooperative if they were treated for wounds.

Different types of contact continued to occur the whole time we worked the 506 Valley. One night as one platoon member was positioning a Claymore mine in the center of the old roadbed after dark, a VC/NVA walked up behind him and began talking to him in Vietnamese. The GI was small in stature, had a dark complexion, and was not wearing his helmet. We figured the VC/NVA mistook him for a VC. The GI had his M-16 lying across his lap as he squatted to access the Claymore, so he grabbed it and turned firing it at the VC/NVA, killing him instantly. The same platoon, moving along the road the next day dropped off an ambush squad before entering a nearby village to question the village chief about the incident the night before. The Chief denied any knowledge of VC/NVA working in the valley. The Chief also claimed there were no VC/NVA in his village and he had no weapons. With that information in mind, the platoon moved on through the village, exiting the opposite side from the ambush squad. That night, the village Chief and several of his villagers were killed in the squad ambush while carrying AK-47s. They were probably on their way to attack the platoon that had interrogated the Chief earlier that day. The network of VC/NVA sympathizers plagued the US Armed Forces throughout the entire conflict in South Vietnam. There were many examples such as the one written above of VC loyalty.

It made it very difficult to believe in or trust the Vietnamese civilian population. How could we tell when the Vietnamese were lying? Their lips were moving.

As we were searching the forested hills in platoon-sized elements, the CP was traveling with second platoon. I do not know what prompted Lt. Austin to ask the captain about commanding the company but I remember the conversation between the captain and the lieutenant almost word for word. Perhaps I recall it because my name was mentioned.

Lt. Austin addressed Captain Welsh, "Sir, I was thinking that if something happened to you, then I would be in charge of the company. Isn't that right?"

"No. If something happened to me, Lt. Ryan would take over the company," the captain answered.

"OK," the lieutenant said reluctantly. "If something happened to you and Lt. Ryan, then I would be in charge of the company. Isn't that right?"

"No, that isn't right," the captain answered again.

"Well, who would be in charge of the company then?" Lt. Austin asked.

The Captain answered, "Muss would be in charge of the company."

With a disappointed whine, Lt. Austin asked, "Muss, how does Muss get to be in charge of the company? I outrank him."

Then the captain delivered the final blow to Lt. Austin. "Yes, but Muss has the right MOS to be company commander." MOS is a military occupation, mine was infantry 11B4P. There were no more questions and Lt. Austin walked away talking to himself under his breath.

In another incident around the same time, we were searching the woods for signs of the enemy and came upon an unexploded bomb. We called in a demo expert to blow the bomb in place. When he arrived and we got him to the bomb's location, he straddled it as if he were riding a horse and began striking the case with a hammer. If he was trying to scare us, he did. We were all ducking for cover as the expert laughed at us running and diving behind rocks and trees. He rigged the bomb with explosives he brought with him and told us to take cover. We went fifty meters from the bomb where there was a shallow gully, and hunkered down there. The expert yelled out to us, "You need to go back farther. That spot is where I am going."

We moved another one hundred meters and hid behind some logs and trees, anything that provided cover or shelter. When the bomb went off, we heard the base plate, which separates the mechanism from the TNT go over the top of us cutting off the tops of the trees as it went. The base plate was three feet in diameter and two and one half inches thick, cutting off trees a foot in diameter or better and dropping them on the ground like twigs broken off in a storm. We could not believe how far the bomb threw the base plate. It passed over us at treetop level and we were one hundred fifty meters from the bomb.

That same day the first platoon patrolling in an area near by encountered an enemy soldier in a spider hole. The VC/NVA engaged the point element killing one of the first platoon members. His name was LeLeaux, a young well-liked individual from Louisiana. The enemy soldier was able to escape unharmed.

The temperatures continued to be unbearable and we stayed as inactive during the day as possible, running our patrols and ambushes at night. Eventually the activity in 506 Valley ceased to be a factor and the command at Uplift moved Alpha Company to a different AO. We were picked up by trucks and transported to a different mountain range. Everybody hated the truck moves; it seemed demeaning for a paratrooper to be moved about in trucks. We were being paid extra money because we were paratroopers but they were treating us like legs by transporting us in trucks.

When we got to our new AO, the CP started traveling with the third platoon at the end of June and the first of July. July was not a good month for Alpha Company. We experienced many casualties in the two areas we worked. I remember sitting at the foot of a mountain on a well-used trail while a squad from third platoon moved up the hill to look for VC/NVA. The point element discovered a trail watcher sleeping in a hammock about half way up the hill. Quietly they maneuvered to engage the unsuspecting enemy. The guy carrying the M-79 grenade launcher fired a round directly at the sleeping trail watcher. When he heard the thump from the grenade launcher, he rolled out of the hammock and the round was caught by the twisted hammock. It did not go off and the trail watcher escaped unharmed. The squad chased the enemy up the trail and discovered a small camp with food cooking and equipment scattered on the ground. Beyond the camp was an open area and the squad held up a short time before moving through the area. As they moved across the opening and the squad was in the middle of the opening, the VC/NVA opened up on them. The point man Davis went down and another member of the squad named Allen was hit in the arm and thigh. Everyone else took bullets in the equipment or through their clothes; it was very close contact. The radio was hit and out of commission.

Since we had no contact with the squad, another squad from our location prepared to go to their aide. When the second squad linked up with the first, they found them waiting to make sure the enemy had moved on before they went to retrieve the point man Davis and the other wounded man Allen. Davis fell behind a rock and was partially obscured from site but the other members of the squad believed they saw him move and thought he was still alive. After holding for two hours, the squads advanced to retrieve their wounded. Allen lost a tremendous amount of blood and needed immediate medical attention. They found Davis was shot through the Adam's apple and died instantly.

The call came in for a dust-off for Allen. I contacted the rear and a dust off with gunships was on the way. Allen lost so much blood by the time the dust off came he was in shock. They let us know he succumbed to his wounds on the way back to the aide station at Uplift. We found out later that he was a hemophiliac and should never have been in the Army. It was a mystery how he passed a physical in the first place. We do not know if he could have been saved if treated right away or if the fact he was a bleeder contributed to him going into shock.

Then came a final blow to Alpha Company. Captain Welsh who had been traveling back and forth from Uplift to the field informed us that he was leaving the field for a job in the rear. His six-month tour as commander of Alpha Company ended. All officers were on a six-moth rotation working six months in the field and then six months in the rear area. The day the captain told us he was leaving Alpha Company no one had to pull guard that night. Captain Welsh, Borchard and I sat up all night and talked quietly and pulled everyone's guard.

I remember Borchard asking the captain, "So Pat, what do you plan on doing back in the world when you get home?"

I chimed in right after Borchard, "Yeah, Pat what are you planning on doing?"

Then he responded, "You know you are the only two I would let get away with calling me Pat, and tomorrow I am Captain Welsh again." That was the relationship we had with the captain. He was not only our commander, he was our friend and he understood where we were coming from with those questions. He just wanted to make sure we did not slip up and call him Pat in front of the others. We understood that and made sure not to call him Pat after that night.

The next day before the new CO arrived, Captain Welsh went to everyone in Alpha Company that was traveling with the CP and shook their hands. He said good-bye face to face because that was the kind of man he was. He cared about the men he commanded and let them know it.

Captain Welsh introduced me to the new commanding officer of Alpha Company as he did everyone in the CP. He told Captain Palmer of my situation in the CP and gave me a complement saying Captain Palmer would not have to worry about anything, "Muss has a good grasp of what is going on and will take good care of you."

I had one last conversation with Captain Welsh before he left the field. As he was saying good-bye, he told me, "I am going to work on getting you a job in the rear."

I told him, "Thank you sir, but you do not have to do that."

"I know I don't have to, but I want to. You deserve it," he told me. Shortly after that, Captain Welsh got on a helicopter and left the field for LZ Uplift. He was going back to the rear to be the Duty Officer in the TOC until his DEROS date. I knew I would be talking with him on the radio when he was on duty. That was comforting to know.

CHAPTER 29

Searching for VC/NVA in 506 Valley with the New CO

We continued to pursue the VC/NVA in 506 Valley with Captain Palmer in charge of Alpha Company. He implemented a few changes in the first days of his command, one of which was taking me off the radio. I was now the squad leader of the CP. Bowles replaced me as the Battalion RTO. I had no radio duties except for calling in our resupply information and dividing the rations and SPs when we received resupplies. For the time being, the CP continued to travel with a platoon for protection, but there was a change about to happen and I could not quite figure out what it was. Because of my job change, I had a lot of time to think about it and I spent some time trying to figure out what was going to change. I got a small example one evening when Captain Palmer came to me and asked me to come with him. I noticed he was not carrying his AR-15, a smaller version of the M-16 with a collapsible stock. I was a short distance from my rucksack and the rest of my gear including my rifle.

He said, "Sergeant Musson, come with me. I want to ask your opinion about something."

I answered, "Yes sir. Just let me get my weapon..."

He broke in before I could finish, "You won't need your weapon. We are not going that far. Come on."

A strange feeling came over me at that point. My mind started processing what the CO had said, "Not going that far." How far was that? Not far from where? Then I got the answers. We went to the edge of the perimeter and I could tell the CO was planning on going farther than that.

As we passed the sentry on guard, I said, "We are going out here, don't fire us up." The CO never hesitated; he just kept walking as if he was not going to say anything to our last point of security before walking past his position. I had to hurry to catch up to him once I let the sentry know what we were doing and not to shoot at us.

After we walked about fifty meters outside our perimeter, I told the CO, "Sir, how far are we going? I'm beginning to feel uncomfortable without my weapon."

He answered, "Not much further. We will be OK."

We walked another fifty meters to a clump of palm trees overlooking some old rice paddies. As we stood on the dike at the edge of the dried rice field, exposed to anyone looking in our direction, my body and mind were gripped in fear. I was one hundred meters from the safety of our perimeter with no rifle for my own or the CO's protection. Silently I asked myself, "How stupid can you be?" The fear that overwhelmed me blocked out the rest of the conversation I had with Captain Palmer. I do not remember any of our talk after we arrived at the edge of the rice paddy. I just wanted to get back inside our perimeter safely.

I must have answered the captain's questions satisfactorily because we started back and reentered the perimeter without incident. I vowed never to make such a stupid mistake like that again, no matter who was insisting for me to follow.

Later that night the first platoon operating in the 506 Valley with us had an incident. Sergeant Fred Greene got up in the early morning hours to take a piss. He was shot and killed by a VC/NVA that had gone undiscovered in the cane breaks near the first platoon laager site. The VC/NVA was able to make his escape unscathed. We will never know if Sgt. Greene discovered his killer, if the VC/NVA's fear of detection caused him to shoot or if Sgt. Greene was a target of opportunity. Greene was well liked in the first platoon and his death was a terrible loss for them and Alpha Company.

We continued to search the 506 Valley with sporadic results. The CP continued to travel within the second platoon for security. One new thing I inherited was responsibility for a mechanical ambush, a term we used because the Army did not recognize booby traps initiated by the US. Everyone that used a mechanical ambush realized it was a booby trap, but we could not call it that. The one I developed was made with two hundred feet of DET cord, two one hundred foot cords with blasting caps on each end. The DET cord or detonating cord is a flexible linear explosive with a core encased in a white or OD green outer jacket. It looks like the plastic clothes line strung between clothes poles in the back yard at home. There were ten baseball grenades that had the pins pulled and handles taped down with enough gaps to run the DET cord between the handle and the grenades. Then the DET cord was strung between three Claymore mines and another Claymore acted as the trigger to set off the whole mechanical ambush. The trigger was rigged to a Claymore electric cord and tied in to an old PRC-25 radio battery. The wires were cut and stripped; the ends were fed through a hole in two plastic spoons taped together. Then a cut off spoon handle was used to separate the two wire ends between the spoons. A trip wire was attached to the spoon handle and run across a trail or suspected enemy path. The wire was positioned in the middle of the ambush for a fifty-foot effective killing range on both sides of the trip wire. When the Claymores and DET cord went off, the handles on the grenades were blown in two and the delayed fuse on the grenades started burning. Then with a short delay of four to six seconds, the grenades all went off along the kill zone of the ambush. The design was clever but intricate; one mistake with the wiring or batteries could kill everyone setting up the mechanical ambush. In order to insure the components arrived intact, we had different people carry them so there were at least four people involved with the set up. I set our mechanical ambush up every night with one helper. I figured the fewer people involved the less chance of a mistake.

We stayed in 506 Valley and our moves became less often. The new CO had no problem with staying at the same laager site for two or sometimes three resupply sessions. That could be as many as twelve days in a row. Despite my efforts to get him to move, he resisted and became more complacent as he directed the other elements in the company from our position. It was very hard for me to believe some of the things he did. He was a former Green Beret and that made his actions more abnormal and hard to understand. Special Forces were extremely disciplined and had a reputation for being undetected when they moved or camped outside their base areas. Captain Palmer was certainly not practicing what I considered

Special Forces tactics or any discipline I would expect from the Green Berets. Twelve days in the same location was incomprehensible, even for a regular GI like me.

I had some support in my efforts. One time the First Sergeant came out on a resupply. We were laagered in at a location familiar to me. I had been on the small hill top when Captain Welsh was our CO. It was a hill twenty meters high, forty meters wide and sixty meters long. It had thick forests of tall old trees on it and some large granite boulders. There was a well-used access trail right in the middle of the long side of the hill. Every time we approached this hill, we met some sort of resistance or had contact with the VC, including this time. After running the VC out, we made ourselves at home. The first sergeant came out on one of the resupply choppers of our second resupply at this location. He got off the bird and sat to talk briefly with Captain Palmer. When he finished he came to see me with lots of questions. He had seen the excess debris that was not normal for a one-time laager.

"Sergeant Musson, how long have you been at this location?" he asked.

"Eight days, Top," I replied.

"Eight days! Have you talked with the old man about that?" he asked with some concern.

"Yes I have, but he won't move," I answered.

"Well I came out prepared to stay the night but I have changed my mind. I will be going back to Uplift on the next chopper," the first sergeant proclaimed.

"I don't blame you Top. If I could, I would go with you," I told him.

"Do you want me to speak with the CO about this?" he asked.

"No, I don't think it would do any good, Top. Your leaving is a big statement that will say a lot," I answered.

The First Sergeant left just as he said he would and the captain came to me asking questions about his departure. I dummied up, claiming I did not know why the First Sergeant decided to go back to Uplift but I was thinking, "Does a tree have to fall on him to get clued in!"

A few days later, the company returned to Uplift for a stand down. Our presence in 506 Valley had stymied the VC/NVA activity in the valley and command pulled us out without replacing us to give the enemy a chance to breathe and feel like they had free reign again. Actually, the electronic monitors were still transmitting from there and would indicate any new enemy activity.

While I was at Uplift, I wanted to take the opportunity to see Captain Welsh again. I knew he was going home soon so I stopped at our local laundry and trinket shop and bought him a new Zippo lighter. Several times when we were in the field, he had asked me to use Bailey to light a cigarette so I knew he needed a lighter. I had our unit patch, the Herd patch engraved on one-side and jump wings with a message on the other. The message read, *Thanks for everything, Muss.* I thought it was simple and to the point. I saw him walking in one of the streets at Uplift and asked if he had a minute. He told me he was on his way to work but to stop by the TOC later and we would talk.

"I need to explain something to you," he told me.

I headed for the TOC about 19:00 hours to link up with the captain. I felt strange as I walked in but he told me to make myself at home. I was still nervous and it probably showed.

Captain Welsh began the conversation by saying, "I need to apologize to you because I told you I would get you a rear job when I got back here. Well, I tried, but I think I overloaded when I recommended you. Major Soland came in the other night to let us know we had an opening in the TOC for a radio operator which I knew would be perfect for you."

The Major asked, "Does anyone have a candidate?"

Captain Welsh answered, "I know a perfect candidate, sir."

"What is his name and what are his credentials, Captain?" the Major asked.

The captain answered, "Sir, his name is Musson and I would say he is the best radio operator we have in the battalion."

"If he is that good he belongs in the field," the major replied.

The captain told me, "That was the end of your rear job and I am sorry. I built you up too much and I don't think the Major believed me."

"That's OK sir. You tried and that's what counts," I told him. Then I handed him the lighter. "I got this for you."

He looked at it and told me, "I don't deserve this."

Just then, a call came in on the radio from a mechanized unit that had been deployed to the area around a local village that was suspected to be a VC stronghold. They were receiving rocket and machine gun fire from the village, and were requesting permission to fire back into the village. Permission was denied. Just then, Major Soland came bursting into the TOC. As soon as he saw me he asked, "Who are you?"

The captain answered before I could say anything, "Sergeant Musson from Alpha Company Sir. I will vouch for him; he is OK to be here."

OK with that, the Major asked everyone to synchronize their watches, "Who has the correct time?" Everyone but Captain Welsh and I started calling out the time. There were a many different times shouted out.

The captain told everyone, "Hold on!" Then he looked at me and asked, "Muss, what time do you have?"

I answered, "23:00 hours, sir."

The captain turned to Major Soland pointed to him then said, "That is the correct time, Sir!"

I think that was the captain's way of getting even with the Major for nixing the rear job. He felt bad about not getting me the rear job but I was OK with it. At the party Alpha Company gave him before he left for home, I heard he stood up holding the lighter I gave him and told everyone that it meant more to him than anything else he received while in Vietnam.

The mechanized unit lost four APCs and a number of men in the battle that raged while I stood listening in the TOC. Toward the end, they were almost begging for permission to fire into the village. Command could not verify that all of the incoming fire was coming from the village so they kept denying any request to engage the village. Finally, the command at Uplift requested an air strike on the village to save the mechanized unit from annihilation. After the air strike, the Major walked to the map in the TOC, pulled the pin out marking the village on the map, and threw it in the trash. I do not know why they never allowed the mechanized unit to fire up the village. It seems the outcome would have been the same. I guess it took the senseless loss of American lives before they retaliated. I said good-bye to the captain and left the TOC thinking about the whole fiasco I just witnessed. I could only hope Alpha Company never experienced any questionable contact and if we did, we would have enough balls to ignore the no fire rule, if nothing else just to save ourselves.

CHAPTER 30

CA to the Basecamp Five Miles Out

On 1 August 1970, the CP and the second platoon of Alpha Company made a combat assault and were inserted in the upper ranges of the mountains southwest of LZ Uplift above the 506 Valley. We were inserted by Huey helicopters while artillery support from LZ Uplift fired 105 Howitzer rounds on the slopes below our LZ location. Once on the ground at the LZ, I remember standing on the edge of the mountain overlooking our objective with Captain Palmer. The captain was talking to me about walking the point when we left our hilltop perch for the forested jungle below. One of the 105 rounds LZ Uplift was using to continue to pummel the suspected enemy base camp below us went off and we could hear the shrapnel from the round cutting the air just above our heads. The captain and I decided to step back from the edge and continue our discussion of forthcoming events on the other side of the LZ. We discussed the order of march off the LZ with the second platoon leader Lt. Ryan. I do not think the lieutenant liked the fact that the CP would point out from the LZ. It seemed strange to me also but Captain Palmer had new ideas he was implementing and the CP operating as a separate body was one of them. My problem with that idea was the CP consisted of the CO, Field First Sergeant, the FO, Como Chief, the medic, a bunch of radio operators with rifles, and me. We had no heavy firepower like a machine gun or grenade launcher and that is why we usually traveled with a platoon.

I was on point as we began our descent in single file from the LZ toward the valley floor searching for a VC basecamp. We found the terrain extremely difficult to navigate with outcrops of solid rock forming vertical cliffs of twenty to thirty feet. We had not anticipated the steep rocky terrain and did not bring ropes to aide our descent although they would have been extremely helpful. I carefully climbed down the rock face to the rock ledge below while some of the second platoon stood guard at the top of the cliff. Once I was down, I moved a short distance away to cover the guys coming down until the CP group had all made a successful descent. Then I continued into the thick jungle that began just after the rocky ledge ended. It began to rain, one of those soft steady rains that marked the beginning of monsoon season.

We had just started a small uphill climb into the heavy forested mountain jungle when a call came on the company radio net. It was the second platoon RTO. One of the platoon members had fallen down the thirty-foot rock face and needed to be extracted by dust-off. Bowles was taking the information on the injury in order to call the rear for the dust-off bird. When his name was sent in the clear, Sienkiewicz, the CO became extremely skeptical of his injuries and wanted to hold off calling the dust –off until he could verify Sienkiewicz's injuries. It seems Ed had just returned to the company from a stay in the hospital for FUO, fever of unknown origin, and the CO thought he might be faking injury to get out of the field, or ghosting, as we called it.

Captain Palmer had several reasons for not wanting to call a dust-off to our location besides suspecting Sienkiewicz of wanting to get out of the field. It compromised our position by letting any enemy in the area know exactly where we were. Another reason, we would have to use a jungle penetrator to make the extraction because the dense jungle did not allow a helicopter to land anywhere near us. That extraction would delay our descent because it took longer for a jungle penetrator extraction. The CO sent word back to have Sienkiewicz come to his location. After Sienkiewicz arrived at our location, everyone realized it was a mistake to have him walk uphill to us. He was walking stiff-legged, not bending his knees. His knees were swollen and completely filled his pant legs making them a tight fit. He told us when he fell he landed on the rock ledge on his knees and he was quick to point out he never dropped the machine gun that he carried on his shoulder. That was no small feat and neither was his walking to our position. The CO seemed put out that he was going to have to call a dust-off to extract Sienkiewicz.

I went about my usual business making sure we had security out on all sides and let Bowles handle the information and calling for the dust-off. I did at least until I heard the coordinates he was calling in for our location. Calling a dust-off allowed us to send the coordinates in the clear so I knew as soon as I heard them, they were wrong.

I immediately said to Bowles, "Where did you get those coordinates? They are not right."

"Yes, they are," Bowles said.

"No, they aren't," I replied. "Who gave them to you?"

"The CO gave them to me and they are correct," he answered, as he continued to call them in to the rear for the dust –off.

We were a twenty-minute helicopter ride from LZ Uplift. When the dust-off helicopter arrived three ridges over from our position and announced on the radio to "Pop smoke."

Without thinking, Bowles repeated the command, "Pop smoke." And someone threw out a purple smoke grenade.

I knew the pilot would never see it but I let the whole scene play out. Finally, the pilot came back on the radio, "I have negative smoke. Over." He was too far away to see the purple cloud of smoke above our location.

I could see the dust-off helicopter in the distance and told Bowles, "Tell the pilot to make a left ninety degree turn from his location right now." The pilot was flying down the ridge toward the valley about a mile from us. Bowles relayed the message and as the pilot turned to come in our direction, I threw out another purple smoke grenade. He flew right over the top of us and identified the smoke color. The smoke identification process was a practice we used to prevent VC/NVA from using a smoke grenade to lure unsuspecting helicopters into a location and ambushing the crew. In cases where it happened and there were two smokes the same color, we would throw out a different color of smoke the second time. Often, the enemy would have an American smoke grenade, but it was rare that they had two smoke grenades.

I do not know if Bowles wrote down the coordinates from the CO incorrectly or if the CO was wrong. I never heard any more about the error because Bowles was stubborn and failed to recognize his own misgivings.

He would never admit I was right. Luckily, the dust-off was not for a gunshot wound or a severe injury. Because of the lengthy delay and the steady rain, we were forced to suspend our search and laager for the night.

The new changes Captain Palmer had made in the CP freed me from some usual duties. I no longer had any radio duties. The guard duty and position for the radios was put together by Sgt. Tiutczenko. While he was letting everyone know when their guard was, I set up my hammock on the edge of the perimeter under a poncho roof. Tiutczenko was talking louder than I liked but while he was talking, I heard someone speaking Vietnamese on the slopes below us. When I would stop the talk from our location, the VC/NVA would also stop talking. I could not convince anyone I heard the VC talking because they never heard anyone talking but Tiutczenko.

I knew the CO had first guard and I was sure I knew where he was located so I crept toward his position to let him know about the talking below us. The pitch black darkness from the jungle, the rain and nightfall made locating the CO's position difficult. When I was sure I was close to him, I began to say, "Sir," in a somewhat soft whisper, trying to get his attention. I continued to take a step and repeat calling for him with each step. I knew I was close and as I took my last step, I stepped on one of his legs that were folded Indian style. Because of the rain, he was completely covered by his poncho and when I stepped on him, he let out a scream that sounded like a woman's scream and began a struggle to remove his poncho as he jumped to his feet in front of me. I was startled to say the least when he suddenly jumped up in front of me. I told him about the talking below us, which he had no reaction to at all. Then I began to slink back to my position straining to hear more of the VC talking if I could. Occasionally I would hear some clanking of pans also coming from the location of the talking. I knew they were close; I did not realize how close at the time.

The following day, 2 August 1970 the second platoon moved through the CP laager position taking over the point while the members of the CP ate chow. A short time later, we received a call on the radio from second platoon; they found a North Vietnamese enemy base camp with about 20 bunkers. The CO became extremely excited and told the members of the CP to get our rucks on. We were going down there. He instructed me to take the point and get him down there. All I did was follow the trail left by the second platoon as we descended toward the basecamp. At one

point, the trail turned and I could see the top of the bunker complex. I
knew it was the top because the VC/NVA always dug their latrine slip
trench at the top of their basecamp. I could see the latrine and I figured
the second platoon entered the basecamp at the top. I could not see any
signs of anyone entering where I thought they should have. Right next to
the latrine there was an area of loose dirt from a 105 hit. That is where the
second platoon turned and continued down the slope. I thought it was a
better Idea to enter the basecamp at the top so we did. There was a dead
tree branch blocking the access to the bunker complex and I removed it
and went in passing the latrine slip trench. We began to secure the area
by establishing a defensive perimeter and contacted the second platoon
to let them know we were above them in the bunker complex. They were
surprised to hear our location because they were playing around, not
paying attention and did not have any OPs out watching, otherwise they
would have known we were there. Since the second platoon had moved
out without their rucks and without eating chow, the CO allowed them
to return uphill to eat and retrieve their rucksacks. In hindsight, that was
a mistake. It left the CP, only nine of us, alone in the bunker complex to
secure over twenty bunkers. We were stretched too thin.

The CO instructed me to organize a patrol and find an LZ large enough
to allow Hueys to land and insert a demo team to blow the bunkers. Two
volunteers, Sgt. James Magee and Sgt. Mike Tuitczenko accompanied me
on the short patrol with negative results for an LZ but I felt we had located
an area to allow a demo team to rappel in to take care of the bunkers. We
returned to the secured area of the bunkers to report the results of the patrol
to the CO, but I could not get eyes on his position so I asked where he was.
One of the RTOs waved his arm in a direction above and to the right of
us and remarked "He's over that way." At the time, it seemed insignificant
that I had stopped next to a large tree and right on top of the VC/NVA
slip trench latrine. Sgt. MaGee moved in front of me and squatted down
to remark about an eight-inch diameter pool of blood on the ground. As
he dipped a leaf in the shallow pool, Sgt. Tiutczenko stepped around and
in front of me to check out Magee's findings. I briefly remember seeing the
blood dripping from the leaf on Magee's finger as he remarked, "Talk about
fresh blood," when all hell broke loose. The initial burst of enemy automatic
weapons fire grazed me in the neck causing an immediate reaction. I threw

my arms up to guard my face and neck as I dropped to the ground for what seemed at the time to be cover. On the way to the ground the bullets were so close I could feel them going by my neck and arms. How I escaped being hit by them was a miracle. Tiutczenko dropped and rolled down the hill. I did not realize at the time that he did so because he was wounded by the incoming bullets. After I was on the ground using the mound of the slip trench latrine for partial cover, the enemy ambush continued pouring small arms fire into my position, the rounds hitting in the dirt only inches in front of my face. The dirt from the top of the latrine hit me in the face and got into my eyes as I looked to see where the enemy fire was coming from. I watched in horror as "Doc" Moss, our medic, ran in front of my position and was hit twice by AK-47 fire in the leg and hip. The two rounds took him off his feet and flung him through the air. As he hit the ground, he tumbled, rolled and finally dragged himself behind another tree slightly above my position and began dressing his own wounds. Everyone but me, Doc and Tiutczenko were returning fire, shooting blindly into the trees above and to the right of us. I was not returning fire because I had decided the enemy shots were coming from the vicinity of the CO's last known whereabouts. I began to scream above the rifle reports to, "Cease fire!"

When everyone stopped shooting, they began to question my decision, "Why do you want us to stop shooting?" they asked.

I explained, "The CO is out in that direction. You don't want to shoot him do you?" I did not want a friendly fire incident. As I continued to explain my decision, I told everyone, "If you have identified a target then you can shoot." When I finished that statement, the CO returned to our position on the run and summersaulted into one of the large open bunkers.

By then the enemy fire had also ceased and I was able to ask the CO, "Did you see them sir?" He responded, "Yes. They were right next to me when they opened fire."

"Did you return fire?" I asked

"No, I thought they were shooting at me," he said.

Then I asked, "Anyone other than Doc get hit?"

Tiutczenko spoke up, "Yeah me!"

I recognized his voice immediately and asked, "You? Where did you get hit?" knowing he had stepped in front of me just seconds before the VC/NVA opened fire.

"I got hit in the ankle," he said. Actually, he was hit in the Achilles tendon through the back of his ankle.

"Do you have a field dressing on it?" I asked him.

He replied, "No, I can't get my boot off."

"Well cut your boot off! You aren't going to need it," I told him.

I also knew Doc Moss was not going to be able to help so it was on us to lend whatever aide was required.

Because Tiutczenko had stepped directly in front of me just before the VC/NVA started shooting, I became concerned and I began to check myself for any wounds. I discovered a large wet blood soaked stain on my pant leg between my knee and ankle. It turned out to be Tiutczenko's blood and some pieces of flesh form his wound. My neck had about a quarter inch diameter wound close to my Adam's apple that another medic, Doc Mooneyham looked at but did not treat because any blood had dried and the wound seemed insignificant even though it stung like hell when it first occurred. I suspect now because the bullets passed so close to me that it was a bullet that hit me or a ricochet off the large tree I was standing next to, maybe a splinter from the tree hit me. When I looked at the tree, it was riddled with bullet holes from the ground up to eight feet on the side facing the enemy's firing position. I often wondered how they missed me and later bragged to anyone who asked me," I was moving so fast, I could see the bullets coming at me in slow motion."

My eyes were full of grit from the rounds that had hit the dirt in front of me when I was taking cover on top of the slip trench latrine. I have had dirt blow into my eyes prior to this occasion so I was not overly concerned about the dirt in them causing me a problem. That was probably an oversight on my part considering the source of the dirt.

When the shooting started, the second platoon cut their chow break short and returned to the bunker complex. We established OPs for security at different spots to cover the rest of us moving about the bunker complex and to prevent a repeat attack. As we searched through the bunkers, we did not turn up much equipment. One bunker with a roof that had been collapsed was suspected of being hit by one of the 105 rounds but I thought from the amount of blood we found it could have been used as a makeshift grave to hide the bodies of any of the VC/NVA killed in the 105 barrage. I found a Thompson sub machine gun buried in the clay outside one of the bunkers. Before I turned it over at arm's length with my M-16, I checked thoroughly for booby traps and found none. I picked up the machine gun, opened the wire stock, released the magazine and pulled the operating handle back locking it in place. It was in good shape for lying in the mud as long as it had. I put my name on it, but the Army did not allow automatic weapons to leave the country so I lost track of it.

Two days after the incident in the bunker complex, I awoke with a red bump in the middle of my left eyebrow that was extremely sore to touch. It was the size of a large mosquito bite but did not itch. Doc Mooneyham looked at it and told me because it was so sore it could be a spider bite and we should monitor it. The next day the sore had doubled in size and moved from the middle of my left eyebrow to the edge of my brow even with the corner of my eye. It was still extremely sore to touch and my question to Doc Mooneyham when I showed it to him was, "Do spider bites move?" He suggested lancing it to see if anything was in it. He was cautious not to open it very much because he did not want to get it infected. He was merely checking to see if it was an infection.

The next day when I woke up, my eye was swollen and sealed closed with a thick yellow-green paste. Because I had a fever, Doc Mooneyham wanted to call a dust-off for me but the CO did not want to compromise our position and told Doc to hold off on the dust-off. This routine was repeated for the next several days with my eyelid now sagging to the bottom of my nose and my eye swelled even with my nose on the left side of my face. My fever continued and my face was so sore I could not touch it on the left side. We were scheduled to be resupplied on 14 August so Doc and I figured I could ride the resupply ship back to the rear for treatment. Again, the CO declined to send me to the rear because, in his opinion, my eye appeared to be getting better. Finally, on 15 August the CO allowed Doc Mooneyham to call a dust-off for me to be evacuated from the field. My eye had gotten worse overnight and my temperature was elevated to 104 degrees.

We called a routine dust-off for me, which means all other dust-offs will go before a routine dust-off. We had to wait about two hours before the rear sent the bird to pick me up. It would have been easier if I could have gotten on the resupply ship going back to Uplift the day before. We were five miles from Uplift. They picked me up and started back to the dust-off pad at Uplift. The pilot began flying along the contour of the ground, bobbing and weaving his way along only feet off the ground and skimming the treetops. I tapped the gunner on the leg and asked, "What is he doing?"

The gunner replied, "He is practicing."

I looked up at the gunner and said in a stern voice, "Tell him to practice with somebody else."

The helicopter went to a higher elevation and leveled off. The pilot got the message and he complied. I was glad because I was not in the mood for aerial tricks. I did not want to become a casualty of a helicopter crash on a routine dust-off because the pilot made a mistake.

After returning to A Company Basecamp LZ Uplift, I visited the first battalion aid station initially because that is where the dust-off lands with the injured. I continued to visit there several more times throughout the day because the Third Battalion Doctor, Capt. Phillip Coleman was in Qui Nhon tending patients at the 67th Evacuation Hospital. The first battalion surgeon lanced my swollen eye but did not do anything to it when nothing drained from the swollen eye.

In between visits to the first battalion aid station and Alpha Company's orderly room, I was fending off questions from guys I would meet that knew me. When they saw me they would ask, "Man what happened to your eye?"

It got so bad, I covered my eyes with a pair of sunglasses but they only delayed the question until the guys got closer to me. My eyelid was at the bottom rim of the sun glasses on the left side of my face. On one of the trips to the orderly room, I was so tired of answering that question about my eye, I told the first sergeant, "I think I am going to deck the next guy that asks me, 'What happened to your eye?'"

A USO show with a band was playing at the first battalion theater so I went over there to watch that. A pretty woman was singing on the stage and she noticed a few of us in the back were injured. I had a Band-Aid covering the place they lanced my eye and a guy next to me had his arm in a sling from a gunshot wound. The woman insisted we come down to the front and was smiling as she motioned for us and pointed to the front row of seats. She was fine until she saw me, then her demeanor changed. She got a look like she was becoming sick to her stomach and she quit smiling at me. She did not look at me the remaining time she was on stage. It was a good show and I was happy she asked me to come to the front. I also understood why she may have been turned off by my looks. My eye was gross.

When Doc Coleman returned to Uplift, I was summoned to the orderly room to have him examine me there. When Doc Coleman first saw me, he asked, "What happened to your eye?"

"I was hoping you could tell me Doc," I answered. I was looking at the First Sergeant and thinking about what I had told him earlier. He had a worried look on his face as if I may try to deck Doc Coleman. I just let it go as frustration with my situation.

The Doc asked me, "How long has your eye been like this"

I told him, "Nine days."

He said, "You should have been in nine days ago". He then called the First Battalion Aid Station to ask what the load looked like going to the hospital in Qui Nhon that evening because he wanted me in the hospital that night. I heard the Doc explain to whoever was on the other end of the phone that he would categorize me as routine, but if it looked like the chopper for Qui Nhon was going to load up, he wanted to change me to urgent priority. I left LZ Uplift at 1800 hours, the only passenger on the Huey going to the 67th Evacuation Hospital in Qui Nhon.

CHAPTER 31

Five Days in the Hospital

The helicopter ride to Qui Nhon was cold. The pilot was flying high enough to prevent a random shot from the ground bringing the aircraft down. I did not complain as it was the coolest I had been for two weeks. The ongoing fever from my abscessed eye was kicking my ass.

We touched down right outside the hospital on a concrete pad marked for dust-offs. Since I was considered walking wounded, I jumped out and headed for the triage room. It was a large open room with many stretchers lined up for working on the wounded when they arrived at the hospital. One of the Army nurses met me, pointed at a row of the stretchers, and said, "Pick one and someone will be with you in a minute."

I walked along the row and hoisted myself up on one of the stretchers about midway down the row. One of the nurses working in the room came over to give me some assistance. The first words out of her mouth were, "Boy, that's a nasty looking eye you got there!"

I responded with, "Thanks. I needed that."

"Oh!" she said, "I was not thinking. That was very insensitive of me. I am sorry."

"That's alright. I have heard a lot of that same thing today," I replied.

Before she could say anything else, the room to the right of me became very busy. Six soldiers with gunshot wounds were carried into the triage. The nurse said, "Sit tight. We will get to you when we can." And she went to help the wounded soldiers.

I watched as they pulled a field dressing off one guy and the blood shot out of his wound in a stream about four feet long. It was then that I had the time to reflect how fortunate I was to have only a bad eye and a fever. I do not know if all of the wounded soldiers made it or not. I was tired and lay down on the stretcher until the nurse was free to take care of me.

When she made it back to me it was about 20:00 hours. This time she said, "We need to get a chest x-ray for you."

I told her, "My chest doesn't hurt."

She responded, "I know, but we have to have a chest x-ray anyway." And she pointed to the x-ray room out the door across the hall and handed me a manila folder.

As I walked in the room, the female attendant took the folder I was carrying and turned to walk to the x-ray machine. She told me without looking at me, "Take off your shirt and tee shirt and stand against the screen." I heard the machine groan and thump. She said, "OK you can get dressed now." But before she went on, she asked, "Did you have that on when I took your picture?" referring to the religious medal I always wore around my neck. My girlfriend gave it to me before I left for Vietnam and I never took it off.

"Yes, mam," I replied, showing respect for her rank. She was a second lieutenant.

"Take off your shirt and stand up there again," she said almost disgustedly. The machine groaned and thumped again and she said, "OK we are done. You can go back over there now," referring to the room with the stretchers.

Once back there, I had many people attending to me. They had me lay down on the stretcher, face up. A doctor came over to me and explained he was going to lance my eye but he did not know where my eyeball was. He then told me he was relying on me to let him know if he was cutting into something he shouldn't. A male nurse lifted my head and placed a gauze pad under my head. Then the doctor took a scalpel and made an incision below my left eyebrow. The hot blood and puss from the abscess ran down the side of my head over my ear, soaking my hair and the gauze pad my head was resting on. The doctor pinched the swollen eye causing more of the hot sticky blood and puss to run down the side of my face. It hurt so bad that I began to take a swing at the doctor but the male nurse caught my arm in mid swing stopping me abruptly. My eye and head started throbbing as the pain continued.

The doctor told me, "I am going to admit you to the hospital tonight. We need to make some tests and monitor your situation. So when you go to the head tonight, I want you to squeeze on your eye to keep the incision open and the fluids draining, OK?"

I told him, "OK," but I was thinking to myself there was no way in hell I was ever touching that sore again, anytime!

A female nurse escorted me up to the ward and showed me around so I was familiar with the layout. I was located on the second floor of the ward I was assigned to. The wards were "H" shaped. Two large rooms with two rows of beds in each room were the legs of the H and the showers and latrines serving the two wards were the bar on the H connecting the two wards together. The showers were all on one side and the latrines on the other. There was a nurse's station right at the end of the bar on the H for each ward. It seemed to be a very efficient design for a hospital.

I made use of the showers as soon as I knew my bed was the first one on the right by the door on the bottom of the left leg of the H. As I stood letting the warm water run over me, the throbbing in my head started to go away. It was 21:00 hours when I got to my bunk. I went to bed and for the first time in Vietnam I was in a clean bed with fresh sheets and I fell right to sleep. Suddenly the huge door to the ward from the deck outside flung open with a thump. The major that came through the door asked, "Did you just come in tonight?"

"Yes sir," I said.

"You are my patient then," he said, "They came and got me at the USO club to come and look at you." The major was an eye infection specialist. It was now 21:30 hours, and I had been asleep for all of fifteen minutes. After I found out who he was, the major continued on to the nurse's station where he gathered some medical utensils. They included a pair of surgeon's scissors, a large gauze pad, a few Q-tips with a single end of cotton and a long round wooden stick, a roll of tape, a tube of what appeared to be bacitracin and a small dark bottle with a screwed cap. He returned to my bed where he told me he had to get a sample to run a culture in order to tell if he had prescribed the right medication.

He inserted the surgeon's scissors in the cut the doctor had made earlier in the triage room and snipped a larger hole below my eyebrow. He removed the scissors and inserted a Q-tip. With a movement like brushing teeth he scrubbed the inner part of the abscess parallel to and just below my eyebrow. It hurt like hell and my eye started throbbing again. Then the major removed the Q-tip, stuck the cotton end in the small bottle, and broke it off even with the top of the bottle. He took another Q-tip, scrubbed the abscess perpendicular to my eyebrow, and put the end in the same bottle as the first. That scrub hurt twice as much as the first and my whole head was again throbbing. The doctor squeezed whatever medication was in the small tube to keep the cut open and draining, then covered my whole eye with a gauze bandage and taped it to the left side of my face. The nurse brought me two brown and yellow capsules and a cup of water. I found out the capsules were an antibiotic so I asked for an aspirin, but she told me I could not have one. I did not think I would ever get back to sleep but was able to doze right off. I think I was on the verge of exhaustion because sleep came very easily to me that night.

I found out shortly after the samples were taken, I had to have blood taken every two hours in order to check on the antibiotic to make sure it was working. Instead of getting rest in the hospital, I was being deprived of the sleep I desperately needed. For the remainder of the night, every two hours a nurse woke me up and took a blood sample.

I was considered walking wounded so I was never restricted to the ward or bed. I could walk down the deck to the snack bar for ice cream or a candy bar, even a sandwich if I did not like the meal they served in the ward. I found out very quickly that travel to the snack bar was dangerous. All the ward doors were on my left side going to the snack bar The doors were very wide to allow beds to be moved in and out of the wards so when they opened, they used up most of the walkway. The first time I went to the snack bar I narrowly missed walking into one of the wide swinging doors. I could not see it, because of the bandage covering my eye, unless I turned my head completely using my right eye to look on my left side. It was very awkward but it was better than being hit in my face with the heavy doors.

On the third day in the hospital I was surprised by a visit from the 1970 Miss America USO Show. Since I was in the first bed by the door two of the girls stopped by right away. They had a picture sheet to hand out and autographed it if you asked them. Susan Anton, who later became an actress, was the first girl to stop at my bed and I got her autograph. I got all the autographs except one, so I chased them to the next ward through the shower hallway. I waited until she was not busy with any of the guys in that ward and then asked her if she would sign the picture sheet. She recognized me and asked," Aren't you from the other ward over there?" as she pointed to my ward.

Yes," I told her, "but I got everyone's autograph but yours and I wanted everybody's autograph."

"Well what is wrong with you? You don't look like you are hurt very bad. Why are you in the hospital?" she asked finally.

I lied to her since she so rudely asked me, "I got my eye shot out."

"OOOH," she said and hugged me, "I am sooo sorry. Of course, I'll sign your sheet." She really felt bad. But I did not. She deserved to be lied to. She was the reigning Miss Oregon. She never learned the truth, so I am telling on myself if she reads this book. Hopefully she learned a lesson in humility and did not treat anyone else like she treated me. I should mention that Miss America was Pam Eldred. She was very gracious and to my knowledge she visited every bed in each of the two wards. She was a good dancer. I learned that from some of the guys that got to see the show the girls performed that afternoon and evening for some of the more critical wounded and the pilots at the hospital. We watched from our balcony but could not see much because we were so far away. The show was in an open hanger on the edge of the airfield where the dust-off pad was located.

A couple of nights I attended the movie that played in the courtyard where the snack bar was located. Some of the nurses had living quarters there on the upper levels of the buildings surrounding the courtyard. They would come out onto their balconies in their pajamas with no robes to cover up with. After the first night I went to the movie, I was wishing I had found out about them sooner. The last night I was there one of the nurses came out on her balcony in her see through baby doll pajamas. She was very popular and according to the crowd she was getting "short" or going home soon. When the crowd asked, "Susie, how many days you got left?"

She shouted out, "Sixty nine, sixty nine!" and bent over showing her ass to everyone in the crowd. It was a better show than the movie that was playing.

The next morning I had a doctor's appointment with the eye specialist. When I went to see him, he removed my full eye bandage and replaced it with a band aide. He said he was releasing me back to the company for full duty. My eye was still a little sore to touch but I was ready to go back. I flew to Phu Cat Air Base and then hitched a truck ride to Uplift. I was back before dark and reported to the First Sergeant at the orderly room. He informed me the company was still in the field and he would arrange a ride for me in the morning. I was OK with that. I had only been away five days but it seemed like a month.

I caught up on my letter writing in those five days. I wrote a letter every day to my girlfriend and told her I was in the hospital. I wrote my parents a couple of times too but I never told them I was in the hospital. My mom would not have handled that well so I neglected to mention it to them.

CHAPTER 32

Rescue in 506 Valley

After getting out of the hospital on 21 August 1970, I returned to LZ Uplift and the next day I was told to get my rucksack ready and draw my weapon and ammo for immediate link up with the company out in 506 Valley. 506 Valley was about five klicks west of Uplift. The first sergeant had arranged a ride with the battalion executive officer on the C&C bird, command and control helicopter. He was going on a routine flight to visit with my CO, Captain Palmer, at A Company's location. I went to the pad where the helicopter was already warming up and climbed into the seat next to the Major. As I sat down on the webbing I made sure I had my weapon pointing at the floor of the aircraft, a routine practice for any rifleman riding in a helicopter. The Major looked me over as if to give me a mini inspection and finally asked if I had a round in the chamber of my M-16. I answered, "Yes sir!" and then he asked me to unload my weapon. I complied without any response but the look on my face must have told him I was questioning that order in my mind. He then offered that it was for the safety of everyone on board. "We don't want to have a round discharge and shoot down the helicopter."

As the pilot lifted off I saw the major talking into his headset and he motioned for me to lean over so he could talk to me. He said, "We are going to respond to a mayday call. A helicopter has been shot down nearby. We are going there to supply security for the pilots and the downed aircraft. When we get there, I want you to secure the front of our aircraft and the downed helicopter. Do you understand?"

I said, "Yes sir!"

He replied, "Now you can chamber a round in your weapon."

I tell you that story because everyone in the infantry knows you seldom have a problem with a round going off that is in the chamber of your M-16 and the selection switch is on safe. The time you could have a problem with a round discharging is when you are chambering a round because the bolt slams closed on the round in the chamber. It was an officer thing so I had to let it go at that and concentrate on looking for the downed helicopter we were about to secure.

Our mission changed in route when we got word that another crew got to the downed helicopter before us. The Major passed the word to me as the pilot turned our ship around and headed back to join A Company in 506 Valley. There was nothing said about the round now in the chamber of my M-16.

Our approach to the LZ that the company had marked with smoke was rough because of very high wind gusts. The LZ identified for us was also in a very tight rectangle of palm trees, barely giving the blades from the helicopter room to clear. What it amounted to was the pilot had to make a vertical landing in a very tight spot and then he would have to make a vertical takeoff, both difficult maneuvers even for a very experienced pilot. I could sense the apprehension in the pilot's control of the helicopter. We were turning and rocking from the high wind and the pilot was trying to control the speed but it was very erratic, increasing then slowing and almost stalling the aircraft. As we came in just above the tops of the palm trees surrounding the LZ, a very strong wind gust caught the aircraft and turned us almost as if the pilot were banking in a turn. The pilot reacted quickly to return us to a normal upright position. I do not know what he said to whoever was operating the radio on the ground but I could see he was not happy about the choice of LZ. He then landed us without incident in the open dry rice paddy next to the palm trees where there were no obstacles and plenty of space. Once on the ground everybody went about business as usual. While the Major had a visit with the CO, I was catching up on things with the field first sergeant. As an NCO in the CP, I was still going to walk point when necessary as I had been before going to the hospital and scouting to identify night laager locations for the CP.

We spent the next week roaming the valley looking for VC/NVA that had been suspected of traveling in random groups throughout the valley. The VC/NVA had been detected moving through the valley by electronic motion sensors that were planted in the area by helicopter. When the VC/NVA were identified by the sensors, a four duce mortar platoon located at Uplift would engage them, catching them off guard and inflicting some casualties among them. Alpha Company had been sent in to disrupt the free movement in the valley. We were experiencing a small amount of sporadic contacts with VC types or NVA. Some were wounded and being transported on stretchers by their comrades. We were able to capture some VC/NVA when the stretcher-bearers dropped their wounded comrades and ran instead of surrendering to us. The wounded had no choice but surrender at that point. We did try to pursue the VC that ran but there were lots of hiding places in 506 Valley. Our efforts to find those that fled were futile so all we could do was contact the rear to come and get the wounded VC and take them back to Uplift for interrogation. There was always a slim possibility that the POWs would give up some information that might help us locate their comrades.

Because of some of the interviews with the POWs, some information was gained on the VC/NVA movement in 506 Valley. Unknown to us, a plan was devised in the rear to open up the valley giving free access to indigenous personnel. In order for that plan to be effective A Company would have to make an obvious exit out of 506 Valley. On 27 August 70 a strange part of the plan was implemented. We were picked up by trucks and driven out of 506 Valley back to Uplift something as paratroopers we rarely ever did. This was all part of the plan devised in the rear to expose enemy movement in 506 Valley. The road the trucks took us back to Uplift on was one that was seldom used and in some places was terribly overgrown. The overgrowth scraped and pulled at us sitting in the back of the deuce and a half truck. As we left in the trucks, two recon squads of seven men each were secretly inserted in the same area we had just departed. In order to remain undetected they humped the five klicks from Uplift. Their mission was to report on the movement of VC/NVA in the valley. There were definite signs of large numbers of enemy moving through the valley but we could not make contact with them or draw them out to fight when we were there searching. The Recon teams only numbering fourteen men much smaller than our company would find out how many there were and what their movements were like.

Relieved to be back at Uplift we unloaded from the trucks, drew our ammo resupply and our rations readying for our next mission. Usually we would return to the rear areas for three days called stand down. During that time, we would go on details and provide security for the rear area. The first night back, I found it difficult to find a place to sleep. I spent the night on top of the sandbags stacked along one of A Company's permanent barracks. The roof had a large overhang, which would keep me dry if it rained. It was very uncomfortable and sleep was almost nonexistent. Our usual assigned barracks for stand down were a group of buildings that used to house the Engineers at Uplift. These buildings were shared by all the companies when they returned to the rear for stand down but someone in their infinite wisdom had them torn down. The company was essentially homeless for our entire stand down.

The second day in the rear we learned that the Recon teams had let over one hundred VC/NVA walk by their ambush because of their much superior force one hundred vs fourteen. The Recon leader also vowed not to let any number by if the opportunity presented itself again.

Because of the lack of housing in the rear, I went to work on the Supply Sergeant to let me stay the night in the supply room. He was getting ready to go home and his replacement was a friend of mine from the third platoon. They were both housed in the rear of the supply room, as was the armor who was also one of my best friends and former company radio operator in the CP. We were three against one in favor of letting me stay in the supply room. In addition, even though we assured him, I would be gone before anyone else was up and around, the supply sergeant kept telling us it was against regulations and if the first sergeant found out we would all be court-martialed. It was a tough sell but we finally got him to agree to let me string my hammock up in the rafters and nobody including the first sergeant, would find out.

At 22:45 hours, there was a knock on the door in the rear of the supply room. The supply sergeant put on his glasses turned on the light and opened the door. In the dark on the back porch of the supply room stood the first sergeant. As I heard the supply sergeant say, "Hi Top, What's up?" I swung my legs out of the hammock so I was sitting up all the time thinking we are caught.

Then the first sergeant asked, "Have you seen sergeant Musson?"

Without hesitation I answered, "Here I am Top."

Then the conversation became a series of questions from both of us.

"Do you have your rucksack packed and ammo ready to go?"

"Yes I do. What's up?"

His reply was, "the company is going out and you need to get to the helicopter pad right away."

I jumped to the floor untied my hammock rolled it up and put it in the pocket where I carried it on my rucksack which was packed on the floor beneath where I had been sleeping. I grabbed my rifle and ammo and hurried off to the helicopter pad about one hundred fifty meters or so from our supply room. As I traveled I was thinking to myself about the many times before I had made this same trip at night only to spend the entire night without sleep on the helicopter pad and return to pull details in the company area the next morning. It seemed like everybody was there before me but I did not think about how long Top may have spent looking for me. I just walked up to where the CO was and asked what was going on. He then told me we were going to CA out to 506 Valley to rescue two Recon teams who were surrounded by an unknown number of VC/NVA. The CO instructed me to take charge of the first helicopter when it landed and sent both company and battalion radio operators with me. Even though I could hear and see the illumination rounds going out to 506 Valley I still was not convinced we were going out. We had a lot of new people in the company and they were asking me what was going to happen. I told them we were probably going to spend the night on the pad and pull details in the morning. I knew helicopters did not fly at night unless they had to or there was something serious going on. The time was 23:15 when we heard the sound of helicopters coming. I was wrong. We were going after all. This would be my first night CA since I came in country almost a year ago.

The rescue force activated totaled thirty-six men comprised from two platoons 2nd and 3rd of A Company and a small element from the CP. The six UH-1 helicopters landed on the tarmac at Uplift in a staggered formation: the lead helicopter in front and then two pairs then the last helicopter. When every chopper was loaded we took off into the night for

506 Valley 5-7 klicks away. There was no time to check or load weapons. You were supposed to have everything taken care of. I was not sure the men riding with me were as ready as I was. I was scared too and was hoping that did not show, although I was sure everyone else was at least as scared as I was. There was no one talking. You would have to yell for anyone to hear you over the jet engine and blades of the helicopter.

As the choppers lifted off from Uplift, the 4th Infantry artillery located on Uplift continued to fire illumination rounds out into 506 Valley. I never understood how they were able to accomplish lighting the LZ with artillery illumination and the helicopters insert troops without hitting the helicopters but they always succeeded without incident. There is a time when they suspend firing artillery just to insure safety of the helicopters and unit going into the LZ. What was a very short distance for the helicopter to cover, the time to get to 506 Valley seemed like an eternity.

As we approached the selected LZ and started to circle you could see people on the ground running around all over. The illumination rounds had the LZ and surrounding area lit up like daytime. As we made our descent to the LZ, about a hundred feet off the ground, I slid out and stood on the skid to speed up the exit from the chopper. I watched almost mesmerized by the green tracers floating up toward the helicopter. They looked like fast moving fireflies on a hot summer night. There were no sounds just small balls of green lights oddly curving as they made their way toward us. Then I realized that we were under fire! The bullets and tracers began to slam into the helicopter all around me and into the tail in the rear of the aircraft. The incoming fire was so intense the pilot immediately pulled the Huey into a steep climb to avoid being shot down. Because I was still standing on the skid the centrifugal force and rate of climb started to propel me from my perch. Luckily for me the door gunner just to my right side was prepared; he grabbed the back of my rucksack and pulled me back onto the floor of the chopper. My heart was racing after grasping the reality of what had just happened to me. The adrenalin continued to surge throughout my body for the rest of the flight.

After the pilot leveled off at a safe altitude, the door gunner tapped me on the shoulder to let me know the pilot was circling back to complete our insertion into the LZ. On a CA, the first helicopter in is always first unless shot down so once again we were the lead helicopter going into the hot LZ. As we started back down making our second approach to the LZ the gunner told me to get everyone ready to jump when we got close to the ground because the pilot was not going to land or stop. I passed the word, we got ready moving once again out onto the skids of the aircraft, and once again the helicopter came under intense fire from the ground. At about six feet above the ground, the pilot flared the chopper and slowed enough for us to jump. I was on the ground with my group of radio operators. We landed in a rice paddy with 4-6 inches of water in it along with the rice plants, which stuck up slightly higher than the water level.

I immediately reached for the red star cluster I had attached to my ruck before we left Uplift, removed the cap placing it on the bottom to ready it for firing, and struck the bottom to launch the bright red cluster of lights to warn the remaining five choppers that the LZ was hot.

There were not enough of us to establish security for the remaining incoming helicopters, so we had to try and link up with one of the Recon teams on the ground. As I looked toward the end of the rice field about 100 meters away, I spotted one of the Recon squad members. He was hunkered down while firing his rifle into some of the nearby hedgerows. I hastily made my way toward him crouching low and splashing through the rice paddy while shouting for the others to follow me. When I reached the Recon squad member I realized that I knew him. He was a former A Company 2nd Platoon member that had requested to go to Recon and was accepted.

As we met up, I asked, "Hobbs, what the hell is going on here?"

His reply came with some concern, "Oh, Larry, be careful. They are all around here. Just before you got here one ran right by me."

I looked back across the rice paddy to our insertion point to see if the other members of the rescue team and the CO were on the ground yet. It was then I discovered the battalion radio operator, Bowles, had never left that sight, exposing himself to enemy fire and leaving me with no radio communication. I yelled for him to link up but I assumed because of the distance and all the automatic weapons fire he did not respond or reply. I then left my somewhat secure position to go back and retrieve him but to no avail, he told me he was waiting for the CO and was not going to leave until the CO got there. I left him standing in the rice paddy again as I ran back to my former position.

I turned once to look as the remaining five choppers landed in typical formation, one behind the other in the middle of the rice paddy. It was hard to tell if they had received any fire as they were landing but most of the VC/NVA had dispersed. The rest of the rescue team unloaded the five remaining choppers and along with the CO came to my position where we established a perimeter for protection and began to assess the situation with the Recon team leader. It was then we learned the other seven Recon team members had not been heard from since the ambush had been initiated. The two Recon teams separated by three hundred meters had strung det cord, claymores and hand grenades along a trail between them to create a kill zone when detonated. Once the ambush was blown, the three hundred plus VC/NVA rallied and surrounded both seven-man teams. The team we linked up with first had a machine gun and was able to repel enemy advances on their position but the second team had no heavy weapons and had not responded to radio transmissions or any other attempts to contact them. To learn of their fate we had to link up with them somehow. The Recon leader also confessed that the exact location of the other team was not known and since there was no communication with them since they blew the ambush, they were presumed lost. They were 300 meters away somewhere at the end of the ambush kill zone.

The CO and the Recon leader decided each element would supply a point man to lead the remaining members of Recon and the rescue element from A Company to the lost recon team. I was the point man selected by the CO for A Company. I met with Recon's point man and the two of us devised a plan to lead the rest of the group to the lost Recon team. We decided not to take the route along the ambush kill zone figuring that may put us in danger of receiving friendly fire. Instead we opted to make a semi-circle approach to where we thought their position might be. That route was a little longer but to us it was a lot safer.

There were a number of hedgerows that we would have to pass through, which was particularly dangerous at night and we did not know if there would be friendlies or enemy on the other side. The Recon point man and I decided to take turns going through each hedgerow: me first, diving to the left followed by him diving to the right. The next hedgerow would be him first, followed by me, and so on until we found the lost team.

As we jumped through to the other side, we would yell, "Don't shoot. We are Americans, " in hope of the lost team realizing we were friendly before they fired us up. We also had to make sure if we were fired on if it was by the enemy not the Americans. This was a pretty terrifying situation since we did not know their location or if any enemy force would greet us as we came through the hedges. The artillery flares that had been lighting the whole area had long since stopped and now we were in total darkness. We had to be prepared and our senses strained to the limit to detect movement between the hedgerows, our eyes keenly trained on the dark shadows with fingers on triggers ready to fire at the unexpected. Our luck held, and although both the Recon point man and I fired our weapons several times after crashing through the hedges, we met no resistance and eventually found the lost members of the Recon team without further incident.

Relief came when in response to our calls came, "we are here!"

All seven of the lost Recon team were wounded, none seriously. Their radio had been a casualty from the first counter attack on their position. A woman burst through their cover, firing an AK-47 on full automatic wounding the radio operator and taking out the radio with two hits. She was killed inside their position by one of the other Recon team members. The other team members were wounded from repeated attempts to overrun their position. They had literally fought for their lives. After an initial assessment of the wounded and accounting for equipment, weapons and ammo we established a perimeter sent out LPs and moved the wounded so they could be treated by the medics. We called in dust off helicopters to evacuate the wounded back to Uplift. We had two medics on the ground; one was a Recon team member and was slightly wounded, the other came in on the first helicopter with the radios and me. They did their usual excellent job of treating the wounded and making them comfortable until the dust off picked them up. Of course the Recon medic did not think his wounds were serious enough to warrant being dusted off, but we sent him back with the others anyway.

Once all the wounded were evacuated we again moved our position to the trail where the initial contact took place. There were nineteen VC/NVA bodies remaining on the trail and traces of several bodies being dragged away were detected in our survey of the kill zone. We collected a number of captured weapons, among them were five AK-47 Russian made assault rifles, sixty Chi-Com hand grenades, twenty-six eighty-two millimeter mortar rounds and numerous 7.62 rounds for the assault rifles. Throughout the night we maintained a fifty percent guard alert meaning half of us were awake while the other half slept. We also had two LP positions out for early detection of movement or counter attack at either end of the trail.

A commotion occurred at one of the LP locations. The LP thinking he was stepping onto a small cluster of vegetation inadvertently stepped on a VC/NVA that had been wounded by one of the gunships covering the Recon team until the rescue team arrived. The courageous pilot hovered right above the hedge row with his mini gun pointed down and traveled the length of the hedge row mini gun blazing to break the VC/NVA intense fire on the lost Recon team. As he approached the end of the hedgerow, he received fire from behind a bush to his front. The pilot looked up at his target behind the bushes and continued to blaze away with his mini gun. The VC's left arm had been taken off completely by the mini gun on the Cobra gunship. After getting him on his feet, the medics also treated him and we called for an extraction helicopter. This extraction was different from a dust off because he was a POW and an interpreter was sent out to take his statement for intelligence purposes. We never heard what happened to him after he was picked up that night.

Sometime in the middle of the night one of the guys along the line of our defensive position reported he heard movement close by. For safety reasons we fired up the area in front of his position and several of the guys next to him fired also. There was more movement and then some moaning. We fired up the area again. The moaning and movement stopped.

Because of the numbers of VC/NVA originally engaged in the ambush site, the CO wanted to make sure the hedgerows and the LZ we came in on remained clear for the night. He asked the battalion radio operator to get some gun ship support on station and have him work over the area. Puff was no longer in operation and Shadow was busy so we settled for a fighter jet and a Gatling gun with 20mm exploding rounds to help us out. The first thing the pilot of the jet asked for was our co-ordinates and wanted us to mark our position. I was carrying a strobe light used for just that purpose so here I was standing at the edge of our position with the strobe at arm's length marking our position. Once that was established we had to let the pilot know which direction from our location we wanted him to fire up. I looked at my compass and called out the direction for the radio operator to pass on to the pilot. The first run the pilot made came in way too close. The exploding rounds stopped about 15 ft. from our location. We asked to have him back that off about 25 meters, we could see clearly there was no enemy within 15 ft. of us. The pilot complied with our request and made runs until all his ammo was spent. We had 50% of the company on guard for the rest of the night.

The next day we searched the area we had fired up because of movement and found a dead VC. He evidently had been wounded in the ambush but could not get away. He had made some attempt to bandage himself but must have been interrupted by our automatic weapons fire during the night.

We ran an expanded search of the whole ambush site and the rescue insertion point just to make sure we had not missed anything. We found definite signs of many wounded or dead being dragged away from the kill zone of the ambush. We secured an LZ for extraction of the remaining Recon team members and bringing in the remaining members of A Company. It seems our patrolling of 506 Valley had been resurrected after Recon's attempt to control enemy movements.

The rescue team that made the CA into 506 Valley miraculously had no casualties from the insertion under extremely intense enemy fire or any ground skirmishes during the night. Recon only suffered seven wounded from the initial ambush, all members of the same team. The numbers of VC/NVA counted by Recon totaled three hundred but an unknown amount of VC/NVA were advancing into the kill zone when Recon initiated the ambush. For that reason we were all very lucky because we were definitely outnumbered. For the superior firepower from the gunships and jets that provided support during the contact we cannot say enough thanks. Also the six pilots that delivered the rescue team were fearless and did an excellent job getting us in under fire. It was an experience I will never forget.

CHAPTER 33

CP Ambushes/The Navy Ends a Problem

We remained in 506 Valley and continued to work the area where Recon made contact with the large body of VC/NVA. Captain Palmer insisted on keeping the CP functioning as a separate unit often separating us from the nearest platoon by twenty five hundred meters. We did not have enough firepower to operate as our own detached force against the superior odds that were moving through 506 Valley. It was a very risky decision made by the CO and it scared me.

Shortly after the rescue, we laagered above the trail where the nineteen bodies of the VC/NVA continued to decay in the hot September sun. I remember seeing two women herding cattle in the dried rice fields below us where some of the encounter with Recon took place. The women obviously did not know we were above them because they both dropped their black pajama pants and squatted to pee in full view of us all. It must have reminded Lt. Mott, our Executive Officer since Lt. Chapla left, of a morning bathroom break because he came by my location and told me not to fire him up, he was going out to shit. When he was done, he came back in and asked Doc Mooneyham for something to help with diarrhea, LT had it bad. Mooneyham was our medic since Doc Moss had been wounded at the beginning of the month. The doc was happy to help the lieutenant and gave him some Kaopectate. That is what he told the lieutenant anyway. He told me he had given him some laxative. Lt. Mott made another trip by me after being medicated by the doc. The lieutenant came back in and asked doc for some more Kaopectate; he claimed the first batch was not working. Doc Mooneyham was more than happy to help and gladly gave him more laxative. After taking it, the lieutenant came by my location in a hurry and said, "I am going out here. Don't fire me up."

A short time later, I heard moaning and groaning from the lieutenant and he exclaimed, "I am going to stay out here for a while!" Then there were very loud moans and groans coming from the lieutenant's location. Doc used to be the third platoon's medic when Lt. Mott was the platoon leader. I assumed he was getting some kind of revenge with the lieutenant's dilemma. Doc thought his prank was funny. I could not bring myself to see the humor in making the lieutenant suffer. We all had diarrhea at some time in Vietnam. The big orange malaria pills we took weekly caused some cases of diarrhea on their own. I do not know if that was the lieutenant's original problem or if it was something else. I tried hard not to dwell any longer on a man with the shits.

I think the lieutenant called the rear to inform the CO of his problem because shortly after he returned to his position in the perimeter, we were saddling up to go to the valley and find an LZ to bring in a chopper with Captain Palmer and take Lt. Mott back to Uplift. The lieutenant moved very gingerly and would let out a moan now and then on our way to the valley. I believe the call from Lt. Mott cut the captain's visit in the rear short. He did not seem happy to be back with us when he arrived. I discussed our next move with the CO. He strangely picked a location we had been in many times before. We were there a couple of times with Captain Welsh and once before with Captain Palmer. It was the small heavily wooded hill the first sergeant came out to stay all night and left because he saw all the trash laying around, recognizing we had stayed there too long. I was not a fan of going back there. We had always had some enemy contact when we went in there and this time I was on point. As I walked up the entry trail toward the top of the hill an errant shot rang out and everyone dove for cover. We moved more stealthily toward the top but whoever fired the shot had left by another route. There was no more resistance so we moved into the old familiar position.

The CO said he wanted to eliminate the problem of the hill so he pointed to another location he wanted me to take him to across the narrow valley. It was a higher hill with more woods and cover but we could still clearly see the problem hill. Once up there he asked to get artillery to put a barrage on the problem hill. We had no artillery forward observer with us at the time so I worked up coordinates and called in a fire mission. The artillery firebase let me know their guns were already firing for someone else but a battleship off the coast would fire for us if we wanted. After a brief discussion with the CO we decided to take them up on the offer. The radioman at the firebase gave me the frequency for the battleship and I contacted the ship directly from our position. We were about seven miles inland off the coast. The Navy could hurl their sixteen-inch shells up to twenty-seven miles so we were within range. The ship's radioman and I talked about what weapons they would fire and how far away we needed to be from the target. We were closer than we liked but the Navy told me it was not a problem for them. I gave the coordinates to the ship's radioman. We all heard a faint boom from the ship's direction. The radioman said, "Smoke out."

I replied, "Roger, smoke out." The smoke round landed dead center in the sixty-meter long, forty-meter wide and thirty-meter high hill. It was a huge white plume with not such a big explosion, a typical smoke round.

Then I followed with, "Fire for effect." That brought on the HE, heavy explosive rounds. Again, we heard the guns on the ship fire the first volley. After that we never heard anything but the rounds exploding as they hit the small hill in front of us. I did not count them but all the rounds the Navy fired hit somewhere on that hill.

After the barrage was over we went down to check the damage. The hill, with very large trees and huge boulders had been reduced to a pile of shredded leaves, wood and gravel not over two feet tall anywhere we looked. I was amazed. It would have taken the Army days to destroy that hill. The navy did it in less than an hour. No shell missed its mark and we had no short rounds to watch out for. I said then I would have the Navy fire for me anytime if they were available. We all witnessed a remarkable feat of expert marksmanship.

We moved back to the hill we had watched the Navy barrage from and laagered for the night. The next day everyone in the field had to have a resupply list to the CP so we could call them in to Uplift for delivery the day after. It was a system we used my whole tour and it worked well most of the time. Sometimes there were misunderstandings that could be fixed with a little effort. One of the misunderstandings was with our first platoon and no matter how many times they were told they never changed their order. If we were out a long period of time we would get a new change of clothes once a month; otherwise the order for clothes should be only for necessities, replacement of ripped or torn articles of clothing. The first platoon ordered a complete set of clothing for each person in the field every resupply. Alpha Company's supply sergeant had complained to me several times to stop ordering total sets because he did not always have enough of them. When he would get our dirty fatigues from a resupply, he had to go through them and destroy the ripped or torn items then request new replacements from S4 and send the rest to be laundered. Since we were not always traveling with the first platoon, I could only turn in what they requested. However, there were other things that the supply sergeant had a problem with on the first platoon's list. He told me to quit ordering the six bottles of hot sauce and six onions that was always on their resupply list. He said the mess sergeant pointed a forty-five automatic pistol at him and told him not to come asking for them again or he would shoot him.

On this particular resupply we were calling the list directly in to the supply sergeant for Alpha Company so I excluded the clothes and the hot sauce and onions. When I had finished the list, the first platoon leader Lt. Miller called the supply sergeant and completed their list for the clothes, hot sauce and onions. When he was done, the CO called him to remind him that all resupply items should be sent to the CP for transmittal to the rear. Lt. Miller told the CO, "I sent the items to your man, but he left them off the list."

The CO turned to me and asked, "Sergeant Musson, is that true?"

"Yes sir," I answered.

"Why did you exclude those items from the list?" the CO asked.

"Sir, because Sergeant Trego told me he could not supply a complete set of fatigues every resupply and he would be shot if he asked for hot sauce and onions from the mess sergeant," I answered.

The CO was pissed, I could tell. He had just called one of his platoon leaders to correct him and I was the problem. It embarrassed him and he told me, "From now on Sergeant Musson, you will call in everything on the resupply list just like it was sent to you. Do you understand?"

"Yes sir. Even the onions?" I asked.

He snapped back, "I just want to get down the hill." He said that because earlier he had asked me to locate another laager site further down the hill so we would be closer to the LZ for resupply the following day. I had done that when he asked but somehow I think he was hoping I would tell him I did not do it so he could continue to vent more of his anger.

Shortly after that incident, the CO took the resupply responsibility away from me and gave it to our new Como Chief, Staff Sergeant Jones. He was a real gem of a guy; after he took over I got complaints from the guys in the platoons that their cigarette ration was all screwed up. Some of the guys were not getting the brands they smoked anymore. When I mentioned it to the CO he told me I was no longer in charge of that and any complaints should go to SSgt. Jones. Sure he would understand. That was like telling the fox that there are chickens missing from the hen house. I did go to SSgt. Jones on behalf of the guys and he told me to mind my business. I found out through a little checking SSgt. Jones was keeping several full cartons of cigarettes for himself and that was the reason the guys were not getting any of their brands.

Those were not the only problems happening in the CP. We were moving less and when we did move we were moving only a short distance from our previous laager site. We spent a whole day next to a good-sized stream. It was twenty meters wide and in some places four feet deep. One of the guys said he wanted to swim and several others thought it was a good idea. I was against allowing it to happen because we did not have enough people for security. Captain Palmer overruled my decision so I had to lay out a plan for everyone to get a turn for a swim. While four of our nine guys went for a swim, the other four would supply security: one upstream, one downstream, one on each side of the stream. The CO was a non-participant in both the swim and security. He read a book along the shore in the tree line. When it was my turn to swim I declined. I still thought it was a bad idea considering the proximity to the Recon ambush site and our rescue CA only a few nights before.

During the swim a call came in on the radio from one of the platoons around the point from us, about twenty three hundred meters away. They had a problem with their Chieu Hoi, or former enemy that switched over to our side. He claimed to be sick but the medic in that platoon had not made the trip to the field with them and they needed the top doc to come to their location to evaluate the Chieu hoi. The CO told me he wanted me to take a patrol with our medic to their location so the doc could determine if they needed to send in the Chieu hoi. "When you get back, I want you to find us a night laager, "he told me. It was going to be a stretch to get there and back before dark. The platoon was almost a mile and a half away from our position.

I took the top doc and two others with me for the long trek to see to the Chieu hoi. The platoon sent a patrol to meet us at the end of the point, which cut a little time off our trip. The doc checked out the Chieu hoi and told the platoon to call a medevac chopper for him. We started back before the dust-off bird arrived because we did not have to be there and I wanted to get back to check for our next night laager. We arrived back at the CO's position at dusk so I wanted to get started to look for a night laager right away. I mentioned to the CO that I would be leaving to begin my search. He told me, "You do not have to worry about that. We found a location while you were gone."

I did not ask who found the new location or how far it was but I should have. We started moving the four hundred meters to the new laager site with the CO leading the way. I was walking slack but I became suspicious of our new laager site when we did not move away from the stream we had spent the whole day swimming in and frolicking around. We were moving in a series of dried rice paddies that dropped gradually as they narrowed. There was a low bluff on our right side that eventually ran up to the stream blocking us from continuing any further. We stopped near a ford in the stream where the rapidly moving water made a lot of noise as it flowed over rocks and boulders in the stream. The bluff was fifteen to twenty feet tall still on our right making our laager a small triangle shape. The CO said, "This is where we will laager tonight."

I did not like the location right off and tried to be diplomatic about my disapproval. "Sir, I think we should look for another laager. This one has some problems."

"What problems would those be?" he questioned, and then I knew he had chosen the site.

"Well, sir, we have high ground on two sides of us and a stream that will mask sounds of anyone approaching from there on the third," I explained. "I have a real problem with that." Then I asked, "Where will the guard post be located?"

The CO pointed to the top of the bluff and said, "The guard post will be up there."

"Can I take a look where you are talking about, sir?" I asked.

"I will show you, Sergeant," he replied.

We climbed the fifteen foot high bluff with a little bit of trouble raising another flag against this location. After we reached the top the CO started to walk into the open grassy field toward what looked to be a well-used trail. We walked one hundred fifty meters across the open field and stopped thirty meters short of the trail. The trail was the same one the Recon team had engaged over three hundred VC/NVA only a few nights before. There was a small bush where the CO stopped. He said, "We will make this the guard post and the ambush will be on the trail."

I was shocked that anyone could devise such a hair-brained plan and expect a reasonable person to go along with it. I began to question the CO. "Sir, you can't be serious about this being the guard post with everyone else sleeping a hundred and fifty meters away?"

"I do not see anything wrong with that," he replied.

"Sir, you are talking about one man leaving the only three radios we have here and walking one hundred fifty meters across an open field to wake up his relief out of a sound sleep. Then that man has to walk a hundred and fifty meters across the open field and find the guard post in the middle of the night while still half asleep. Shall I go on?" I argued.

"Well, what do you suggest, Sergeant?" he asked.

"I suggest we move the laager to another place." I answered.

His answer was, "No. I do not want to do that."

"You are determined to laager there and have the guard and ambush up here is that what I understand?" I asked.

"Yes, unless you have a better idea," he answered.

"Sir, with all due respect to your rank, you are stupid if you think I would agree to this situation. If someone comes along the trail, you can kiss the guard's ass and the radios good-bye because we would never get here in time to save him," I said.

As we argued back and forth at some length, I finally proposed to either move the laager up to the area where the radios were or I would stay awake all night with the guard for added security on the guard and the radios. I don't think the CO would have accepted either idea if Sgt. MaGee had not said, "I have to agree with Sgt. Musson on this one, sir."

The CO looked at me and said, "You realize what this means, Sergeant?"

I answered with, "I think so sir, but I don't care what it means. I am only thinking about our safety."

I set up the ambush and everyone moved up to the area where the radios were located for guard duty. There were enough bushes around the area so everyone had some kind of concealment for the night. All of the bickering back and forth did not matter, because at 0100 we received word on the radio to move our position. We were given a set of coordinates and told we would be picked up at that location at first light. I had the ambush rigged this time as mechanical, meaning it was on automatic. A mechanical ambush was an intricate mixture of explosives that when put together and set up correctly would trigger itself and cause extensive injuries to the person or persons who set it off, so I had to be careful when I picked it up. The mechanical ambush worked like a charm but was dangerous because it was easily tripped if you forgot where everything was located. I collected all the explosives then I packed the Claymores and grenades in my ruck and we headed for the coordinates the rear sent out. The pickup of course never happened. We were up all night arguing and moving around 506 Valley and all of us were irritable as hell.

It appeared that we were going to be in 506 Valley for quite a while. There was enough enemy movement to keep us alert. Then we started getting incoming mortar rounds around 18:00 hours every night. That told me the VC/NVA were watching our movements somehow and that was scary. We moved into a creek bed for the day to rest near water until night when we would move to our next laager. The creek was not too far from a round hill. The hill was not high or big, it was just an average round hill. At the base of the hill, there were tall palm trees and a well-used trail ran among them. I decided to set up the mechanical ambush on the well-used trail. My ambush had four Claymores, eight to ten hand grenades, and a hundred foot of det chord. The det chord exploded so fast, it triggered the Claymores at the same instant and blew the handles off the grenades so four to six seconds later there were delayed explosions to pick up stragglers. The triggering device was a trip wire with a plastic spoon handle fitted between two spoons back to back with electric wires connected to an old radio battery. It set off the electric blasting cap placed in the nearest Claymore.

As I was connecting the wires to the battery, five Vietnamese kids walked toward the triggering device. I had to expose myself to prevent them from walking into the ambush. The two guards I had for protection while I assembled the ambush also started yelling at the kids. The kids just laughed and ran away. What we did not realize at the time was the kids were spotters for the VC/NVA that were stalking us. Later that evening around 18:00 hours we started receiving mortar rounds near our laager site. We moved to the top of the round hill. We discovered a large trench on the top of the hill that was dug for a petroleum pipeline years earlier. We left the ambush in place for the night and used the trench for a laager that night. We had no other type of contact the rest of the night.

The next day under the CO's direction, we moved across the open rice field near the site where I set up the mechanical ambush and spent the whole day there. The CO informed me we would laager there for the night. That information upset me because we had already been mortared in the field, and this was a set up for a second night of mortars.

Late that afternoon a helicopter brought in the battalion commander and the new Command Sergeant Major, CSM Green. While the colonel and the captain conferred, CSM Green came and talked to me. He asked me some interesting questions about the amount of time we had been at our present location and where we had come from to get there. He did not like my answers and said he was strongly recommending the colonel make the CO move our night laager. In spite of CSM Green's urging, the captain refused to move. I went out in front of our position and rigged the mechanical ambush explosives to be manually set off. There was a gully about seventy-five meters in front of our position, which would provide a large force some natural protection if we were in a firefight. It was close enough to run a Claymore wire and connect it to a regular firing device. I left the firing device at the guard position.

Again, that evening at 18:00 hours we received incoming mortar rounds on our position. They were very accurate so we made a hasty retreat to a thickly covered hill behind us. The cover was small trees about ten to twelve feet tall. They were similar to willow trees and were covered with small oval green leaves. There was a gulley washed into the small pebbly clay soil that we followed to the top of the hill. We had covered a distance of about three to four hundred meters and needed to make sure everyone made it together. We took a head count to confirm that we were all safe.

Once the head count was complete, I realized I had left the ambush and the firing device at the old laager site in the valley below. I went to the CO to let him know about the mistake. He told me I had to go retrieve it. I knew I was going to have to go back but I thought I could just get the firing device and blow the ambush in place. Captain Palmer insisted I gather up the whole ambush and bring it back to the top of the hill. I told him I could not do it by myself; I would need someone to stand watch while I recovered the Claymores and grenades. The CO informed me he would not send anyone to help me. I would have to ask volunteers to go with me. I got only two but they were enough. There were a total of nine of us in our patrol. I would be taking a third of our security with me back to the valley. Before we left, I made sure everyone knew the route we were taking down and back up. I did not want any problems with our own guys shooting at us. We would use a password and identifier in order to be cleared coming back on top of the hill. I also let everyone know we would be gone a long time. I was not comfortable with what we were doing and was not rushing myself or taking any chances.

I walked away from the group on the top of the hill with no radio operator accompanying me. I was on point, leading the two volunteers and had my ears tuned to the front of us. Colon taught me that. He always said, "Keep your eyes and ears out in front of you. Your slack man will take care of what is behind you." We moved slowly listening alertly to check for movement in front of us. As we left the scrub trees, I hugged the contour of them following them until I found our former laager. I found and picked up the Claymore firing device tucking it into my ruck. I then moved to the trees at the top of the dike wall that surrounded the dry rice paddy and the gulley where the ambush was located. I tried to stay low, using the grass in the dry rice paddy to maneuver our way into the gulley. I kept thinking, watch your ass and that I should have blown the ambush and told the CO that it went off when I picked up the firing device. If the three of us had run into anyone recovering the ambush, we would have been history. There was no one to save us if we made contact and we had no radio to call for any help. I had one of the guys that came with me cover the end of the gulley away from where we entered it. The other guy covered the open end of the rice paddy after the gulley, and then I started disassembling the ambush. I noticed that I was starting to hurry like there was an urgency to be done. I told myself to slow down and I did but my mind kept thinking in a fast pace, trying to think ahead so as not to miss anything.

I finally had all of the ambush components disassembled and lying in the grass. I quietly called the two guards in to help me carry the Claymores, grenades and det chord. Once we had the explosives loaded up, I started for the hilltop laager where the CO and the others were waiting for our return. We were very lucky we did not encounter anyone while we recovered the ambush. Now all we had to do was make it back to the laager safely. Again, I was very cautious moving up the hill this time. I tried to keep from making any noise and kept myself alert for any unusual noise in front of me. When I thought we were close enough to the others at the laager site, I softly called out the password and got the proper response. We made it back. I was grateful to the guys that helped me and thanked them for volunteering. They settled in and went to sleep anticipating some guard duty before morning. I did not sleep at all that night. I was still expecting something to happen but it never did.

CHAPTER 34

Battle for Our Lives

After spending the night on top of the low hill we escaped to from the valley, we moved right back to the same area we left the night before. We crossed the dry field and gulley where I had set up the mechanical ambush to a small abandoned village. It was nestled in among some tall palm trees and we found signs of recent use in the typical thatched roofed hootches and the bunkers that surrounded them. There were footprints in the soft dirt made by someone wearing Ho Chi Mihn sandals. Ho Chi Mihn sandals were a popular footwear with Vietnamese people especially the VC/NVA. They were made from old tires and inner tubes. The soles were made from the tire treads and the straps to hold them on were made from the inner tubes. The tire tread footprints were all over the old village indicating recent enemy activity in the village. The village was located on the opposite side of the round hill we took refuge on the first time we were mortared.

The first platoon moved to our location for some added protection. I guess the CO finally realized nine of us were not winning our part of the war. Now with first platoon's help we were able to put out OPs during the day and make our position more secure. We ran patrols out from the village to check the hilltop and the surrounding areas. There was a well-used trail running uphill out of the village that led to the old trench on top of the hill. The trees that lined the trail were the willowy type about eight to ten feet tall with trunks two inches in diameter. I was concerned about the tall palm trees being a problem during a mortar attack. The trees would cause airbursts when the mortar rounds would hit the tops of them and send shrapnel cascading down on anyone below. I checked one of the bunkers in the village for booby traps I found nothing so I had a good place to go before 18:00 hours if there were a mortar attack. I think I told everyone a couple of times that I would be in that bunker by 18:00 hours.

Sometime during the late morning, Captain Palmer returned to Uplift. A Huey helicopter brought Lt. Mott out to our location and left with the CO on board. I do not think there was a special reason for the CO to go back to LZ Uplift; I think it was his decision to leave. He spent much more time in the rear than Captain Welsh did when the company was in the field. By early afternoon, it started to rain so Captain Palmer decided to stay at Uplift overnight, leaving Lt. Mott in charge of the company in the field. He also left instructions for what he wanted us to do come nightfall.

The rains were part of the incoming monsoon season, which normally started in September. The rain was soft and steady, soaking everyone who remained outside. I made a trek up to the OP location to check on them. I wanted to make sure they had rain gear with them and while I was there, I asked if there was anything I could do for them. They seemed to be fine and let me know they were OK. The OP location was in a shallow wash just to the right of the trail leading to the top of the hill. By lying in the wash, the OPs could see any movement on the trail through the base of the scrub trees. When I came back from the OP visit, I checked the bunker I had identified as my refuge during a mortar attack. I wanted to make sure the narrow opening had not been blocked off. When I first checked the bunker it was a bit of a struggle to get through the narrow entrance.

I went from the bunker to a long narrow hootch that was keeping six members of the first platoon dry and out of the rain. The hootch was built out of a bamboo frame covered by grass bundled together for the sides and roof. I squatted in the door of the hootch, talking with the guys inside, and reminding them that the time was approaching 18:00 hours. At 17:55 hours I said to the group huddled in the hootch, "I am going to my bunker." As I started to stand up a B-40 Rocket Propelled Grenade, or RPG, hit the back corner of the hootch. The blast burned my eyebrows and eyelashes and hurled me up in the air and down into the mud outside the hootch. I was on the ground face first but not for long. I got to my feet and ran to the bunker sailing through the opening without touching any of the sides. Most of the members of the first platoon were firing in the direction the RPG came from. The RPG left a smoke trail, which is a telltale sign of its origin. No other rounds came in to our location so I left the bunker to check on the guys in the hootch. Amazingly no one was injured in the blast. The guys were still collecting themselves and checking for wounds but the only injury was to the hootch.

I found out the guys that had fired at the smoke trail from the RPG used up all of their ammo. That included the M-60 machine gunner who shot all his ammo at the smoke trail. A mechanized squad of APCs and a Sherman tank was not too far from our location and they came rolling up ready to fire on any enemy location. As they rolled in to our position just outside the tree line we heard them ask, "Where did it come from?" Everyone's hands pointed toward the hill across the rice paddy. Before the tank stopped rolling the gunner put two or three rounds of high explosives in that direction with precision accuracy.

We needed a resupply of ammo right away. When we contacted the rear to request an emergency resupply, they told us the choppers had made their last run for the day and were returning to their base. All that meant to us was we were not getting any ammo.

The guys in the mechanized squad chipped in and gave us some M-16 ammo and two hundred rounds of M-60 ammo. They gave us coordinates where they were laagering for the night in case we had more problems and then as quickly as they arrived, they were gone.

Lt. Mott contacted Captain Palmer at Uplift to keep him apprised of the situation. I do not know if the captain changed his original plans for us or if he gave Lt. Mott new direction but we made ready to move up the trail toward the top of the hill. We set up a mechanical ambush in the middle of the village and added some canisters of CS gas or tear gas crystals. If the ambush was blown, the CS gas would be spread out in the explosion. The canisters we were using were so strong, the crystals would render the village useless for some time afterward.

I do not know if my distrust for Captain Palmer's decisions affected my suggesting to Lt. Mott that we not take the trail up the hill or if it was instinct, but I thought it was better if we did not go up hill at night. I know Lt. Mott considered my proposal of moving to the rice paddy and skirting the hill along the tree line to link up with the mechanized squad that had come to our aide when we took the RPG. I told the lieutenant that I was sure they would welcome our presence for security for one night. I felt as though he wanted to do what I was suggesting but he kept saying the CO wants us to go up the hill. I finally gave up my request and set the triggering device on the mechanical ambush.

First platoon was leading out when we left the village with SSgt. Ken Hammock walking the point. The column seemed to be moving very fast, too fast for a night move in the environment we were working. Lt. Mott passed the word up the column to slow down. When the word reached SSgt. Hammock, his slack man, James Waldron told him, "You are doing my job. I should be walking point." Waldron was on his second tour so he certainly understood what a point man should do. The two men discussed the pace a little more and then Waldron moved past SSgt. Hammock to take over the point. He took a couple of steps before shots rang out and he fell back in Hammock's arms. He was killed instantly and the rest of us began to move into defensive action taking cover where we thought we would be safe. There was not much cover to be found. Mostly we hugged the trees on the edge of the trail or went to ground seeking the security of a prone position. Because I was getting short, getting ready to go home soon, I was sent to guard the rear. I found out it was a terrible place to be. I did not know who was winning, them or us. I had to watch both directions because the enemy may come up behind us or come down the trail from the top of the hill if they got past our guys there. Occasionally someone would come to my location asking for ammo and I was freely handing it out. Since I had been off the radio I was carrying a double load of ammo and magazines. The gunfire was a constant roar and sometimes a round would go by me into the scrub trees. I heard of daring exploits by the first platoon leader, SFC Walker. He would wait until he could see the muzzle flashes from the VC/NVA's AK-47s, then he would jump into the bushes where they were firing from and open up with his M-16. Hammock was busy directing the others and tending to casualties. We lost another first platoon member, Dennis Gentry, when a Chi Com grenade exploded next to his head where he was lying returning enemy fire. Three others were wounded when Robinson, the machine gunner experienced a short round with the gun. He set the barrel in the mud instead of the toe of his boot to clear the obstruction.

When he lifted the gun to fire it, the barrel blew up, wounding him and two others.

When it came time to assault the hill I went up with everyone else as we fought our way to the top of the hill trying to reach the trench that was at the top. This was the old trench that had been dug for a petroleum company years before. When we reached the safety of the trench, Bowles called the rear for a dust-off. We had to evacuate the wounded and the KIAs in case we would have to move in a hurry from our defensive position. We did not want to leave anyone behind but we knew the KIAs and the wounded would put us at risk if we had to move them along with us. It was better to get them out now while we had the chance and there was no contact with the enemy.

While we were waiting for the dust-off helicopter, everyone counted their ammo. The results of the ammo check shocked all of us. No one had any ammunition but me. I had two full magazines, thirty six rounds and that was all. We hunkered down in the trench with a Claymore on either end for protection. The guards on the trail where it crossed the trench took a magazine each. We had a few grenades for the defenders lying in the trench. For the rest of the night we were on fifty percent guard, half of us awake at all times. Everyone knew if the VC/NVA came back we would be using our hand-to-hand combat skills. We had nothing else to repel them with but the few grenades we passed among us. The night went by very slowly. It was probably the longest night I spent while I was in Vietnam. It passed without any more incidents and we were all grateful for that.

Early the next morning we started cautiously down the hill back into the village. We had to be extra careful of the mechanical ambush, checking it for tampering before dismantling it. We quickly put together a resupply list with ammo being the number one priority. We had to be constantly vigilant because we did not know the disposition of the enemy and we were essentially taking refuge in a place where they had already launched two attacks against us.

The CO came in on the first resupply bird to the relief of Lt. Mott. He left on the same bird once the supplies were unloaded. I was uneasy all day, reliving the events of the night before and thinking about what might happen next. My nerves were shot. I could not relax and I know I was making others in our group uneasy. I finally went to the CO and told him I was going in on the last resupply bird. I was short and I told him I was not helping the morale by being out here with them. He cautioned me not to go but my mind was set. I needed a break; the contact we had experienced in the last month and a half had surpassed all I had experienced in the previous eleven months. I knew I was no longer effective as a leader nor could I be unless I took the pressure off myself. I had seen others leave the field with more time left in country than I had. When the final resupply bird left our location to return to Uplift, I was on board. I had spent my last day in the field and I was looking forward to going home.

CHAPTER 35

In Country R & R at Phu Cat Airbase

When I got back to Uplift, I reported in to the first sergeant at the orderly room. I explained my reasons for being there and I could tell by the look on his face he knew where I was coming from. He told me to go to our barracks and get some rest. Later that afternoon, First Sergeant Soto sent for me to come to the orderly room. He realized that every NCO in Alpha Company had recently gotten a three day in country R & R except for me. He told me to go clean up and put on a new uniform and he would get the paperwork ready for a three day in country pass. It did not surprise me that I was overlooked knowing how my luck ran, but I was happy that Top caught the error and corrected it. The pass was exactly what I needed to get my head straight.

Since I did not have time to plan something at one of the beach resorts like Bung Tao or China Beach, I figured I would make use of the 173rd barracks at Phu Cat. It was close to the swimming pool and had hot running water. The mattresses were thick and no bedding or blankets were required with the hot weather we were having. The NCO club on the air base had food and entertainment every day and the trip there was short enough to take advantage of a three-day pass. There was another reason for the Phu Cat trip. For the last two months, I had only been paid ten dollars a month for some unexplainable reason. The way Lt. Mott explained the pay shortage to me was that I got no pay but he was authorized as paymaster to give me ten dollars to tide me over. No one had any explanation for why I was not receiving any pay. I was lucky I saved seventy-five dollars from each pay period and there was no place to spend any of that money. I had a little over one hundred dollars to go on my in country R & R but I could have been going on a three-day pass with only twenty bucks!

I hitched a ride from Uplift to Phu Cat only twenty-five miles away the morning after I came in from the field. By now, the Airbase had a good program for checking weapons at the gate before entering the base. Since I went alone if they had not had a system, my whole time off would have been spent watching my weapon. I was happy about the change in their policy recognizing visitors had weapon issues.

When I was free of my rifle, I headed straight for the BX to buy some swim trunks and a towel, then I went to the 173rd barracks to make sure I still had a place to stay. It was just the way it was when we first discovered it, hot running water and all. I went from there to the swimming pool to relax and swim in water other than a river or stream. The Air Force swimming pool set up was much like one back in the states. When I arrived at the locker room, I received a basket for my clothes and a padlock. In the locker room, there were empty lockers the basket slid into and once the lock was on, my valuables were safe. All I had to do was remember the number on the locker. Of course, the sun was out and the weather was hot so the pool water felt great! I spent the whole first day at the pool. They even had a snack bar with hot dogs so I ate lunch there.

After the pool, I went back to the barracks, showered, and got ready to go to the NCO Club. They served steaks like in a restaurant, with waiters and the whole bit. The steaks were good and after the restaurant closed, there was a floorshow on the stage in the club. If there was no USO Show touring, they had a number of local bands that were just as good. The difference between them was a USO group usually included women and the locals were just a bunch of airmen that started a band. Either way I knew I would enjoy whoever was playing that night.

When I arrived at the NCO Club, I had dinner, and then moved to a table in front of the stage to watch the show. It was a bunch of local guys but they played good music. I heard someone calling my name and turned to see who it was. There was Doc Mooneyham sitting with a couple of guys from the airbase. They invited me to join them so I went to their table and Doc introduced me to his friends. Both of the airmen were firefighters working at the fire station on the flight line. I only remember one of the guy's first names, Joe. As Doc and I got to know the airmen better, they invited us to come to the station the next day, take a tour of the flight line, and look at their fire equipment. I did not have anything to do but swim at the pool so I was in. Doc was AWOL from Uplift and just out enjoying himself, so we both agreed to meet Joe at the firehouse the next morning.

Joe and the other airman were off duty. The Air Force worked their fire fighters the same as in the states. The crews worked two days on and two days off. A day was twenty-four hours with the crew sleeping at the firehouse. The tour started in the firehouse with Joe leading us around. We saw the sleeping quarters, showers, exercise room, the kitchen and dining room. They even had a traditional fire pole from the second floor to the garage. It was all very interesting and both Doc and I felt like VIPs on the tour. However, the best part was when we loaded into one of the squad trucks and went right out to the flight line. We saw jets close up in their protected bays and larger aircraft like the C-130 Hercules parked on the tarmac. Then Joe treated us to a special tour of a Shadow Gunship. Shadow was replacing Puff the Magic Dragon, a WWII vintage C-47 aircraft. Puff had one mini gun mounted in the left rear door and a flare launcher in the right rear door. Shadow was a C-119 Flying Boxcar painted with camouflage patterns and had mini guns mounted in each of the windows on the left side of the aircraft. In the left rear door was an infrared camera and the right rear door had the flare launcher. One of the crew on board when we toured Shadow told us the aircraft actually moved sideways in the air when all the mini guns were firing. He also showed us the scoop shovels used to scoop shell casings from the floor of the aircraft when the mini guns fired. There was a neat saying painted on the outside of the plane, "What evil lurks beneath the jungle canopy? The Shadow Knows." What a fantastic firsthand look at the aircraft used to support us when we were in contact with the enemy!

After the tour of the flight line, I stopped at the BX, Base Exchange, the Air Force version of the PX, or the military general store. All of us had agreed to meet at the movie theater on the EM side of the base to take in an afternoon matinee before going to the NCO Club for dinner and another live show. A blacktop road through a hollow called No Man's Land led to the EM side of the post. It was a long stretch of road with nothing on it but the bog in the bottom of the hollow. No one walked through No

Man's Land at night. It was the unwritten rule on the air base. It was such a long stretch; I hitched a ride to the EM side of the base during daylight.

The EM side was like a mini mall, with clubs that served beer and food. They also had games like pinball and slots to keep the young airmen occupied. The pride of the EM side was the theater. It was built similar to a small town theater in the states: doors on both sides of the box office allowed entry and exit into the lobby and big screen theater. The chairs were metal folding chairs bolted together with clamps on the legs so they could not be moved or misaligned. There was a big sign right under the movie screen that apologized for the seats. The regular cushioned theater seats were ordered but had not yet arrived. The Air Force was apologizing for the seats, but I was happy to be in an air-conditioned theater under a real roof in a real building watching a movie on a regular screen. We had wood benches outdoors at LZ Uplift with four sheets of plywood painted white for a screen.

We met up with Joe and went in to watch the movie playing in the theater. To us it did not matter what movie it was. We were happy to watch whatever was playing. At LZ Uplift, there was a different movie every night. On the airbase, they played the movie at night, then again the next afternoon as a matinee. After the movie was over, everyone was outside looking for rides. It was starting to get dark and no one wanted to make the walk through No Man's Land. Joe told us he spotted a guy he knew in one of the big trucks, a duce and a half. He flagged it, waving his arms and the truck stopped.

Joe told Doc and me, "Get in the back and I will fix it with my buddy."

Doc and I went to the rear of the truck and were in a small line waiting to climb in the back. Joe got in the cab with his buddy. The truck started to move slightly.

I told Doc, "Come on, Doc. We got to get on the truck." The truck started to move faster. Doc was just stepping on to the tailgate hinge guard on the rear of the truck. The hinge guard on duce and a half was one quarter inch plate steel formed in a rounded corner square shape and welded to the back bumper to protect the hinge on the tailgate. It measured six inches square by four to six inches high. It was a heavy-duty hinge guard and stuck out prominently on the back of the truck.

I was hanging on to the tailgate with one hand and had the bag from the BX in the other hand. I was running behind the truck and encouraging Doc to hurry and get in. I heard the driver shift another gear and I knew I had to get in or be dragged down the road. I was running faster now trying to make up my mind to jump for the hinge guard or let go. I was at a full run when I jumped for the hinge guard and barely made it. Doc was in the bed of the truck helping me over the tailgate while the other passengers seated on the sides were laughing. We must have appeared to be performing a comedy routine. When I stood up grinning at the group in the back of the truck, I was still holding the plastic bag of goodies I got from the BX earlier.

Since the seats were all taken, Doc and I went to the front of the back of the truck and stood next to the canvas-covered cab. The plastic window on the rear of the cab was scratched but we could see the three passengers up front. When we reached the end of the road that came out of No Man's Land, a right turn would have taken us to the NCO Club. Instead, the truck turned left taking us to the barracks area of the base. Doc and I started pounding on the top of the cab and yelling at Joe.

"Joe, what are you doing? We are going the wrong direction," we called to him. The truck driver stayed on his course and eventually stopped outside a large barracks. Doc and I jumped quickly from the back of the truck and ran to the passenger side door. We jerked the door open yelling, "Joe, what is going on?" Then we realized the guy was not who we thought he was. "Hey, you are not Joe!"

We did not know what happened to Joe, so we walked from the barracks through several others and stopped to ask directions to the NCO Club. It was already dark and we found ourselves wandering through several areas that were unfamiliar to us. When we arrived at the NCO Club, Joe was sitting at a table in the middle of the showroom. When he saw us, he stood up and waved us over to the table. Doc and I were anxious to find out what had happened back outside the theater.

Joe told us, "I thought I knew the guy in the truck but I did not, so I never got in the vehicle. I rode over here with another guy. What happened to you guys?" We told Joe the whole story and had a good laugh about it. We had drinks and watched the floorshow, another local band. Before I left for the evening, Doc hit me up for a loan. He was going to stay as long as he could and since he did not have a pass, that could be for a while. I gave him forty dollars and left for the 173rd barracks. The next morning I went back to the swimming pool for a final swim then headed for the base steam bath house. I got a good rubdown and a steam bath, then back to the barracks and a shower before I went to the gate to pick up my rifle and head back to LZ Uplift. It was easy to get a ride from the gate to Highway 1. From there it was a tossup if someone would stop even if they were going through Uplift to English or further north.

On my way out of the gate at Phu Cat, I got a special treat. An older good-looking woman was taking a sponge bath in one of the Vietnamese hootches off the side of the road. She had her top off and was washing her more than ample breasts about twenty feet from me. It was a nice view to end a good trip to the airbase.

I arrived back at LZ Uplift in the late afternoon of my third day on my pass. I was a little early but there was really nothing left to do. When I reported in at the orderly room the first sergeant told me the CO had charged me with insubordination on an article fifteen. An article fifteen was a disciplinary action taken at the company level and was part of the company records only. The article fifteen would not follow me outside the company if I were going to another duty assignment with the Army.

The Co was back in the rear again while the company remained in the field. The first thing the first sergeant wanted to know was if I could take the time right then while the CO was in his office in the rear of the orderly room to sign the paperwork for my article fifteen. I was not on any duty that night so I obliged him and said OK.

Then he asked me, "Do you know how to report to the CO for an article fifteen?"

I answered, "Yeah, I am pretty sure I do, Top." He went back to tell the CO I was reporting for my article fifteen. I was not sure if it was for the incident when I called him stupid or if it was for leaving the field after the 13 September battle. Since the article read insubordination, I assume it was for me calling him stupid.

The first sergeant returned to where I was standing and told me, "OK, the old man is in his office go and report to him. Make sure you do it correctly." That meant that I knocked on his door and waited until he asked me to enter. Then I would walk to within two feet of the front of his desk that was opposite the door. I would come to the position of attention, salute, and wait until he returned the salute, then follow his instructions to sign the article fifteen in twelve places throughout the document. Then he would explain any fines or loss of pay incurred, and I would again come to the position of attention, salute, do an about face and leave the room. He would give the paperwork to the first sergeant to file in my company records. That is the way it was supposed to happen. It really happened this way.

I went down the hall to the CO's office. He did not have a door; a bunch of beads adorned his doorway. I knocked on the doorframe but I could already see the CO was not behind his desk. He was lying down in a lounge chair just to the left of the door. He said, "Come in." I stepped into the room that was his office and quarters, came to the position of attention, and started to salute.

He stopped me saying, "We do not have to do that. The paperwork is on my desk, sign it and give it to the first sergeant on your way out. I am not going to reduce your grade, you are too good of an NCO, but I am fining you the maximum pay, sixty five dollars." With that, he got out of the chair and left the room, walking past the first sergeant and not saying anything to him.

I signed the articles in the twelve locations for my signature, returned the document to the order it was left for me, and carried it to the first sergeant. He was standing behind his desk looking at the CO walking across the compound. He looked back at me asking, "What is with him?"

I answered, "I don't know, Top."

He looked at the article fifteen I handed him and asked, "Did you sign it in all the appropriate places?"

"I think so, Top." I answered.

He flipped through the pages of the document checking for my signatures. Then he leaned to his right, held the article fifteen by the corner and dropped it into his wastebasket. When he looked up at me, his mouth turned down and he shrugged his shoulders. That was the last I saw or heard of my article fifteen. Once again, he proved that there is no getting over on the senior NCOs.

CHAPTER 36

The Last Detail/Exit Uplift

I had a grueling schedule once back at Uplift after my in country R & R. I was in charge of the bunker assigned to Alpha Company and pulled guard duty every night. I was allowed to send one person on the bunker to the movie every night but because I was in charge of the bunker, I was not permitted to attend any movies. Being in charge does have its drawbacks sometimes. There were only a select few of us in the rear, so we all had the duty every night. That made choosing who would go to the movies easy. We drew straws, shortest one first and so on. If our guard duty lasted longer than three days, we repeated the order of attendance. Those were the rules. It did not take me long to think them up or for the others to mess them up.

The first night was messed up when Witte, a private in Alpha Company who had been busted for using speed, decided he was going to attend the movie before he reported to the bunker for guard. I spoke to him about how he just cut his friends out of a night at the movies and we eliminated the longest straw when the other two guys drew for the next two nights. Witte argued that he should still be included because he was not aware of the agreement to draw straws when he made the decision to go to the movie first. I told him, "Witte, we all have to live with our decisions. You chose to go to the movies tonight so you are the first one in the rotation. Live with it." I guess I made my point; he never brought it up again.

We got relieved off guard duty after five days and I was finally going to get to see a movie, maybe two if I was lucky before I left for home. The first night off guard, I showed up and got a good seat at our outdoor theater.

They moved the theater from its old location by our old barracks, now torn down. The new theater was behind the orderly rooms in an unused open area. We still had the screen made of four sheets of plywood painted white. When it was dark enough, the projectionist showed up and started to load the film into the projector. Suddenly someone shouted, "Look!" and pointed behind and to the right of the projector. Everyone standing or sitting looked to see two 122 mm rockets traveling parallel about seven feet apart and fifty feet in the air flying over us. They were obviously intended to hit the theater area but they flew over and landed in the area between the ARVN base and Uplift with two almost simultaneous loud explosions. Well, again with my luck, that episode canceled the movie for the night and Uplift went on fifty percent security, meaning the bunkers with four men each, would have two awake at all times. I guess I was glad I was not on the bunker that night.

The next day I spent working a group of Vietnamese filling sandbags. SSgt. Trimm, Alpha Company's NCOIC of the rear, Non Commissioned Officer in Charge, gave me a bunch of work permit vouchers to take to the gate and pick up some volunteers that would come to the gate every day for work because we paid them for the work. It was easy to pick them because as soon as they saw I had pay vouchers they were climbing all over me. I just had to make sure I picked the same number as I had vouchers. If I picked one less, a voucher was wasted. If I picked one more, I would have to pay him myself. We had a quota for the number of sand bags that had to be filled. I had to stay with the Vietnamese and keep track of them every minute until those numbers of bags were filled. Then I would escort them back to the gate and I was done for the day. I pushed hard to get them to fill the bags so I could get off the detail as soon as possible. When I was done, I took a brand new uniform to the tailor and laundry to have it washed and all my patches sewn on the jacket. I needed the uniform to leave the company and travel to Cam Ranh Bay to go home. Sometime during that day I found out the company was out of the field and relaxing on Sky Soldier Beach. That evening I planned to attend the movie at the theater behind the orderly room.

I was attending the movie, the one that was canceled the previous night. The movie was about a third of the way complete when the projectionist stopped the film. When the film stops for any reason, including a projector problem, everyone got upset. Of course, after the film stopped, my name was called by the projectionist, "Is Sergeant Musson in the crowd?"

I froze in place, not wanting to answer in anticipation of the consequences, "Yes, I am here," I replied. Then there was a hail of crushed beer cans, pop cans, and crumpled boxes and papers flying through the air at me. In 1970, the beer and soda cans were still made from tin, not aluminum and could hurt if hit in the right place. I ducked and dodged as best I could but managed to take a couple direct hits that stung.

The projectionist exclaimed, "Sgt. Musson, you are to report to your orderly room right away." I decided not to answer to prevent another fusillade of incoming cans, but there was an increase in the volume of projectiles as I left for the orderly room anyway.

The first sergeant met me at the back door of the orderly room and explained the MPs were bringing in a prisoner from Alpha Company. They were summoned to the beach to pick up a guy that fired up SFC. Ramsey as he returned from the neighboring village to the beach after closing the local whorehouse. The first sergeant wanted me to meet the MPs at the helicopter pad and stay with our guy from Alpha all night. It was the policy of the MPs that the company the individual was from had to furnish a twenty-four hour guard for those individuals. I drew the short straw again.

When he got off the bird at the helicopter pad, I could see a guy I knew only as "Pip". The MPs had him hand cuffed and as I walked with them I asked if they would remove his handcuffs. Pip was a very likable guy and as far as I knew, he had never been in any kind of trouble before, especially the kind to keep him in handcuffs. The MPs refused to remove his cuffs and told me it was policy while a prisoner was in custody. I argued that he was in my custody now, and neither Alpha Company nor I had such a policy. I think they considered me a smart ass and they continued their use of handcuffs on Pip. We arrived at the MP station on Uplift. The MPs took one handcuff off Pip and put his arms on either side of a large wooden post. Then they put his free wrist back in the handcuffs and locked it. He was essentially tied to a post in the middle of the room. If he wanted to sleep, he had to lie on the floor, which was difficult to do with his hands in the cuffs. I tried with no success to get the MPs to release him so I could take him to our barracks where we could both get a good night's sleep. Their only excuse was they could not be responsible if they allowed him to be freed. Since I did not have a key to the handcuffs, I even used the excuse that if we were mortared or rocketed, how was I supposed to get him to a shelter outside the MP building. All they would tell me is, "He should have thought about that before he got in trouble." The next morning I was relieved of my guard because the MPs were taking Pip somewhere. That was the last time I saw him and I never heard the outcome of his case.

The next day I had to travel to LZ English to register weapons I was planning to take home. I had two, the fifteen inch Bowie knife I had purchased long ago when I was with the second platoon and a captured Chinese Communist hand grenade from the night we rescued the Recon team in 506 Valley. The grenade was homemade and the Chinese C-4 explosive and blasting cap were removed. The clerk registering the weapons did not have a problem with the knife, but when I laid the Chi-com on the table he freaked out! He slid his chair backwards all the way to the wall and yelled, "Get that out of here! You cannot register that!"

I took the grenade apart to show him how it was disarmed but he insisted that I could not register it. I put it back in the bag I was carrying and went back to Uplift without a registration for it. I planned to take it home with or without a certificate.

The last full day I was at LZ Uplift I was assigned one last detail. I worked it with one of the guys, a PFC from A Company 2nd Platoon. His first name was Lanny. The NCOIC, SSgt. Trimm told us we had to paint the three latrines throughout the company area. I asked him if that was the only detail we had to do. He looked at me funny and said, "Yes, that is all you have to do." I wanted to make sure, so I asked the same question again which resulted in the same answer. The sergeant told us there was enough work to keep us busy all day. I knew there was a lot of work, but SSgt. Trimm did not know me.

I told Lanny if he would go along with me we would be done in about an hour or so. He questioned me, "How you going to do that? The sergeant said it would take all day."

I told him, "Trust me, I can find a way." I had an idea to shorten the detail, but I had to have cooperation from the other guy to pull it off. We went to the supply sergeant and asked him for the largest brush he had. He gave me a 4" paintbrush. "Not big enough," I told him.

"Then go to S4 and see if they have what you want," he replied. I did just that and got a wallpaper brush, about 8" wide and exactly what I was looking for. I also got a paint roller, handle, and pan. Lanny and I went back to get the paint, anxious to get started.

All of the latrines were built the same way; some were larger than others because they had more holes. The biggest latrine we had to paint was a six hole latrine on the main street going to the mess hall. The other two were four hole latrines. The buildings were tall and narrow. The top half was screen wire right under the sloped flat roof. The bottom half in the front and sides were six-inch lapboards with corner, top and bottom trim boards. The back lower half was a group of plywood doors used to remove the half barrels sitting under the holes. One of the punishment details was burning shit in those half barrels. Luckily I never had that detail my entire tour.

As we walked up to first latrine, I laid out the plan to Lanny. I told him all he needed to do was paint the bottom of the lapboards. I showed him what I was talking about and demonstrated how to paint the entire bottom so there was no mistake. I poured the gray paint into the roller pan and told him I would take care of the rest. At first I do not think he believed me or maybe it was mistrust because I was a sergeant. He seemed hesitant, but when he saw how much painting I was doing he picked up his pace. The roller worked well on the plywood doors. The wallpaper brush handled the lapboards fine and Lanny took care of the half-inch bottom of the lapboards with the four-inch brush. We completed all three latrines in one hour and fifteen minutes, a little over my estimate but in plenty of time to enjoy a whole day off without details.

SSgt. Trimm saw us cleaning up the brushes and roller pan. He came over and asked, "What are you guys doing? I know you cannot be done painting yet."

"We finished everything you asked us to do," I replied.

"I cannot believe that. You don't mind if I check it out do you?" he asked.

"Be our guest," I answered.

He walked to the first latrine to check it out. The thing he was most interested in seeing was the bottom of the lapboards. I told Lanny before we started he would have to make sure he covered everything with the four inch brush because Trimm would check it. Lanny did a good job and we passed inspection on all three latrines. SSgt. Trimm hated to give us the rest of the day off but he was true to his word. Lanny kept thanking me but I told him he did a lot too. Instead of fighting me or questioning me, he trusted me and working together we got an early trip to the steakhouse.

I had time to pick up my new uniform from the laundry and make sure everything was sewn on right and my name was spelled correctly. I also worked on the polish on my boots. I talked to my buddy Hendricks from Headquarters Company. He and I entered the Army on the same day and were leaving LZ Uplift together. He also stored my duffle bag under his bunk in his room or I would not have any personal items. When the supply sergeant told us we could no longer store anything in the supply room, I had to find a place to store it or throw it away. Hendricks took it knowing he could get in trouble himself for having two duffel bags. He told me I could leave it overnight with him and he would bring it with him when he left his room. Hendricks also arranged to have the colonel's jeep and driver take us to the gate early the next day.

I did not think about going to the movie that night, I was too excited. I went over toward the theater but ended up in the screened porch on the back of Alpha Company's orderly room talking to the two new lieutenants in the company. They were asking questions about how to survive in the field and whom in their platoons could they trust. I tried to tell them honestly what my opinions were. I suggested they pay attention to the guys that had been here the longest when it came down to advice. I avoided questions about the CO's competence because everyone's opinion varies and they would have months to figure out what they thought of the CO.

I bundled the last of the letters from my girlfriend and put them in a large envelope to send home. Before I sealed it up, I read the very last letter I got from her for the last time. It came about a week before and she was filling me in on what she was doing at school. I don't remember too much of the main body of the letter, but I remember she signed it, Love, JoAnne and wrote, P.S. Hurry home. I'm waiting. After I finished reading it for the last time, I put the letter in the big envelope. Then I put the big envelope in the mail clerk's basket with a note back to her, confident the letters would beat me home. I let her know how anxious I was to see her again and begin to get on with the rest of our life together.

The night turned into day. I do not remember sleeping that night or if I did, where I slept. On my way to the orderly room, I passed a group of guys sitting on the back porch of the supply room. I asked them if they wanted me to call anyone for them when I got home. I got no takers on that but when I asked if I could do anything for them, Benny Singleton said, "When you pass the first civilian bar, go in and order three fingers of scotch and say this is for Benny"

"I will be happy to do that. Consider it done, Benny," I told him. Then I took a picture of the group and bid them farewell.

I was signing out at the orderly room and I saw Hendricks walking toward his orderly room next door carrying both of our duffel bags. The first sergeant gave me a new colored 173rd Airborne patch for my uniform and a fifth year yearbook commemorating some of the things we did in the thirteen months I was in country. 1970 was the fifth year the 173rd had been in Vietnam. As I saluted the first sergeant to leave, I heard the jeep that was taking me to the gate pull up outside. Before I loaded my duffle bag, I put the things the first sergeant gave me inside the duffel bag and set it in the back of the jeep next to Hendricks' bag. The driver, George Farris, was headquarters company driver. He rigged two purple smoke grenades, one on each of the two long radio antennas in the colonel's jeep. Hendricks and I loaded in the jeep. Farris pulled the pins on the smoke grenades and we headed for the gate leading to Highway One outside LZ Uplift. We were on our way, the Last day at LZ Uplift. The first day of our journey back to the United States. Man, it felt good!

CHAPTER 37

Hendricks Saves the Day

After we left Uplift, travel was on us to get down to Cam Ranh Bay on time to get a flight back to the states. There were a lot of stops we had to make and things we had to do to get out of Vietnam. First place we had to go was back to Cha Rang Valley to get our personal gear we stored there when we first came in country. When I cut the bands on my footlocker and opened it, I could not remember putting any of the items I found in there. It was almost a wasted trip when I thought about the value of everything in the footlocker. There was nothing in the footlocker I needed for the Army or for civilian life.

From the jungle school at Cha Rang Valley, we went to Phu Cat Airbase for a little rest before we headed for Phu My where our orders were for going home. Phu My was the financial and document base for all of the 173rd Airborne. It was a critical stop but we needed the entire day to complete all of the checking out phases at Phu My.

I was able to show Hendricks around the airbase some, letting him in on the 173rd barracks where I was planning for us to stay. Hendricks reaction when he saw the 173rd barracks was about like mine the first time; he could not believe that such a lavish place existed. He really liked the hot running water and the thick mattresses on the bunks.

We started planning the rest of our day and evening. I suggested a movie at the theater on the EM side of the base after we made a trip to the BX. From there we could take in the band or USO show at the NCO Club. Hendricks was surprised I knew so much about Phu Cat Airbase, but I told him I had done all of what we were going to do less than a week ago.

We hitched a ride to the BX where Hendricks picked up a few items he thought he might need. I just settled for some licorice candy and we went outside to catch a ride through No Man's Land to the EM theater. It was not long before we were in the back of a truck headed for the theater. Once we were there, Hendricks was amazed again by the theater building and the air-conditioned theater. I was really spoiling him with all the plush amenities on the airbase. He even got a charge out of the sign apologizing for the metal folding chair seats inside.

When the movie was finished, we went outside where the usual crowd was maneuvering for rides to the NCO Club. Hendricks and I got close to the road and were able to flag an officer driving an extended cab pickup. When he stopped, there was a rush for the pickup from the others waiting for a ride. Hendricks and I went for the tailgate. I let Hendricks go in front of me. He had some difficulty climbing in to the bed of the truck because of all of the people trying to do the same. I was having flashbacks to the last time I was in this situation. The pickup started moving and I kept encouraging Hendricks to get in, "Come on, Tom. Get in the truck. I don't want to be left behind."

The truck started to move faster and I heard the driver shift the standard transmission into second gear. I was beginning to run almost at full speed yelling, "Come on Hendricks. Get in." Just then the rear bumper became available and I took a stab at it with my right foot. One of the other guys in the bed of the truck was helping Hendricks drag me in over the tailgate.

When I turned around, I said, "Wow, Hendricks, I didn't think I was going to make it." I looked up and saw it wasn't Hendricks who was helping me. I looked around quickly and he was nowhere in the back of the truck. "Hendricks, where the hell are you?" I called.

"See you at the NCO Club, Muss," he answered waving from the center of the blacktop road in the middle of No Man's Land.

I had no idea what happened other than I was running behind a truck again and jumping for the bumper to get a ride just like with Doc the week before. No one could have convinced me it would happen twice but it did! The only difference was the size of the trucks and this time the driver dropped us off at the NCO Club. I went inside the club anxiously waiting for Hendricks to arrive. I had to find out what happened with him. When he showed up, I already had a table at the restaurant. He explained that when he was helping me, he dropped his bag from the BX and jumped out to retrieve it. We laughed about our misfortunes and ate a good steak dinner before moving into the showroom to watch two of the local bands perform. I remember one of the bands played and sang Dave Dudley's "Six Days on the Road" that seemed fitting even though we would be home before six days were up. Regretfully, we left the NCO Club early for the 173rd barracks because we had to get an early start for Phu My the next day.

We were at the gate at Phu Cat before first light to catch any truck leaving in order to get to the corner at Highway One, only a few miles away. It was not likely that a truck from the airbase would be going to Phu My directly so we had to be at the intersection of Highway One as early as possible to insure we had enough time to complete checking out at Phu My. The first truck out of Phu Cat dropped us off at the intersection on Highway One. We were lucky and did not have to wait long for a ride to Phu My. I remember the early morning sun shining brightly as we walked up to the first building at Phu My to start the process of going home.

The first building had our orders to leave the country and our finance records. I let Hendricks lead the way; he was a clerk and knew more than I about the records and orders. The buildings had different stations set up for the different processes. Hendricks got his orders at the first station and was breezing right through the other stations. I was having a bit of difficulty; the clerk at the first station told me he had no orders for me. He looked through some file drawers at the end of the room. I thought he was looking for my orders. When he walked back to the desk where I was standing he said, "I got some bad news for you, Sarge. I found your name in the finance files. They put a hold on your pay because you are listed as KIA." That explained why I had not been paid for the last two months.

"What does that mean? You can see I am not dead, can't you?" I asked.

"We can't do anything for you. Without orders we can't process you out, Sarge," he told me." Would you mind taking a seat outside so we can process the next person in line?"

315

LARRY J. MUSSON

I went outside, took a seat on a bench and waited for Hendricks. When he came out, he was shocked to see me already outside. "How did you get past me?" he asked.

"I didn't. They don't have any orders for me and I am listed as KIA," I told him.

"That's impossible," he said. "I'll tell you what you do. You see the guy sitting on the steps over there. That is the IG, Inspector General. You go tell him your problem and he'll get it straightened out."

"You think so, huh?" I asked.

"I know so. That is his job. The Inspector General handles all the problems in the Army."

I walked over to where the E-8, Master Sergeant was sitting on the steps of a building marked, Inspector General with a name of Captain Paul under the title. As I approached, he stood up. He was a mountain of a man about six foot eight inches tall. His arms at the biceps were as big around as my legs. He had a Special Forces patch on his left shoulder and I could not help but wonder how he got a job in an office. I saw his name embroidered on his fatigue blouse. It was Green. When I was close enough he asked, "What can I do for you, Sarge?"

"I am having trouble getting my orders to go home. They told me over at records, I was listed as KIA so they could not help me," I explained.

"Well, obviously I am not talking to a ghost, so let me see what I can do."

He went inside and made a phone call. During the call, he asked for my name and DEROS date. I heard him tell the person he was talking to that he wanted orders prepared so I would be able to leave on the bus for Phu Cat that afternoon. He hung up the phone and pointed to another building saying, "When you get over to the clerks' office, ask for Specialist Jacobs. He is preparing your orders."

"Thanks a lot, Sarge," I said to him as I left his office for the clerks' building across the street.

When I walked inside, I did not have to ask where Specialist Jacobs was, I recognized him from jump school. We were on the same floor of the barracks in 44th Company at Fort Benning. After a short reunion, he told me he had a lot of typing to do on my orders and for me to come back in forty-five minutes. I left to see how Hendricks was making out. He was

316

now in the next building over from where we started. When he saw me, he asked if everything was OK. I told him I was waiting on my orders to be typed.

"See, I told you the IG would take care of you," Hendricks told me.

"So far, so good," I told him as I left to pick up my newly typed orders.

Jacobs had the orders sitting on the corner of his desk when I walked in. He worked in an area that resembled a secretarial pool at any office. There were a lot of clerks sitting at desks all doing the same thing. Jacobs explained to me that I had to take the orders he typed to the print shop at the end of the street and have twelve copies made. The Army never did anything in print without making copies.

I left the clerk's office pool and headed for what they told me was the print shop. It was the last building on the same side of the street. I walked in with my orders and was greeted by a Private First Class. He was standing behind a long counter with a metal basket at the end of it. There was another guy scurrying around the office like he lost something and was in a hurry to find it. I told the PFC, I needed the orders I had with me printed so I could leave on the bus. I was heading home today. He looked at the metal basket that was already piled high with papers and said, "In order to get these printed today I will have to put them on the top of the pile. That way yours are the next orders we print."

As I started to thank the PFC for his help, the other guy behind the counter came over saying, "What was that I heard? We print the orders in the order we receive them. Yours go on the bottom of the pile. You can pick them up tomorrow afternoon." He was a staff sergeant so I had to word my response carefully.

"I am sorry, Sarge, you must have missed the part about me needing these so I could leave this afternoon," I told him.

"No, Sergeant. I did not miss anything but I will tell you, I run this office, not you. You get your orders when I say so and that is tomorrow afternoon. Are we clear on that, Sergeant?"

"I hear what you are saying, but I need some help here, Sarge, so I can go home. I need these orders today. Can you help me out?" I explained.

"I do not care what you need, Sergeant. Come back tomorrow. Now get out of my office," he bellowed.

I left and went to wait for Hendricks to let him know I was not going to make it. He came out of the building he was processing in and saw the dejected look on my face. "What's wrong now? Did you get your orders?" he asked.

"Yeah, I got the orders, but I have to have twelve copies made and the staff sergeant that runs the print shop told me there was no way I was getting them today," I explained.

"Go back and see the IG, Muss," Hendricks told me. "He can help with that, too."

I walked back over to the IG office to see if the Master Sergeant could help me. When he saw me, I could tell he knew there was another problem.

He asked, "What's the problem now, Sarge?"

I began to explain the situation with the staff sergeant at the print shop. Master Sergeant Green listened intently. Then he remarked, "I know that staff sergeant. He is new in country. Only been here a couple of weeks. Let me give him a call." As he dialed the phone, he told me, "Have a seat, this won't take long."

I sat in the chair across from MSG. Green and listened to the one sided conversation. "This is MSG. Green. Let me talk with SSgt. Hudson. Sergeant Hudson, MSG. Green from the IG's office. I have a Sergeant Musson in my office. He told me he dropped a set of orders off for you to print up for him." There was some response from the Staff Sergeant in the print shop and then, "I am acting on Captain Paul's behalf while he is away from the office. That does not matter. What matters is I want this sergeant's orders printed and in my office by 15:30 hours today, so he is able to go home." There was more rhetoric from the staff sergeant. Then the MSG continued, "It is not a favor for him, it is an order from me, Sergeant, and if you want to keep your stripes, I suggest you have his orders on my desk by 15:30 hours. I will expect your full co-operation. Thank you." He hung up the phone then looked at me, "Come back at 15:30 hours and I will have your orders."

"Thanks again, Sarge," I told him as I turned and left his office.

Now another problem presented itself. I was supposed to be on a bus out of Phu My at 16:30 hours and I had not started to process out. I went back to the building where I started earlier in the morning. There was no one waiting in line so I entered the building and approached the clerk that told me he could not help me without orders. I asked him if there was anything he could do to help me now. I explained to him that if I did not start processing out now I would never make the bus on time. He sympathized with me, and asked if my orders were being processed. I told him they were in the print shop but would not be ready until 15:30 hours. He told me, "We will get you started, but I need those orders as soon as you get them." As I went through the motions of checking out, I found out some frightening news. The clerk helping me told me the bus I was trying to get on left Phu My at 16:30 hours with no exceptions. The drivers would not wait for anyone. That fact weighed heavily on my mind. I only had one hour to deliver my orders and then make it to the final process point at the bus stop. That all had to be completed before 16:30 hours.

I bumped into Hendricks and found out he was done processing. He told me he was sitting on a bench at the bus stop. He offered to take my duffel bag so I could move around faster and I gave it to him. I did not know it then but letting him have my duffel bag really paid off later.

It was approaching 15:30 and I had to get to MSG. Green's office to get my orders. I went to the door of his office and knocked. It was 15:25 hours. I was five minutes early. MSG Green was sitting behind his desk in his tee shirt. He told me, "Come in, Sarge." As he stood up he slipped on his fatigue shirt. "I do not have your orders yet, but I am expecting that staff sergeant any minute. Here he comes now."

I turned around to look out the door and there he was. He was running as fast as he could go without losing the papers he carried under his arms. He came into the office huffing and puffing and apologizing for being late. He set the papers on MSG Green's desk and could not get outside fast enough. It was funny but I did not laugh. I picked up my orders and thanked MSG Green once again and headed for the first checkout station building. I was on a tight schedule but I had to make this work and get on that bus before 16:30.

Since I was literally hand carrying my orders I had to hand carry them to the last stop in the checkout system: the building at the bus stop, the last station. I ran from the building that was the first station in the checkout system where the clerk had helped me. I estimated it was a little over a quarter mile straight-line distance. I gave the guy manning the last station my orders and watched as he looked through them. The bus was already there and some of the GIs going home were already loaded. Hendricks was still on the bench with both duffel bags beside him.

The guy at the last station called me over to the service window in the small building. He told me, "You are missing one form that I must have to let you process out." At that point I was not surprised that I was missing one form to send me home. He gave me the number on the form but I do not remember what it was. He also told me that I would have to get the clerk's office that prepared the orders for me to fill out the form. I turned to Hendricks and told him of my plight and that I was returning to the clerks' offices to get the form. It was 16:00 hours, I had a half hour to get the completed form and return to the bus stop.

I ran for the buildings where the clerks prepared my orders. I went to Jacobs' desk and asked about the form. He said he was familiar with the form but another guy in the office always prepared that form. Jacobs told me he was on a meal break but he always took his break in his barracks. He walked me to the door of his office building and pointed out the barracks. Jacobs told me, "His name is Stewart, Specialist Stewart."

I ran to the barracks, entered the first floor and yelled, "Specialist Stewart!"

An answer came back from someone on the first floor, "He's upstairs."

I climbed the stairs to the second floor and again yelled, "Specialist Stewart!"

I saw a guy about three quarters of the way back in the room sit up on his bunk and answer, "Yeah, what can I do for you?"

I explained what I needed and asked if he would help me, "I know you are on break but I need this so I can go home today and the bus leaves in fifteen minutes."

"OK, let's go then,." he said. He stood up, put on his shirt and we ran down the stairs. We headed for his office in the clerk's building. When we got there, he told me, "Stay close because I am going to need some information from you." As he typed the form he asked some questions, pulled the completed form out of the typewriter and said, "Good luck."

Exactly what I needed was luck. I did not ask if I needed copies of the form, I just ran for the bus stop. It was 16:30 hours as I ran at full speed toward the little building at the bus stop. I could see Hendricks with his boot up on the first step of the bus. He was bent over tying his boot. Our duffel bags were on the ground next to him. He saw me running toward him and yelled to me, "Come on, Muss! I don't know how much longer I can hold him up." I heard the bus driver yelling obscenities at Hendricks and trying to close the door of the bus on him. Hendricks kept pushing the door back when it touched his leg as he leaned into the door.

I delivered the form to the guy at the last station and got my orders to DEROS back from him and headed straight for my duffel bag. Hendricks and I got on the bus with the driver still yelling obscenities and the others on the bus were laughing uncontrollably. The time was 16:40 hours. The bus was ten minutes late for the first time in history but I did not care, I was exhausted and lucky to have a friend like Hendricks.

The bus headed for Phu Cat Airbase where we would get on a flight manifest for Cam Ranh Bay. From there we would be on a chartered flight back to the United States.

We arrived at Phu Cat and we had to check in at the base hotel so the Army could keep track of us. If we stayed at the hotel any other time there was a two-dollar room fee. This time the Army paid and it cost us noting but we could not leave the hotel.

Bright and early the next morning we loaded a small bus in the front of the hotel and headed for the flight line where we boarded a C-130 Hercules plane for the flight to Cam Ranh Bay. We were on the next to the last trip home.

CHAPTER 38

Getting Out of the Army/Going Home

We landed at Cam Ranh Bay where a bus picked us up and took us to an area with many barracks and an open area for formations. There were boardwalks on the sides and between the barracks because the surface was loose sand all over in the barracks area. The formation area was the only concrete area. We found out the names on the flight manifest for planes going back to the United States were called at the formations. The difference between coming over and going home was there were no details to work going back to the States. If your name was not called in the formation one time, it may be the next.

I was contacted by a senior NCO after the first formation I attended. He approached me because he was looking for E-5 type individuals to escort someone with a general or undesirable discharge back to the States. Everyone carried their own orders going home except anyone with a general or undesirable discharge. An E-5 or above had to carry theirs for them. The senior NCO explained the process to me, and then added that I would be given a priority status going home and be put on the next flight out. He also told me there were more escort positions available, so if I knew someone else they could get the same deal as me. This was a great opportunity to pay back Hendricks for all his help. I introduced him to the senior NCO. The NCO hesitated and then told me the escorts were required to be hard stripers. Hendricks was an E-5 but he was a Specialist Fifth Class and did not qualify for an escort. I told the NCO I would agree to do it if Hendricks could be included on the next flight with me. He agreed so we were added to the manifest on the next flight.

I had to be introduced to the person I was escorting home so I was given a time and a place for that. In the meantime, I had to go to supply and requisition my uniform. Everyone leaving Vietnam left in the dress uniform specified. We were leaving during the transition from kakis to greens so they issued us kakis, the light tan summer uniform. Along with the uniform with my sergeant stripes sewn on, I received the decorations listed on my discharge papers and my nametag. The Army was trying to make us presentable for the eighteen to twenty hour flight home. After we were issued the uniforms, we did not have much time to make our flight. I went back to the barracks, stripped off my jungle fatigues, took a quick shower, and got into my new dress uniform.

I went to the office to pick up my escort and then to the bus that would carry us to the flight line to get on the plane for home. Hendricks was with me through the whole preparation for the flight. It seemed funny that nothing had happened to make our effort more difficult. Everything was running smoothly so far.

As we were boarding the plane, I talked with the guy I was escorting and told him he could sit anywhere he liked. "I am not going to watch you every second, but when we stop and get off the plane, I expect you to be back before it is time to take off again. I do not want to have to look for you. Do we have an agreement on that?" He agreed and I took him for his word. I looked to see where he was sitting on the plane; it was with some of the others that were being escorted. That did not surprise me, because I talked with one of the other NCO escorts and told him my plan for getting my escort home. He seemed to like the idea and evidently used the same method as me.

Everything was working as planned on the way home. We made a few stops for reasons that were unannounced to all the troops. Most of the stops were on military installations operated by the United States. I remember we stopped on Okinawa. I bought my dad a watch at the PX there. One of the other islands where we landed, the wings on the plane were over water on both sides at the end of the runway. The pilot told us that during some storms, the runway would be under four to ten feet of water. Another time the pilot pointed out ships in a harbor that were sunk during WWII. One of the last stops we made was in Hawaii. We landed there and deplaned onto the runway. I checked and saw my escort get off the plane with the other two guys he was sitting with. Again, I do not know if it was a refueling stop or why we did stop but we were there a lengthy period of time. We reloaded the plane to leave but when I checked the three seats occupied by my escort and the two others, they were empty. I asked the other NCO that had talked with me earlier if he had seen them. He had not seen them since we got off the plane.

I went to one of the flight attendants and said, "I have a problem. I am escorting an individual back to the States. I have his orders here but he is missing along with two others. We have to hold the plane until we find them."

The flight attendants informed the pilots of the situation and we started searching the airport. We did not deplane and only a handful of us began the search. Names of the three individuals were broadcast over the airport's PA system. It was a very tedious procedure for all involved. We started the search in the main terminal, looking in every restroom including the women's facilities. If they were trying to evade discovery, they could have been anywhere. We systematically went from one end of the terminal to the other. I finally found them sitting together on a bench outside the airport in the furthest point from our aircraft. I made it clear to them I was not happy. We had delayed our flight back to the States or world as we called it, for two hours. The pilots were not happy either.

The only excuse the three gave was they did not hear the call for the flight. I told them I would believe them but after a while, I would have thought they would go to a gate and ask questions. Their only concern was if their action was going to change anything for the rest of the flight. Since we were bound straight for McCord Air Force Base in Washington, I told them nothing would change as far as I was concerned but I could not speak for the other two escorts. When we saw them, they concurred with me. McCord was the end of the flight home.

There was nothing left to do at this point but sit back and enjoy the flight. My mind started to think about getting home and seeing my girlfriend for the first time in thirteen months. I was listening to the music being piped through the airplane's system. One song I thought was appropriate was "Hitchin' a Ride" by Vanity Fare. Another I was particularly fond of was "Suspicious Minds" by Elvis Presley, but I listened to all the songs they played over the system.

I had a particular mission in mind as we approached the airfield at McCord. I wanted to know exactly what time I landed in the United States. Some had told me we were in Hawaii but I wanted to know when we were back in the continental United States. It was very important for me to know the exact time for some reason. As the plane started down for the final landing, I watched the hands on my watch. When the wheels touched the runway, it was five minutes before seven PM on October 3, 1970. I was home. I had not planned well enough to have my girlfriend's phone number and I did not have it memorized so I called my mom and dad, to let them know I was safe. I would call them later to tell them when I would be coming home to Chicago so they could pick me up. I was expecting a surprise from my girlfriend. I figured she would be there to pick me up but not tell me. She did that to me once in high school when I came home from Springfield, Illinois on the train after attending two weeks of an American Legion function called Boy's State. She came up behind me and I was very surprised.

Because I was escorting an individual, I bypassed the lines of normal checks when a soldier returned to the US. An officer greeted me and took charge of the documents I was carrying for the individual I was escorting. The officer then told me I was free to move to the customs area for a final check of my duffel bag before being released to continue to Fort Lewis, Washington. During that time period, I lost track of Hendricks for a while since he had to stand in line with the other group of transits on the plane.

I walked up to the customs area where there were several large tables with a customs agent standing by each table. None of the agents were smiling or welcoming us home. They just stood by the table with a blank stare on their face. That made it hard to select an agent that might go easy on me, although I was not trying to sneak anything through Customs. I had never been through Customs before so I did not know what to expect. The agent I selected was an older gentleman with snow-white hair. He had me place my duffel bag on the table and remove the padlock so he could go through it. He also checked the papers for registered weapons and wanted to see the Bowie knife. He removed the top six or eight inches of clothing from the duffel bag, then asked, "Is there anything in here that will poke, stick or cut me?"

I answered, "No, sir."

He stuck his arm in the bag up to his shoulder and moved his hand around inside then he asked, "Do you have any photos of dead bodies on your person or in this bag? If you do, you need to surrender them now. If you surrender them, we will confiscate them as contraband and no charges will be brought on you. They are illegal for you to possess or bring into the United States. If you do not surrender them and I find them, you will be prosecuted to the full extent of the law. Now, do you have any photos of dead bodies?"

Again, I answered, "No sir."

He moved his hands around in the bag some more and then he stopped and asked, "Do you have any contraband or weapons in your bag that I missed or you do not have papers for?"

I answered, "Yes sir."

"What is it?" He asked.

"A Chinese Communist hand grenade," I answered.

"Show it to me," he said firmly.

I reached in the duffle bag and pulled the grenade out in the cloth I had wrapped it in. I unwrapped it and as I handed it to the agent, I said, "It is disarmed."

The agent took it from me and rolled it in his hands a couple of times looking at it intently. Then as he handed it back to me, he said, "Show me how it is disarmed."

I took the grenade with the metal jacket in one hand and the bamboo handle in the other, gave a twist and the two pieces separated exposing the now empty metal jacket where the Chinese C-4 had been and the cut off blasting cap in the end of the bamboo handle. The agent took the two pieces back from me and examined them.

"OK," he said. "You can keep it." And he handed it back to me. "Anything else I should know about?"

"No sir," I answered.

His final words were, "You can put your things back in your bag and thank you for your honesty. That grenade is a nice souvenir."

I walked outside and got on the bus to Fort Lewis, hoping Hendricks would make it through and catch the same bus. When he showed up, I had a seat saved for him. The bus took us to the fort and our first stop was the mess hall. Everyone returning home from a combat zone got a steak dinner. Ours was a steak and egg breakfast because we were too late to get the dinner. We told them how thick and what kind of steak we wanted. I chose a three quarter inch ribeye medium rare with a ham and cheese omelet and hash browns on the side.

After breakfast, they herded us into a large room and asked for someone to volunteer to lead the group. I learned a long time ago not to volunteer for anything in the Army. As they went through the ranks, they determined the highest rank in the group was E-5. When the person looking for volunteers saw my stripes, he said, "How about the tall sergeant in the back. You want to be in charge of your group? It has benefits."

What kind of benefits are there?" I asked.

"Come up here and we will discuss them," he said.

I walked to the front of the group and he motioned for me to lean in so he could say something without the group hearing it. As I leaned forward he said, "You will be the first person through the line for everything. Your name will be called first for all the checkout stations.

"I will do it on one condition," I answered.

"What condition is that?" He asked.

"I am number one and my buddy is number two to check out."

"What is his name?" He asked.

"Thomas Hendricks," I told him.

"Done." he said "Congratulations, Sarge."

Before we went to the first station, which was medical, the person that selected me to lead the group came and told me they had overlooked a Staff Sergeant that was in the latrine when we chose you. "He wants to lead the group."

"I'm OK with that," I said.

"We are going to let you go first for everything like we agreed, OK?" He quizzed.

"OK." I said smiling. The staff sergeant never knew about the deal I made so Hendricks and I went through all the stations numbers one and two. Medical was a farce. They told us if we had no injuries or pains and we did not want a doctor to examine us all we needed to do was sign the release form. They reminded us that if we did not sign the release, a doctor's exam would be scheduled for the next day. The clock had already rolled over to October 4, my DEROS date so I signed the form.

The last thing we did was go to finance to get our last paycheck, any back pay and sign out of the Army. When I went to finance, they told me I had two months back pay coming. It amounted to over nine hundred sixty dollars. What a pleasant surprise that was! The two months I had not been paid caught up to me, I was rich! Other guys that signed out of the Army went to the bus station to wait on the next bus going to Seattle Airport. I told Hendricks we were not riding a bus or waiting for one either. We were taking a cab to the airport in Seattle. It was only twenty-five dollars for both of us and I wanted to get home as soon as I could. I gladly paid the fare. Hendricks came up with the idea he wanted to stop by the PX before we left the fort. That cost was an extra ten dollars but I did not care, I had the money.

We arrived at the Seattle Airport at 11:30 A.M. and as I headed for the ticket counter, I passed a bar in the airport that was open. I told Hendricks, "Wait here; there is something I have to do." I walked into the bar and holding out three fingers, told the bartender, "Give me a glass and put that much scotch in it." The bartender filled the glass to the top of my third finger. I lifted the glass and said, "This is for you Bennie Singleton." I downed the whole glass, the first drink I had since the night I got drunk on the four fifths of 100 proof "Old Grandad" with Tiutczenko and two other guys at Uplift. I went back out and joined up with Hendricks and we found a ticket counter.

I explained to the agent at the counter that I wanted to fly military standby on the first flight going to Chicago, Illinois but if it looked like we were going to be bumped off the flight I wanted to buy a full fare ticket. She kept insisting that there would not be a problem and assured me there was no chance I would be bumped off the flight. The flight we booked left Seattle at 2:50 PM arriving in Chicago at 9:30 PM. I wanted an earlier flight but there was none so we settled for the 2:50 flight. I called my folks to let them know and we waited for our departure time. Hendricks was going to Chicago with me and then on to Rockford, Illinois with a connecting flight.

We boarded the plane for Chicago and I could see why the ticket agent had insisted there would not be a problem. It was one of Pan American's new 747s. It was a huge airplane and there were many empty seats on our flight. We were lucky and got the seats directly across from the flight attendant's seats so while taking off we had some pleasant good-looking company. Her name was June and she told us she had recently done some promotional work for the airlines and was featured in the Pan Am Magazine. We found the picture and article in a copy in one of the seat pockets. June was explaining about the new 747 aircraft and let slip that there was a piano bar on the second floor of first class. We decided to ask her to take us on a tour so we could see it ourselves. She said she could not do that because of the passenger riding in first class. We tried to get her to approach him to see if he would mind us touring the first class section but she refused. Even our coaxing and pleas referencing us being combat veterans would not budge her. After that we noticed she spent a lot of time out working the other passengers in the cabin and not so much time talking to us. Maybe we should have asked her to autograph the magazine article.

The plane was right on time landing in Chicago. We were next to the exit door, so after the first class passenger exited the plane, we were next. Back then, family and friends were allowed to go to the gates to meet incoming flights. I saw my mom and dad right away and my brother and a friend of ours were there to meet me also. Coming home from Vietnam was different than soldiers returning from the war zones today. There were people standing around with smiles on their faces when I hugged my mom, but there was no applause or cheering from the crowds in the airport like you see today. No one spit on me either like so many GIs returning from Vietnam said they experienced when they walked through the airport. I continued to look around to see if my girlfriend had made the trip also and asked if she had come. My mother told me she was at school and did not make the trip home from Southern Illinois University in Carbondale at the other end of the state. It would have been a long trip so I was not too disappointed.

On the trip home, I gave my mother a view of her son she had never seen. I was sitting in the back seat with my brother and friend. They were asking questions about the war. "Did you shoot anybody? Did you see any enemy up close?"

I answered with a recollection from the rescue mission to save the Recon teams in 506 Valley saying at some point, "The fucking VC were all over the place!" It rolled out of my mouth as if I was telling it to some of the guys back in Nam. I did not realize I had said it until my friend and brother told me to clean up my language. My mom, never flinched. I am sure she heard it but she never said a word.

When we got home, I started asking about a car to make a trip to Carbondale to see my girlfriend. If one were not available I would rent one to make the trip to see her. I had to see her as soon as possible. Then I got the news, on October 3, 1970 at 7:00 PM she was married to someone else. The ceremony took place in the Catholic Newman Center at Southern Illinois University. Mom did not tell me that way, she just said, "She is married." I could not say anything; the pain in my heart was unbearable. I was a soldier home from the war, hardened by extreme combat, yet tears were streaming uncontrollably down the sides of my face. During all of the years I had known her, dated her, we had experienced break ups before but they were nothing compared to this. She had been my childhood sweetheart since the third grade. She had the pre engagement ring I gave her before I left for Vietnam. She told me to hurry home, she was waiting and it all ended with the three words I never expected: she is married.

AFTERWARD

I have to admit, the strangest thing that happened in writing my story was finding an editor. The editor for this book was my longtime former girlfriend. Yes, the same one that got married the night of October 3, 1970 when I got back to the United States. I had the idea that since she was a Professor of Education at the University of Wisconsin Stevens Point, I would ask her to edit my book for me. She told me she was not a professional editor but she accepted my request to edit my book. I have been sincere when I have told her many times throughout the process; I could not have done it without her guidance. She accepted the role of non-military advisor and kept me focused on all readers, military and non-military that may choose to read this book. It was my pleasure to work with her on this book. I will admit, by destroying the letters I wrote to her about all of my activities in Vietnam, it made writing the book more difficult, but my memory served me well. When she reviewed the chapter with the Donut Dolly, she said she had read the story in another chapter. She thought I was repeating myself. I assured her the only other time I had written her about the Donut Dolly was in my letters. She must have remembered the incident from forty-five years ago.

All of the events I have written about in this book are true, and if they did not happen to me personally they happened to the person I wrote about in the book. I know some things seem unbelievable and if they had not happened to me, I may not believe them either. Everything that happened in Vietnam took place between September 1969 and October 1970. When people ask me where I went to school, I tell them the school of hard knocks. I cannot put a value on the education I received by going to Vietnam. It was priceless. There is no amount of money, however, anyone could give me that would be great enough to do it over again.

Since beginning to write this book, I experienced the loss of two friends the book was dedicated to, John Chapla and Patrick Welsh. I say friends because they were great friends but they were also great leaders. I sent the dedication to John shortly before his death. That was the only part of the book he read. I sent it to get his approval on how I worded the dedication. Even then, he was encouraging me to write my story. As we talked about him doing some chapter reviews of my writing, I told him I wanted to get his opinion on the book as I wrote it. He told me, "Better get crackin'." I knew then that he knew the end was near. He passed away a little more than a week later.

Pat Welsh came to the 173rd Airborne Brigade's annual reunion at Fort Bragg, North Carolina in 2014. When I saw his condition, I knew he was not medically fit to be there but he had made a commitment to come and he was there. I had copies of the first chapter I wrote which is chapter 32. I let him read it because I wanted his opinion on my writing. He told me it was good and he was looking forward to reading the completed book. Chapter 32 was the only chapter he read. Several months after seeing him at Fort Bragg, he passed away. I attended his funeral in Louisville, KY and was honored when his wife asked if I would say something about him. How could I refuse, he always told me I was the son he never had. When his brothers and sisters present learned I was writing a book and Pat was featured in it I was overwhelmed by their response. I met both of his daughters in Louisville and told them some of the accounts that are written here. I hope I have met their expectations when they have seen my story of Pat's help and leadership. He saved my life more than once and I wish he were here to comment on my writing. Pat was an avid reader and encouraged me often to write my story.

Occasionally, members of the first platoon have their own reunions and they have graciously invited any members of the command position to attend. I try to make any of those I can. It is a way of regaining the comradery we experienced in the jungles and rice paddies of Southeast Asia. The platoon also gathers for memorials when one of the members passes. Unfortunately, that is becoming more frequent as we get older.

However as long as I am healthy and capable I will continue to "Drive on" with the first platoon whenever possible. ATW!

As for the second platoon, I have contact with my two platoon sergeants Bill Andersen since 2000 and Samuel Richardson since 2014 when I met him after a forty four year absence. I also continue to stay in touch with Bill Borchard, the company RTO who always has been a dear friend and close companion. He saved me from being left behind on March 17, 1970 while I was directing rockets on our position to break off contact with the enemy. He still has a great since of humor and continues to tell me jokes I have never heard before.

Lt. Tim Austin is a good friend and the Brigade Association secretary. I fondly remember the humorous incidents he participated in described in this book. He and Nick Grumbos rekindled their friendship in 2012 at the annual reunion in Lexington, KY.

Last but not least, I am sure Bill Borchard would agree with me is our friend Nick Grumbos, who lives a short distance from me. We see each other regularly. He never ceases to amaze me! He has been a great inspiration to me since I returned home.

The only other thing I can think of to say is when you see the men and women of today's military or armed forces show them some respect. They do and have performed a great service to this country for a lot less money than they deserve. The next time you see or hear of a member of the U.S. Congress wanting to vote themselves a raise, write them to give that percentage to the individuals in the military instead.

GLOSSARY OF TERMS

Term	Definition
105	105 mm cannon/ round
50 Cal	50 Caliber machine gun
AIT	Advanced Infantry Training
Ammo	Ammunition
AO	Area of Operation
APC	Armored personnel carrier (track)
AR-15	Small Carbine Similar to the M-16 Automatic Rifle Carried by Officers
ARVN	Army of the Republic of Vietnam, South Vietnamese army regular
B-40 Rocket	A shoulder held RPG, Chinese or Russian made
Beauquop	A lot or many
Bird	Slang for Helicopter
Blocking Force	Identifies a US element inserted to block VC /NVA escape or penetration
Booby Trap	Explosive and non explosive devices used by the VC or NVA triggered by various means to injure or kill US soldiers some very primitive some very sophisticated
Boonie Hat	military soft hat with 360 degree brim
Boonies	Slang term for the jungle

Bunker Line	Outer most fighting positions of an established basecamp, LZ or firebase. Bunkers encircle the entire camp and are manned 24 hours a day
C-4	Plastic explosives
CA	Combat assault, helicopter assault into unprotected area usually comprised of 6 UH-1 Huey helicopters or more with 6 GIs in each helicopter
Canteen	Plastic water carrier, 1 or 2 quart size each had its own cover
Cat Codes	3 letter Alpha code to identify words or phrases on the radio. These were referenced in a cat code book used to send messages on the radio from the field to the rear or from the rear to the field. All radio operators carried the cat codes in the field. These were considered secure documents and were controled by the commo chief in the field or the batallion radio operator.
Charlie	US slang for Vietnamese indigenous person (enemy)/ Also term for Phonetic Alphabet letter C
Chi Com	Chinese communist hand grenade, the local manufactured type was more powerful than US grenades but was unpredictable, it had a delay time of 0 minutes to never exploding
Chinook	A large two rotor helicopter capable of hauling heavy loads in the cargo bay or slung under the aircraft and up to 33 men with 6 crew members. It could land or take off like a normal helicopter or use a runway like an airplane. The runway was used for rapid unloading of cargo carried inside the aircraft on pallets.
Chopper	Another term for helicopter
Chow	Food, term is used in the field or in the rear
Chieu hoi	Words mean surrender, also can be a person who surrendered

Clacker	firing device for the claymore mine, produces 1-1/2 volts of electricity
Claymore	US anti personnel mine, C-4 packed with 4500 BBs set off by a firing device sometimes called a clacker.
Clover Leaf	Type of ambush prevention run by large patrols in areas where ambush is expected or jungle is thick and visibility is limited. Two small elements move in circular movement parralling the main body of the force as they move through a suspect area. This manuver is repeated as long as conditions exist.
CO	Commanding Officer or Company Commander
Coke Girl	South Vietnamese girl selling sodas in the field to GI's
Cold LZ	Landing zone with no incoming fire of any kind
Company Street	The street in front of the Company's Orderly Room, used for Company formations and roll call.
CP	Command Position/Reference to the element the commanding officer is traveling with in the field. The CP consisted of mostly radio operators and the forward observer, commanding officer, top doc/medic and anyone else related to the command of a company traveling outside the base camp
CQ	Short for "Charge of Quarters" when the orderly room is usually manned by an NCO from the Company in the rear area after regular hours. Every night occurance.
C's / C rations	US Army's canned rations consisting of various meals none as popular as beans and franks
DEROS	Date eligible for return from overseas
Det cord	long thin flexible cord loaded with explosives
Drive On	Black triangular piece of cloth with unit patch and your name on it worn around the neck
Dust-Off	Medevac evacuation helicopter, also the radio term to summon one

Elephant grass	tall sharp edged grass found in the highlands of Vietnam
EM Club	Enlisted mens Club. For the privates in the Army but anyone that wasn't an officer were allowed to use the facility
Field	anywhere outside the basecamp or LZ
Fire for Affect	Artillery/mortar term used for a barrage when rounds are on target
Flight Manifest	The list of names/equipment selected for a particular flight #
FO	Artillery/mortar forward observer
formation	Formal Army gathering of troops in an organized group, usually in columns /rows from left to right with the leader in front of the first row
Getting Over	Ghosting/ being able to apply one's skills for not going to the field or not doing details
Ghost	Slang term used by GIs for getting out of details or doing nothing (Ghosting) Not being seen by anyone in charge
GI	US Soldier (ground infantry)
Green Machine	Encoder/decoder used to scramble/unscramble messages sent in the clear over the radio. Carried by the como chief in the field. Connected to the PRC-25 radio by a short flexible cable. The signal for sending the messages would be activated by the person initiating the call by "go green"
Green Smoke	color of smoke grenade used to identify a cold LZ
Green Tracers	Bullets tipped with green phosphorous that glow green when fired are usually loaded every 4th or 5th round and used during night time to detect direction of fire. Green tracers were only used by VC and NVA
Heat Tab	Fuel Compressed Trioxane Tablet, 2 in a package. Took your breath away if you smelled the fumes but was a low illumination heat source for cooking chow or heating water for LLRPs in the field

Hootch	House, hut, Living quarters
Hot LZ	Landing zone where the helicopter or troops received incoming fire
Hump	Slang for carrying your ruck in the boonies
indigenous personnel	the enemy, VC or NVA
Iodine tablets/ pills	Small tablets used to purify water. Almost no one used them because of the iodine taste in the purified water.
Jungle Penetrator	Medical evacuation device used to extract wounded in thick jungle when it is impossible for the dust off helicopter to land
Jungle Sweater	OD Green light weight sweater used at night or under fatigue jacket for warmth
KIA	Killed in action
Klick	Term short for Kilometer - 1000 meters
Laager	Night time position usually in the shape of a circle (or as close to it) for protection
Lifer	Slang for career army person usually a senior NCO or officer
Light 'em up	Slang term for shoot at the enemy
Long John	Term for Long Rigid Radio antenna that breaks down into several pieces each about a foot long
LP	Term for listening post, night time forward position for 2 people listening for enemy movement in the night. LPs were always located outside the perimeter and established after the perimeter is set up for the night. The object of the LP was to detect the enemy and not disclose your position.
LRRP	Short for Long range reconnisense patrol - also for the freeze dried meals which were more popular than C rations but required hot water to eat
LT	Short for Lieutenant

LZ	helicopter Landing Zone, also identifies some base camps (LZ Uplift)
M-16	Preferred rifle for US infantry. It fired semi and automatic by selection
M-60	US light machine gun
M-79	40 Millimeter Grenade Launcher
Mad Minute	Term for time when all weapons on the perimeter of a base camp or firebase free fire for one minute
mechanical ambush	US version of a booby trap set off by electricity from a used radio battery and some improvised common GI devices which could easily be found at every laager site.
melamine cans	Large thermal containers with lids used to send hot chow to the field on resupply day
Mess Hall	US army cafeteria serving three meals a day
MOS	Military Occupation
MSG	Master Sergeant E-8 Senior NCO
NCO	Non Commissioned Officer, E-5 thru E-9
NCO Club	Non Commissioned Officer's Club. Club for Corporal and above. Not for officers
NCOICR	Non Commissioned Officer in charge of the rear area, each company had one
Net	Radio term for frequency assigned to each Company
Number 1	Slang Vietnamese term for Best
Number 10	Slang Vietnamese term for worst
NVA	North Vietnamese Army Regular
OD	Olive Drab, the Army's favorite color of green
Old Man	Slang nickname for company commander
OP	observation post, daytime forward position to watch for enemy
Out	Radio term for I received your transmission, good-bye
Over	Radio term for I have completed my transmission back to you or what is your reply

Phonetic Alphabet	The Army ABCs. Every letter was given a name that began with the letter used (Alpha, Bravo, Charlie, Lima, Mike, November for ABCLMN)
Point	The front of the column/ can be a reference to point man
Point man	GI walking in the front of the column. This individual is usually selected for his special skills and alertness. This is a key position in advancing any sized element in all types of terrain and conditions.
Police	Term used in the army for picking up trash
Poncho	US issue OD rain gear we were not allowed to use in the field. It made too much noise when walking and the jungle version ripped to shreds very easily.
Poncho Liner	Light weight insulated nylon liner for the poncho. Usually used at night for a field blanket without the poncho.
PRC-25	Portable radio carried by RTOs in the field for communication between squads, platoons, companies and the rear.
Prick 25	Slang term for PRC-25 Radio. Radio weight with 2 batteries is 27 pounds
Priority	Medevac term for dust-off priority goes before routine and can be bumped by a higher priority (Urgent)
Push	Slang term for radio net (Frequency)
PZ	Identified pickup zone
Recon	Small squad sized unit (7 men) operating by itself to locate enemy movements, size and location of enemy elements. Recon was assigned to E Company. Also a term used to check out an area of interest.
Red Smoke	color of smoke grenade used to identify a hot LZ
Red Tracers	Bullets tipped with red phosphorous that glow red when fired, are usually loaded every 4th or 5th round and used during night time to detect direction of fire. Red tracers were only used by US troops
REMF	Rear echelon mother fucker

Resupply	Term used to replenish food, water, ammo and necessities for troops in the field. Sometimes would include a hot meal prepared by the mess hall in the rear area and delivered to the troops in the field in melimine cans.
Roger	Radio term for I Understand
Routine	Medevac term for dust-off lowest priority goes if no other priority is waiting and can be bumped by a higher priority
RPG	Rocket propelled grenade
RTO	Individual identified to carry the radio for the squad, platoon, company, battalion or FO
Ruck	Short for Rucksack, the infantryman's suitcase. Everything a GI carries to the field is in his rucksack
Rucksack	GI backpack supported by an aluminum frame for comfort. Everything a GI carries to the field is in his rucksack
Runner	Term for person to deliver messages on foot
S1	Battalion Admin responsible for all personnel
S2	Battalion Intelligence
S3	Battalion Operations
S4	Battalion Supply
Shape Charge	Bell shaped explosive designed to create a certain sized hole
Shit Burner	an individual selected to burn half barrels of latrine waste. Used as punishment detail or was given to South Vietnamese contract workers in the rear areas
Skid	Ski shaped pipe mounted under the UH-1 helicopter on both sides used for landing
Slack	walks behind the point man
Slick	Slang term for UH1 huey helicopter
Smoke	Short term for smoke grenade. Colors of smoke are red, green, yellow and purple.

Smoke Out	Radio term when a smoke round is fired so observer can adjust rounds, reply on the radio is smoke out over
SP's	Short term for Sundry Pack a supply of cigarettes, candy, writing paper and pens, envelopes, bars of soap, boot laces and other essential items for GIs.
Squelch	Radio term a dial on the PRC-25 radio controls the constant static heard if you don't use the squelch dial. While on guard at night radio transmissions were acknowledged by pressing and releasing the call button 2 times or "break squelch twice"
Star Cluster	a self contained rocket/ fireworks for marking positions at night. When making a CA at night the lead helicopter had one person carry a red and a green star cluster, red indicating a "hot" LZ and green indicating a "cold " LZ. Notifies remaining helicopters of LZ status.
Starlight Scope	Night vision instrument that works by starlight, must be a clear night to work properly
Steak House	Club on LZ Uplift run by senior NCOs. You could buy a steak and plate of beans for $1.50, coke for $0.10 and beer for $0.15. The steaks were siphoned off the Mess Hall which never served steak.
Sundry Pack (SP)	a box of goodies received every other resupply included cartons of cigarettes, various candy, pipes, tobacco, soap, shaving cream, writing tablets, pens, boot laces, buttons and sewing kits
Take Five	term for taking a break
Tarmac	Term for helicopter landing area in the rear basecamps
TOC	Technical Operations Center (building in the rear area where all radio transmissions are monitored and command decisions are made for troops in the field)
Top	Term for Top Sargent or First Sargent

Trip Flare	Small bright ground flare activated by a trip wire used in laager defense
Trip Wire	thin wire used as perimeter protection because it is hard to see to activate flares and explosive devices
Uplift	173rd basecamp for the 1st and 3rd Battalions, located on highway 1 between Bong Son and Phu Cat. Also called LZ Uplift or Landing Zone Uplift
Urgent	Medevac term for dust-off highest priority first to go
VC	Victor Charles, non regular army north Vietnamese enemy. Usually born in the south and recruited or forced to fight for the North
Water Blister bag/ Bladder	Large rubber container used for resupply to carry water to the troops during the hot season
Water Proof Bag	most all belongings carried in the field were in a waterproof bag in a rucksack
WIA	wounded in action
WP	short for "Willie Pete" or White Phosphorus Grenade. Can be a mortar or artillery round also. Smoke is brilliant white and burning shrapnel is very hard to put out

Printed in the United States
By Bookmasters